Communities

ADVENTURES IN TIME AND PLACE

James A. Banks

Barry K. Beyer

Gloria Contreras

Jean Craven

Gloria Ladson-Billings

Mary A. McFarland

Walter C. Parker

NATIONAL
GEOGRAPHIC
SOCIETY

GEORGE WASHINGTON WAS OUR COUNTRY'S FIRST PRESIDENT. THIS PAINTING OF HIM BY THE ARTIST JOHN TRUMBULL IS IN THE WINTERTHUR MUSEUM IN DELAWARE. IS THERE A PLACE NAMED FOR GEORGE WASHINGTON NEAR YOUR COMMUNITY?

Macmillan
McGraw-Hill

New York   Farmington

PROGRAM AUTHORS

Dr. James A. Banks
Professor of Education and Director of the Center for Multicultural Education
University of Washington
Seattle, Washington

Dr. Barry K. Beyer
Professor Emeritus, Graduate School of Education
George Mason University
Fairfax, Virginia

Dr. Gloria Contreras
Professor of Education
University of North Texas
Denton, Texas

Jean Craven
District Coordinator of Curriculum Development
Albuquerque Public Schools
Albuquerque, New Mexico

Dr. Gloria Ladson-Billings
Professor of Education
University of Wisconsin
Madison, Wisconsin

Dr. Mary A. McFarland
Instructional Coordinator of Social Studies, K–12, and Director of Staff Development
Parkway School District
Chesterfield, Missouri

Dr. Walter C. Parker
Professor and Program Chair for Social Studies Education
University of Washington
Seattle, Washington

NATIONAL GEOGRAPHIC SOCIETY
Washington, D.C.

PROGRAM CONSULTANTS

Daniel Berman
Asian Studies Specialist
Coordinator of Social Studies
Bedford Central Schools
Bedford, New York

Dr. Khalid Y. Blankinship
Affiliated Scholar, Council on Islamic Education
Fountain Valley, California
Assistant Professor of Religion
Temple University
Philadelphia, Pennsylvania

Dr. John Bodnar
Professor of History
Indiana University
Bloomington, Indiana

Dr. Roberto R. Calderón
Department of Ethnic Studies
University of California at Riverside
Riverside, California

Dr. Sheilah Clarke-Ekong
Asst. Professor, Department of Anthropology and Research Associate, Center for International Studies
University of Missouri, St. Louis
St. Louis, Missouri

Dr. John L. Esposito
Professor of Religion and International Affairs
Georgetown University
Washington, D.C.

Dr. Darlene Clark Hine
John A. Hannah Professor of History
Michigan State University
East Lansing, Michigan

Paulla Dove Jennings
Project Director
The Rhode Island Indian Council, Inc.
Providence, Rhode Island

Dr. Henrietta Mann
Professor of Native American Studies
University of Montana, Missoula
Missoula, Montana

Dr. Gary Manson
Professor, Department of Geography
Michigan State University
East Lansing, Michigan

Dr. Juan Mora-Torrés
Professor of Latin American History
University of Texas at San Antonio
San Antonio, Texas

Dr. Valerie Ooka Pang
Professor, School of Teacher Education
San Diego State University
San Diego, California

Dr. Joseph R. Rosenbloom
Professor, Classics Department
Washington University
St. Louis, Missouri

Dr. Joseph B. Rubin
Director of Reading
Fort Worth Independent School District
Fort Worth, Texas

Dr. Robert M. Seltzer
Professor of Jewish History
Hunter College of The City University of New York
New York, New York

Dr. Peter N. Stearns
Dean, College of Humanities and Social Studies
Carnegie Mellon University
Pittsburgh, Pennsylvania

GRADE-LEVEL CONSULTANTS

Rob Allen
Elementary School Teacher
Two Mile Prairie Elementary School
Columbia, Missouri

Elaine Culton Braucher
Third Grade Teacher
North Side Elementary School
Harrisburg, Pennsylvania

Glenda S. LaFavers
Third Grade Teacher
Windsor Elementary School
Amarillo, Texas

Mary Ann McGrath, Ph.D.
Third Grade Teacher
Lyman Elementary School
Lyman, South Carolina

Vicki Mirabal
Elementary School Teacher
Chelwood Elementary School
Albuquerque, New Mexico

Donna Yamada
Elementary School Teacher
Booksin Elementary School
San Jose, California

CONTRIBUTING WRITERS

Karen C. Baicker
New York, New York

Linda Scher
Raleigh, North Carolina

Acknowledgments

The publisher gratefully acknowledges permission to reprint the following copyrighted material:

From "The Channel Tunnel" by Adam Westgarth from **Connexions** by Adam Westgarth and others. Reprinted by permission. From "Coyote Gets Turkey Up a Tree" from **And it is Still That Way** by Tina Naiche-collected by Byrd Baylor. Reprinted by permission. From "The Express Train" **More Sounds We Found** by Barbara Mariconda and Denise Puccio. Copyright 1988 by Wide World Music, Inc. (ASCAP), a division of Shawnee Press, Inc. International Copyright Secured. All rights reserved. Reprinted by permission. From "The Light at the End of the Chunnel" reprinted by permission of National Geographic Society. From **Uncle Jed's Barbershop.** Text copyright 1993 by Margaree King Mitchell. Illustrations copyright 1993 by James Ransome. Simon and Schuster. "Open Range" (Poem) from **Cowboys and Indians** by Kathryn and Bryon Jackson. Copyright 1948 by Simon & Schuster, Inc. and Artists and Writers Guild.

(continued on page R40)

Macmillan/McGraw-Hill

A Division of The **McGraw·Hill** Companies

Macmillan/McGraw-Hill
1221 Avenue of the Americas
New York, New York 10020

Printed in the United States of America

ISBN 0-02-146558-4

5 6 7 8 9 VHJ 02 01 00 99 98 97

CONTENTS

iii

UNIT THREE
140

Building a Government

v

UNIT FOUR Communities on the Move

204

REFERENCE SECTION

FEATURES

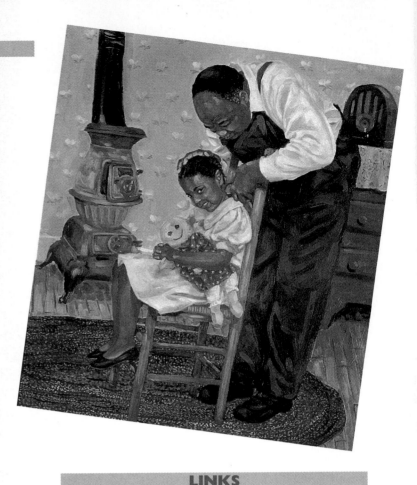

CHARTS, GRAPHS, & DIAGRAMS

TIME LINES

MAPS

YOUR TEXTBOOK at a glance

Your book is *Communities: Adventures in Time and Place.* It has twelve chapters and a special section, as well as many other parts to study and enjoy.

NATIONAL GEOGRAPHIC

Look at Your World

How do people travel from one place to another?

What are some things that help make the Southwest special?

▲ **Special pages from National Geographic bring you ideas and Adventures in geography.**

MANY VOICES — MUSIC

America

Good citizens care about their community and their country. When people sing the song "America," they show pride about living in the United States. In what ways do you show pride in our country?

My coun-try, 'tis of thee,
lib - er - ty, Of
fa - thers died,
From ev - ry -

Living with the Environment

In the last chapter you read about how the Anasazi used natural resources to survive in the dry environment of Mesa Verde. But the Powhatan's environment around Jamestown was different. There was plenty of rain for plants and trees. The area around Jamestown is a coastal plain. A coastal plain is flat land along the coast. It was good for farming. The Powhatan grew corn, beans, and squash. They also hunted deer and other animals.

The English also liked Jamestown's environment. They saw the location as a good place to build a community. Their boats had a good port in the deep waters of Chesapeake Bay. The waters, which surrounded the English on three sides, helped to protect the English against attack. The Native Americans and the Spanish often used land routes for attack.

Links to CURRENT EVENTS

Catch of the Day!

What are new ways people use natural resources?

Virginia's waters have long provided people with food. Today fish and shellfish are not only found in the water, but also on land! They are now raised in tanks on fish farms in Virginia.

Where do the foods you eat come from? Keep a list. Then compare your list with others from your class.

The Bettmann Archive

LESSON 1

Ben Franklin and Philadelphia

READ ALOUD

"Most of the shop fronts were painted red, blue, green, or yellow, and the big swinging signs in front of them were brilliant with paint. . . . The people of Philadelphia wore bright colors and had a taste for fine clothes."

Welcome to Philadelphia!

These are the words of a writer named Margaret Cousins. She describes what life was like in the city of Philadelphia, Pennsylvania in the early 1700s. At that time there were 13 English colonies in America. The colonies had many cities. The biggest, busiest city of all was Philadelphia. About 38,000 people lived there, more people than in Boston and New York City put together.

Philadelphia became one of the most important communities in our country's history. Many things happened there that led the colonies to become the United States of America. Let's take a look at what Philadelphia was like back in colonial days.

Focus Activity

READ TO LEARN
How did Ben Franklin make a difference in Philadelphia?

VOCABULARY
almanac
tax
American Revolution
Declaration of Independence

PLACE
Philadelphia, Pennsylvania

PEOPLE
Benjamin Franklin
Thomas Jefferson

146

◄ **Some lessons have Links or Did You Know—activities and facts to share. You will also see Many Voices—songs, writing, and art by many people.**

Look at the special lessons and features shown at right. They build your **Skills** and bring you interesting subjects from the past and present. ▶

CITIZENSHIP
VIEWPOINTS

Three DIFFERENT Viewpoints

Legacy
LINKING PAST AND PRESENT
Our Country's

GEOGRAPHYSKILLS

Reading Grid Maps

USING THE SKILL
Look at the grid map below. You can see two sets of lines. One set runs across, the other set runs up

Look in the index for the Library of Congress. Find D13 next to its name. D13 is the letter

HELPING Yourself
• Grid maps have crisscrossing lines that help you find places.

map. To find the Capitol, look in the index. What grid boxes is it in? Find the Capitol on the map.

Infographic

A Day with the Anasazi

Pretend you are standing across from the cliff house where Little Rabbit and his family lived long ago. What might you see?

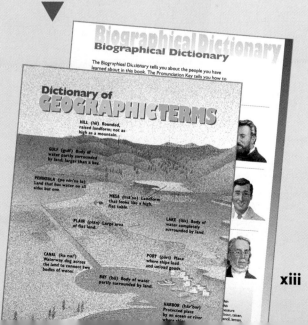

Many storage rooms are used to hold crops and grain.

Women and children are grinding corn.

Swift Raven is making clay pots for cooking and storage.

Strong Deer is sharpening an arrow for hunting.

Meet Ben Franklin

Everyone in Philadelphia was talking about one person—Benjamin Franklin. He seemed to be everywhere, doing just about everything.

Ben Franklin grew up in Boston, Massachusetts, in a family of 17 children. When he was 12, his father sent him to live and work with his older brother James, a printer. Ben quickly learned a lot about printing. But he did not get along with his brother. When he was 17, he left for Philadelphia.

When he arrived in Philadelphia in 1723, Ben found an exciting city. He talked to everyone and soon made many friends. He loved his new city, and he set out to make it even better.

PENNSYLVANIA
Philadelphia

As a young man, Ben Franklin learned to use the printing press.

147

Your book has a **Reference Section** at the end. Use it to look up words, people, and places as you study them. ▼

Biographical Dictionary
Biographical Dictionary

The Biographical Dictionary tells you about the people you have learned about in this book. The Pronunciation Key tells you how to

Dictionary of
GEOGRAPHIC TERMS

HILL (hil) Rounded, raised landform; not as high as a mountain.

GULF (gulf) Body of water partly surrounded by land; larger than a bay.

PENINSULA (pe nin'su la) Land that has water on all sides but one.

MESA (mā'sa) Landform that looks like a high flat table.

PLAIN (plān) Large area of flat land.

LAKE (lāk) Body of water completely surrounded by land.

CANAL (ka nal') Waterway dug across the land to connect two bodies of water.

PORT (pôrt) Place where ships load and unload goods.

BAY (bā) Body of water partly surrounded by land.

HARBOR (här'bər) Protected place by an ocean or river

xiii

▲

Each lesson begins with a **Read Aloud** selection. A **Read to Learn** question and a list of important words, people, and places will guide your reading.

NATIONAL GEOGRAPHIC

Look at Your World

How do people travel from one place to another?

What are some things that help make the Southwest special?

What makes this place different from other places?

How does mail get to exactly the right place?

What foods do people get from trees?

GEOGRAPHY SKILLS

PART 1
Using Globes

VOCABULARY
North Pole
South Pole
equator

What are globes?

- A globe is a small model, or copy, of Earth.

- Find the North Pole and the South Pole on the globe. The North Pole is the farthest place north on Earth. The South Pole is the farthest place south on Earth.

- Find the equator on the globe. The equator is an imaginary line circling Earth, halfway between the North Pole and the South Pole. On a globe the equator is shown as a real line. The equator divides Earth in half. At the top is the northern half. What half is at the bottom?

NORTH POLE

EQUATOR

SOUTH POLE

PART 2

Using Maps

VOCABULARY

continent   map key   locator

ocean   cardinal directions

symbol   compass rose

What are maps?

- A map is a flat drawing of a place. This map shows Earth's seven continents. A continent is a very large body of land. Find the continents on the map. What are they called?

- The map also shows Earth's four oceans. An ocean is a very large body of salt water. Find and name the oceans.

More Practice

There are other maps that show continents and oceans in this book. For examples, see pages 58, 59, and R10-R11.

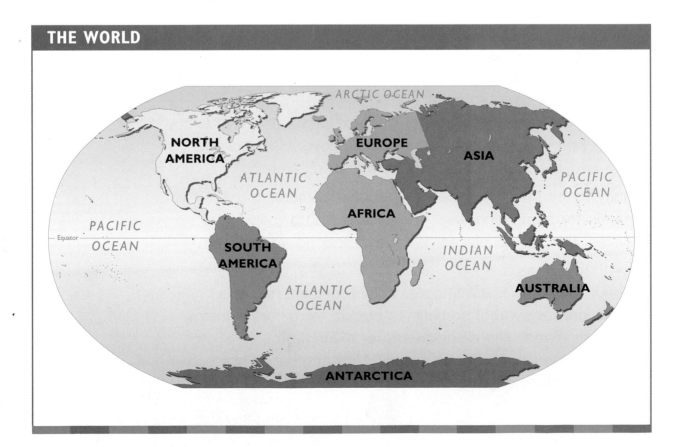

THE WORLD

ARCTIC OCEAN

NORTH AMERICA

EUROPE

ASIA

ATLANTIC OCEAN

PACIFIC OCEAN

AFRICA

PACIFIC OCEAN

Equator

SOUTH AMERICA

INDIAN OCEAN

ATLANTIC OCEAN

AUSTRALIA

ANTARCTICA

Why do maps use symbols?

- Look at the map at the top of the next page. It is a map of the real place shown in the photo above. How are the map and the photo alike? How are they different?

- Many maps have symbols. A symbol is something that stands for something else. The symbols on a map stand for real things and places. What symbols do you see on the map?

- Symbols can be lines, shapes, colors, or pictures. The same kind of symbol sometimes stands for different things on other maps. The color green, for example, could stand for parks on one map and farmland on another. What might a picture of a cow stand for?

Pool ⬭   House ⬦   Tree 🌲

Sidewalk ▭   Road ⬭

Why read a map title and map key?

- A map title tells you what the map shows. What is the title of this map?

- To find out what symbols on a map mean, you can look at a map key. A map key tells what the symbols on a map stand for. Look at the map on this page. What does the blue circle stand for? What symbol means tree?

More Practice

You can practice working with symbols and map keys on many maps in this book. For examples, see pages 25, 249, and 302.

What are cardinal directions?

- There are four cardinal directions. These directions are north, south, east, and west.

- North is the direction toward the North Pole. When you face the North Pole, you are facing north. South is directly behind you. East is to your right. Which direction is to your left?

What is a compass rose?

- How do you find directions if a map does not show the North Pole? You can use a small drawing on a map, called a compass rose, to help you find directions.

- Look at the picture of the compass rose below. The compass rose shows cardinal directions. North is shown by **N**. What letters stand for east, south, and west? Find your home state on the map of the United States at the bottom of the next page. What lies to the north of your state? What lies east, south, and west?

More Practice

You can practice finding directions and using a compass rose on most maps in this book. For examples, see pages 126, 243, and 257.

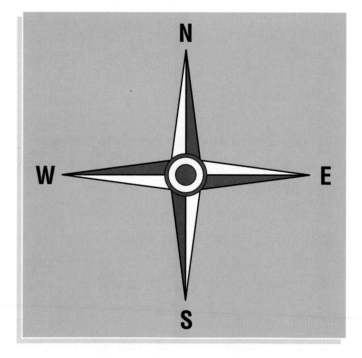

What is a locator?

- A locator is a small map included on a bigger, or main, map. A locator shows where the area in the main map is located. The area of the main map is shown in red on the locator. Find the locator on the map below.

- Study the locator. What does it show? Find the red area on the locator. On which continent is the red area? What country does the red area show? Now look at the main map. What does it show?

More Practice

There are other maps with locators in this book. For examples, see pages 53, 79, and 293.

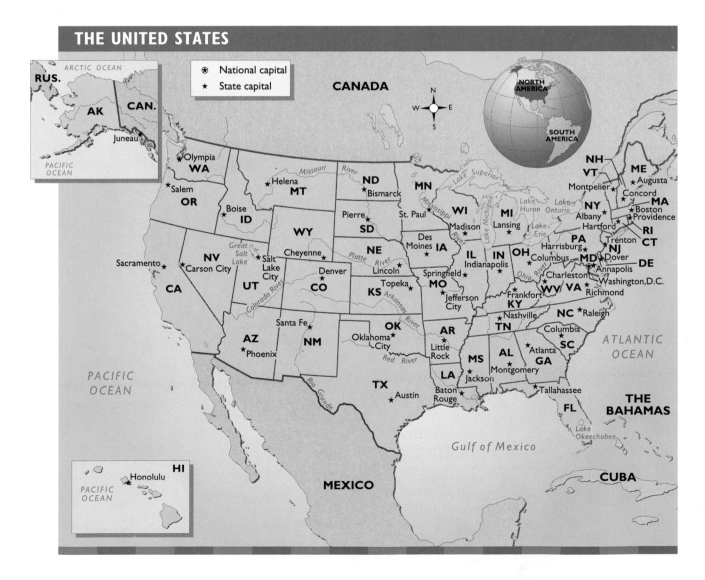

THE UNITED STATES

⊛ National capital
★ State capital

RUS.

ARCTIC OCEAN

AK   CAN.

Juneau★

PACIFIC OCEAN

CANADA

NORTH AMERICA

SOUTH AMERICA

★Olympia
WA

★Salem
OR

Boise
★ID

Helena
★MT

Missouri River

ND
★Bismarck

Pierre
★

SD

MN
Lake Superior

Mississippi River

St. Paul

WI
Madison★

Lake Michigan

Lake Huron

MI
Lansing★

Lake Ontario

Lake Erie

NH
VT
Montpelier★

ME
★Augusta
Concord★

NY
Albany★

MA
★Boston
★Providence

Sacramento★

NV
★Carson City

Great Salt Lake

★Salt Lake City

Cheyenne
★WY

Platte River

NE
Lincoln
★

Des Moines
★IA

IL
Springfield★

IN
Indianapolis
★

OH
Columbus★

PA
Harrisburg★

Hartford
RI
Trenton
★NJ

CT

CA

UT

Denver
★CO

Colorado River

KS
Topeka
★

MO
Jefferson City
★

Ohio River

MD★Dover
Annapolis★
Washington,D.C.

DE

Santa Fe
★

AZ
★Phoenix

NM

Oklahoma City
★OK

Red River

Arkansas River

AR
Little Rock
★

Frankfort
★
KY

WV
Charleston★

VA
Richmond★

Nashville
★TN

NC
★Raleigh

PACIFIC OCEAN

TX
★Austin

MS
Jackson
★

LA
Baton Rouge

AL
Montgomery
★

Atlanta
★GA

SC
Columbia
★

ATLANTIC OCEAN

Rio Grande

Gulf of Mexico

★Tallahassee

FL

Lake Okeechobee

THE BAHAMAS

HI

Honolulu

PACIFIC OCEAN

MEXICO

CUBA

G9

PART 3

Different Kinds of Maps

VOCABULARY
landform map
grid map

What is a landform map?

- The map below is a landform map. This kind of map shows the different landforms on Earth. Many landform maps use different colors to show the different kinds of land. Look at the map key. What color shows mountains? What other landforms are shown?

More Practice

There is another landform map in this book. See pages 40-41.

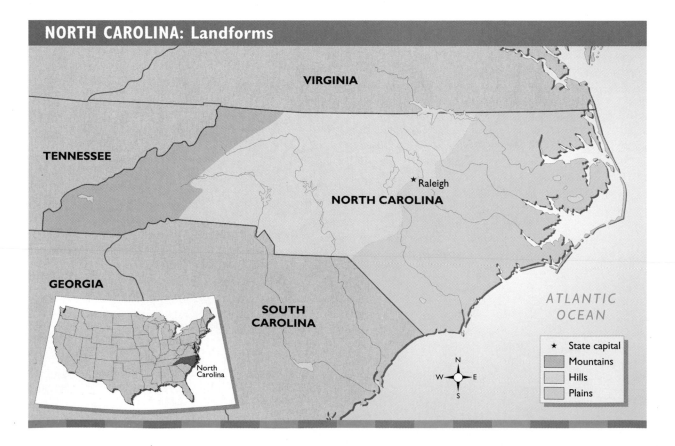

NORTH CAROLINA: Landforms

VIRGINIA

TENNESSEE

★Raleigh

NORTH CAROLINA

GEORGIA

SOUTH CAROLINA

ATLANTIC OCEAN

North Carolina

N
W　E
S

★　State capital
　　Mountains
　　Hills
　　Plains

What is a grid map?

- When you visit a new place, a grid map can help you find your way around. A grid map uses a set of boxes, or grid, to locate places.

- Look at the grid map below. The boxes on a grid map have letters and numbers. All the boxes in the first row across are As. All the boxes in the first row down are 1s. So the first box to the left in the top row is A1. What is the second box in the second row? What place is located in C3?

More Practice

There are other grid maps shown in this book. For examples, see pages 176–177 and 179.

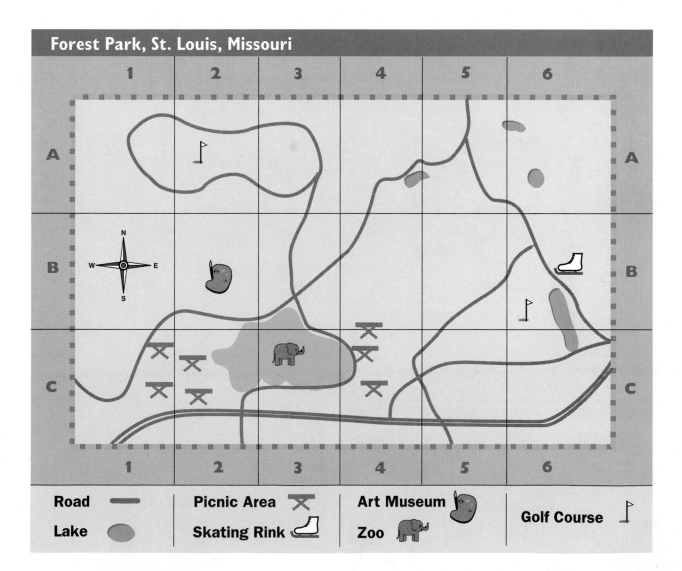

Forest Park, St. Louis, Missouri

| Road — | Picnic Area | Art Museum | Golf Course |
| Lake | Skating Rink | Zoo | |

Living in Communities

WHY DOES IT MATTER?

How would you describe where you live to someone who has never been there?

You could describe your family, your friends, your street, and the land and water nearby. In doing so, you are describing your community.

Your community is special. In this unit you will find out about communities across the country and around the world. Some may be like your community, and some may be very different. All are shaped by where they are located. And in their own ways, all communities are special.

SunBank

4

CIRCUS SCHOOL

You'd flip for a chance to go to this school! It's for kids who perform with the Ringling Bros. and Barnum & Bailey Circus. These kids are part of a tumbling troupe that travels all over our country with the circus. Since they can't go to a regular school, they study in a trailer called the "Little Red Schoolhouse." And yes—even circus performers have to do homework.

GEO JOURNAL

The circus school is part of a community. Write about a special place in your own community.

Understanding Communities

THINKING ABOUT GEOGRAPHY AND CULTURE

What is special about your community's people? Perhaps they live on farms or maybe they work in tall skyscrapers. To find the locations of the communities shown, match the colored triangles on the map with the triangles by the pictures.

In Chapter 1 you will see several different types of communities. One of them might even be like yours.

Anaconda Range, Montana

Chicago, Illinois

Boca Raton, Florida

This rural community is located in Montana.

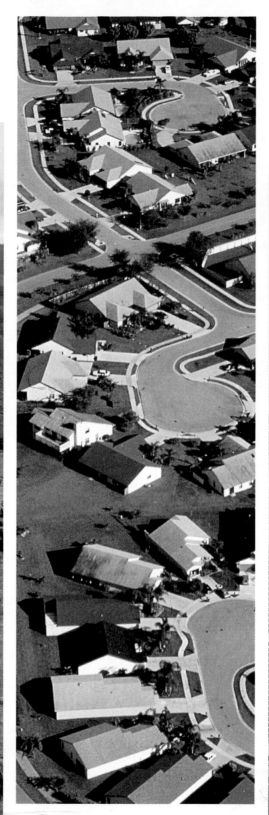

Chicago, Illinois, is an urban community.

Boca Raton, Florida, is a suburban community.

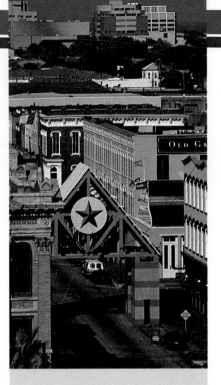

Looking at a Community

READ ALOUD

It's the start of the school year for Mrs. Roy's third-grade class in Galveston, Texas. Students want to write to other third-grade classes around the United States and the world. Today they are writing postcards describing Galveston.

People and Places

Before writing the postcards, Mrs. Roy's class discussed life in their community. "What *is* a community, anyway?" asked Mrs. Roy.

Max said a community is a special place. It is made up of many neighborhoods where people live. Karen said it is a place where friends and family have fun. And Marcus said a community is libraries, schools, and businesses.

"In a way each of you is right," said Mrs. Roy. "A community is usually made up of several neighborhoods. It is a place where different people live. It's also where people work and have fun together. People make communities special."

Focus Activity

READ TO LEARN
What is a community?

VOCABULARY
community
island
port
hurricane
citizen
pollution

PLACES
Galveston, Texas

Living Together

"We have a lot of people living here in our community," said Karen. "I think that our community is big."

"That depends," Mrs. Roy said. "What community are you comparing it to? Say you lived in a big city. Galveston would then seem very small. If you lived in a small town, it might appear very big."

Galveston, Texas, has about 60,000 people. But no matter what its size, every community is special. Think about your own community. What is special about it?

A community is:

a place
people
neighborhoods
families
schools

houses of worship
working together
friends
helping each other
having fun

Mrs. Roy's class learns about communities.

9

Central business district

Seawall

Port of Galveston

Galveston Island

Gulf of Mexico

Galveston Island State Park

0 3 6 Miles
0 3 6 Kilometers

TEXAS

Galveston

Galveston is on an **island**.

1. Along what body of water is the seawall located?

2. Is the port of Galveston east or west of the seawall?

3. Why do you think the central business district is located near the port?

Ships from around the world load and unload goods at the port of Galveston.

Working Together

One thing that makes each community special is the way people can make a living there. Look at the map on this page. Since Galveston is on an island, many people have jobs in shipping. An island is land that is surrounded on all sides by water.

The port of Galveston is a busy place. A port is a place where ships load and unload goods. At the port you may see dockworkers unload bananas. They will be sold in stores in Galveston. Other boats are loaded with cotton, rice, and wheat. They will be shipped to countries far away.

Galveston has one of the "fastest" ports in the country. Boats can dock quickly. Boat captains and dockworkers work together. They load and unload goods so that boats are out in record time.

People in Galveston work at the port and many other places. What jobs do people have in your community?

Helping Each Other

Communities need people to solve problems. Here's what one woman said about people helping each other during the great Galveston hurricane of 1900. A hurricane is a storm with very strong winds and heavy rain.

I grew up on stories about 1900. Everything about who we are today was shaped by that hurricane. We worked together to rebuild Galveston. People wanted to help each other.

The great hurricane almost destroyed Galveston. But the citizens of Galveston refused to give up. A citizen is a member of a community or a country. The citizens of Galveston rebuilt their community. To make sure Galveston would be safe, they built a 17-foot seawall to protect the city from flooding. It still stands today.

Today some citizens are working together again. They are helping to fight air pollution in Galveston. Pollution is anything that spoils land, water, and air. Cars can cause a lot of pollution. To help, some citizens in Galveston are driving together in car pools. In the years ahead Galveston will be an even cleaner place to live.

Building the seawall required hard work and cooperation.

The Rosenberg Library

Having Fun

Look at the picture of the seawall below. You can see what it has become. It is now more than a wall to protect Galveston from the sea. Along the seawall is a sidewalk. People stroll there and ride bicycles. They also roller-skate and jog. Below on the beach, people come to relax in the sand and swim. These are just some of the things that people in Galveston do for fun.

Galveston Island State Park is nearby. Many people go camping there. They also enjoy birdwatching, swimming, and fishing.

In many communities the land and water shape how people have fun. This is also true of Galveston.

For people in Galveston and other communities, having fun also means just being with friends and family. What are some ways you and your family have fun in your community?

Along the seawall and at Galveston Island State Park there is much to see and do.

WHY IT MATTERS

By learning about Galveston with Mrs. Roy's class, you now know what a community is. As you read this book, you will explore how people in different communities live and work together.

One way to see how people live and work together is to visit the main street of a community. Around the United States the main street is often the center of community life. Turn the page and you too can visit "Main Street."

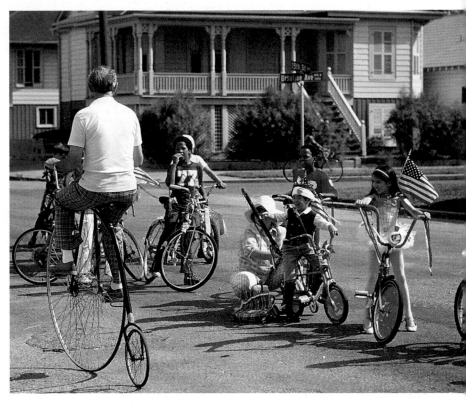

Having fun in Galveston means sharing good times with people.

Reviewing Facts and Ideas

SUM IT UP

- A community is a place where different people live, work, and have fun together. There are usually several neighborhoods in a community.

- Galveston, Texas, is a place where people live and work together to take care of their community.

- A community needs people who care about it and each other.

THINK ABOUT IT

1. Describe Galveston's location. What are two ways location is important?

2. **FOCUS** What is a community?

3. **THINKING SKILL** How is your community _different_ from Galveston? How are they _alike_?

4. **WRITE** Suppose Mrs. Roy's students had written to your class. Write a postcard to them describing your community.

Main Street, U.S.A.

Where do you go to get a library book or to meet a friend? You might go to the main street of your community.

Many communities have a main street. In the past Main Street was often the center of a community. Today people still go there to shop and to meet each other.

Because the main street is part of a community's past and present, you can call it a **legacy** (LEG uh see). A legacy is something that we value in our lives today and that is also a valued part of our past.

A main street in Madison, New Jersey, 1913

Madison Public Library, New Jersey

A dogsled race down a main street in Anchorage, Alaska

Main Street in Marshall, North Carolina

A community event along a main street in Galveston, Texas

Communities Across the United States

READ ALOUD

Hello. We are a third-grade class in Galveston, Texas. We want to know about your community. What is it like? What do you do for fun? Where do people work in your community?

Focus Activity

READ TO LEARN
What types of communities does our country have?

VOCABULARY
urban
suburb
rural
transportation

PLACES
New Orleans, Louisiana
Bothell, Washington
Rochester, Indiana

Hello from Around Our Country

This postcard was written by Mrs. Roy's class. They sent it to different schools around the United States. A few weeks later they received responses from all over the country. The students were very excited. Let's see what they found out about communities around our country.

A Letter from New Orleans

The following letter and photos came from a third-grade class in New Orleans. It is a city located in the state of Louisiana. New Orleans is an urban community. An urban community includes the city and its surrounding areas. What does this letter tell you about urban life?

The French Quarter is a neighborhood in New Orleans known for its music.

New Orleans is a big city. People come from all over the world to hear our jazz music. We even have a park named for one of our famous musicians, Louis Armstrong.

Our sidewalks are full of people. We walk or take streetcars to get around the city. Sometimes it gets crowded. Over 500,000 people live here!

Some of us live in big buildings. Others live in houses that are close together. There are many tall office buildings here. But we have many beautiful old buildings, too.

P.S. What kind of music do you like?

Hello from Bothell

Another letter came from the community of Bothell (BAHTH ul), Washington. Bothell is near the city of Seattle. Communities like Bothell are called suburbs. A suburb is a community located near a city. What does this letter tell you about living in a suburb?

In suburbs like Bothell, many people work in large business parks (top), and relax at places like Bothell Landing (bottom).

Hello! Things change quickly here in Bothell. There used to be a lot of open spaces for playing. But now our suburb is growing. Houses are closer and closer together. Even our roads are more crowded with cars. It sure is a problem!

Bothell has many business areas, like the one in the picture above. People work together and live near each other. We make things like airplanes. We even make video games!

For fun we also like to go with our families to walk and relax at Bothell Landing.

P.S. Our teacher helped us write this!

Regards from Rochester

Have you ever seen a round barn? Well, near Rochester, Indiana, we have them.

Rochester is a farming community. Some of our families have farmed here for a long time. We still raise corn and cows. But it's getting harder to make a living. Land and farm equipment are becoming more expensive.

Our houses are far apart here. There are not many stores nearby. But these things are changing as urban areas grow our way.

Maybe one day you'll come and see us and our neat barns!

Bye-bye.

You can see from this letter that Rochester, Indiana, is a rural community. A rural community is a place of farms or open country. Distances between places are far in rural communities. Can you think of other types of rural communities? A small town in the mountains and a fishing village on the ocean are two other examples of rural communities.

In Rochester cars and trucks are the main form of transportation. Transportation is the moving of people and products from place to place. On the next page you will find a song about another type of transportation.

No matter what shape the barn is, farming requires hard work and long days.

WHY IT MATTERS

The way we live depends on where we live. In the United States we live in different types of communities. We also have different types of houses, jobs, and transportation. We have different ways of having fun as well.

Some communities are near each other and some are far apart. As communities grow closer together, contact between people increases. To get along with each other, it is important for us to understand neighbors and communities other than our own.

Freight trains carry goods to and from communities across the United States.

Reviewing Facts and Ideas

SUM IT UP

- The United States has different kinds of communities.

- New Orleans, Louisiana, is an urban community.

- Bothell, Washington, is a suburban community.

- Rochester, Indiana, is a rural community.

- Transportation is the moving of people and products from place to place.

THINK ABOUT IT

1. What is a rural community? How is it different from an urban community?

2. **FOCUS** What types of communities does our country have?

3. **THINKING SKILL** In which _group_ would you place your community: urban, suburban, or rural? Why?

4. **GEOGRAPHY** Draw a map showing the route from your community to another one.

GEOGRAPHY SKILLS

Using Map Scales

VOCABULARY
scale

WHY THE SKILL MATTERS

Say you want to visit Rochester, Indiana, and other communities in the state. You start in Rochester, and you want to learn how far it is to Indianapolis. One way to do this is to read the scale of a map. The scale helps to measure the real distance between places. It shows that a certain distance on the map stands for a certain distance on Earth.

USING A MAP SCALE

Look at Map A. The scale is the line with marks that stand for miles. It shows that one inch on Map A stands for 100 miles.

One way to use map scales is to make a scale out of a paper strip. Look at the scale below. Place the long edge of your strip along the top of the scale. Mark every 1/2 inch to show 50 miles. You have just made your own scale. Use it to measure distances on Map A. How far is it from Rochester to Indianapolis? To find out, place the strip so that the **0** is at the dot for Rochester. Now read the number closest to Indianapolis. The distance from Rochester to Indianapolis is about 50 miles.

USING DIFFERENT SCALES

Not all maps have the same scale. Maps have different scales because they show larger or smaller parts of Earth. Even though the scales are different, the real distances remain the same. The scale on Map B is different from the scale on Map A. How many miles are shown by one inch on Map B?

Make a new strip to match the scale on Map B. Now measure the distance from Rochester to Indianapolis on Map B. Once again, the distance is about 50 miles.

TRYING THE SKILL

As you continue to use map scales, look at the Helping Yourself box for reminders. Try measuring some other distances. Use your scale for Map A. Measure the distance from Uniontown to Indianapolis. Place the **0** on your strip at the dot for Uniontown. Line it up so that your strip reaches Indianapolis. How far apart are these two places? Now use your scale for Map B. About how far is it from Louisville to Cincinnati?

HELPING Yourself

- **A scale** is used to measure distances on a map.

- **A map showing fewer miles per inch will show less area.**

- **A map showing more miles per inch will show more area.**

REVIEWING THE SKILL

Use Maps A and B to answer these questions.

1. What are map scales? How are they useful?

2. How many miles is it from Scotland to Indianapolis? How do you know?

3. Which map shows a larger area of Earth? Which scale shows more miles per inch?

4. Other than a paper strip, what could you use for a scale?

MAP A

MAP B

A Community in Mexico

READ ALOUD

"I like living near Mexico City. There is so much to do and see here. There is a mixture of the very old and the very new. It's a special community to me."

"A mí me gusta vivir cerca de la Ciudad de México. Hay mucho que hacer y ver aquí. Hay una mezcla de lo viejo y de lo nuevo. Es una comunidad muy especial."

Focus Activity

READ TO LEARN
What are communities like in Mexico?

VOCABULARY
culture
national park

PLACES
Cuajimalpa, Mexico
Mexico City, Mexico

A World of Communities

These are the words of Ana Laura Flores, a ten-year-old girl who lives in Mexico. She wrote a letter to Mrs. Roy's class in Galveston.

As you know, there are urban, rural, and suburban communities in our country. The same types of communities can also be found in other countries.

A big city in the United States has a lot in common with big cities in other countries. The same is true of farming communities as well. But there are also a lot of differences.

In this lesson you will read about some communities in Mexico. As you read, think about how they are the same and different from communities near you.

Living in Mexico City

Ana lives with her family in Cuajimalpa (kwah hee MAHL pah). It is a suburban community near Mexico City. Mexico City is the largest city in Mexico. In fact more people live in or near Mexico City than any other city in the world.

Mexico City has a lot in common with big cities in the United States. It is an exciting place. It has a rich past. Mexico City is the oldest city in North America.

Mexico City is also different from our cities. It has its own special culture. Culture is the way of life of a group of people.

Look at the map of Mexico City below. El Zócalo (el SOH kah loh) is the main square. What can you tell about the names on the map? Most of them are in Spanish. It is the main language of Mexico. Language is an important part of culture. In Mexico you may also hear people speaking many different native languages.

Built in the 1500s, La Catedral still is a popular place on El Zócalo.

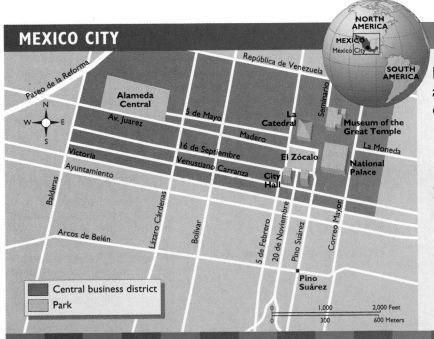

MEXICO CITY

Paseo de la Reforma
República de Venezuela
Alameda Central
Av. Juárez
5 de Mayo
Seminario
La Catedral
Museum of the Great Temple
Madero
16 de Septiembre
El Zócalo
La Moneda
Victoria
Venustiano Carranza
National Palace
Ayuntamiento
City Hall
Balderas
Lázaro Cárdenas
Bolívar
5 de Febrero
20 de Noviembre
Pino Suárez
Correo Mayor
Arcos de Belén
Pino Suárez

Central business district
Park

0   1,000   2,000 Feet
0   300   600 Meters

MAP WORK

In Mexico City, culture is an important part of everyday life.

1. What are some places in the central business district?

2. About how far is it from El Zócalo to Pino Suárez?

3. Why do you think many different types of people can be seen at El Zócalo?

Many Faces of Mexico City

What can a ride on the subway teach you? In Mexico City a trip on the subway will tell you a lot about Mexicans!

The city once built a subway station called Pino Suárez (PEE noh SWAH res). The remains of a very old Aztec Indian temple were discovered there. Today the station includes a display of an ancient stone. It was once used for religious ceremonies by the Aztecs.

What does this tell us about the people of Mexico City? It says they have a long, rich past of many different peoples and cultures.

Many people move to Mexico City every day. They come from different parts of Mexico. Like many cities in the United States and around the world, there are not enough jobs and homes for everyone. Some people in Mexico City live very well. Many are poor. People will have to work hard as they try to solve these problems.

Remains of an old Aztec temple were found while building the subway in Mexico City.

A Suburb Grows

Cuajimalpa is about 14 miles from downtown Mexico City. It used to be a rural village. Farmers, coal miners, and woodcutters lived there. Families like Ana's have lived and worked there for many years. But just as Mexico City has grown, new people have also moved to Cuajimalpa.

Slowly the community of Cuajimalpa is changing. New homes and buildings are being built on what used to be farms. People like Ana's father must find jobs in the city. Cuajimalpa is changing from a rural to a suburban community.

Mr. Flores works in Mexico City. He takes a bus to get there. The bus trip used to take him only 15 minutes. Now, because of increased traffic, the trip takes almost an hour.

Ana's mother takes care of her four children. She also works for a different family in another home nearby. Ana and her three sisters take a bus to school. During their free time they like to go to the town square to meet their friends.

As Cuajimalpa grows, Mr. Flores's bus ride to work takes longer and longer.

27

Communities Change

"What makes Cuajimalpa special," says Mr. Flores, "is the blend of the old and the new."

In the center of Cuajimalpa is an old marketplace. But the town also has modern supermarkets. While many new people now live in Cuajimalpa, most people have lived there for a long time.

Many people want to move to areas similar to Cuajimalpa. They like the beauty of the land. Near Cuajimalpa there is a large pine-tree forest. It is a national park. A national park is land that is set aside by a government for all people to enjoy. Making the pine forest a national park will protect it. The forest won't be "eaten up" by the growth of Mexico City.

As Cuajimalpa and Mexico City grow, people worry about air pollution. They are using their cars less often to help solve this problem. By working together, the people of Mexico are making their communities better places to live.

People can enjoy hiking in a national park near Cuajimalpa.

WHY IT MATTERS

Like communities in the United States, communities in Mexico are changing. Many urban and suburban areas are growing out toward rural areas. With this growth old ways of life change and cultures change.

All communities face problems as they grow and change. To solve these problems people must work together.

Outdoor markets are popular places in Mexico to buy food and other products.

✓ Reviewing Facts and Ideas

SUM IT UP

- Communities in other countries have a lot in common with communities in the United States. They also have differences.

- Culture is an important part of what makes each community different. Mexico has a special culture.

- Cuajimalpa is a suburb of Mexico City. It used to be rural, but it has grown as Mexico City has spread out. Communities change.

THINK ABOUT IT

1. What are some special parts of Mexican culture?

2. **FOCUS** What are communities like in Mexico?

3. **THINKING SKILL** What do you _predict_ will happen as urban areas continue to grow?

4. **GEOGRAPHY** Use the map on page 25 to measure the distance from Pino Suárez to the National Palace.

29

CITIZENSHIP
VIEWPOINTS

In Kenya, Africa, people can see animals in a type of zoo called a game park.

WHAT DO PEOPLE SAY ABOUT ZOOS?

In communities around the world, many people visit zoos to learn about animals. Many scientists who work with animals believe zoos are important. One person who agrees with this viewpoint is Elijah Kemp. You will read his words on the next page. He says that zoos protect endangered animals. Endangered animals are animals that are in danger of dying out.

Other people do not like zoos. They believe animals should be free in their natural environment. Ned Marsen's words explain this viewpoint.

Some people are not against all zoos. The best zoos, says Elisabeth Turbow, give animals room in a place similar to the animals' natural environment.

Read and think about the three different viewpoints on the next page. A viewpoint is what a person thinks about something. Then answer the questions that follow.

Three DIFFERENT Viewpoints

1 **ELIJAH KEMP**
Third Grader, Cerritos, California
Excerpt from Interview, 1994

I think zoos are very educational because kids get to see animals firsthand. You're looking at them. But they are safe and you're safe. Watching animals in the zoo is not like anything you see on television. It's real! Zoos are also good because they raise endangered species. They protect these animals. That's how they grow!

"... zoos are very educational ..."

2 **NED MARSEN**
Fourth Grader, Teaneck, New Jersey
Excerpt from Interview, 1994

There aren't zoos for people, so why should there be zoos for animals? We have lots of space, but animals in zoos don't. They should be able to live wherever they want. The best place for them is where they have always lived.

"There aren't zoos for people ..."

3 **ELISABETH TURBOW**
Fourth Grader, Rochester Hills, Michigan
Excerpt from Interview, 1994

The way I feel about zoos is mixed. Having animals in cages is bad because they can't move a lot. But in many zoos animals are healthy. They get exercise and care. We enjoy seeing them. We're happy and the animals are happy. You also get to see animals like zebras that you wouldn't see if zoos weren't here.

"The way I feel ... is mixed."

BUILDING CITIZENSHIP

1. What is the viewpoint of each person? How does each person support his or her view?
2. How are these viewpoints alike? How are they different?
3. What other viewpoints might people have on this issue?

SHARING VIEWPOINTS
Discuss how you agree or disagree with these and other viewpoints. Make sure you give reasons to support your opinion. Then as a class write one statement about the purpose of zoos that everyone in the class can agree on.

CHAPTER 1 REVIEW

THINKING ABOUT VOCABULARY

Number a sheet of paper from 1 to 10. Beside each number write the word or term from the list below that matches the description.

citizen
community
culture
rural
island

national park
pollution
suburb
transportation
urban

1. The way of life of a group of people
2. A member of a community or a country
3. A community located near a city
4. The moving of people and products from place to place
5. A place where different people live, work, and have fun together
6. Land that is surrounded on all sides by water
7. A type of community with farms or open country
8. Land that is set aside by a government for all people to enjoy
9. Anything that spoils land, water, or air
10. A type of community that includes a city and its surrounding areas

THINKING ABOUT FACTS

1. Name three things that make up communities in our country.
2. How did the people of Galveston, Texas, help each other in 1900?
3. How has the community of Bothell, Washington, changed in the past few years? Why are these changes taking place?
4. Why do people in Rochester, Indiana, need cars to get from one place to another?
5. How are the communities of Cuajimalpa, Mexico, and Bothell, Washington, alike? How are they different?

THINK AND WRITE

WRITING A PARAGRAPH
Write a short paragraph describing how people in your community have come together to solve a problem.

WRITING ABOUT CHANGE
Think about a rural community where the drinking water makes everyone look young. Write a paragraph describing how this community might change if people from other communities learned of its water.

MAKING A LIST
In communities across the United States, Main Street is changing. Make a list of three stores or places in your community that were not around long ago. Write a sentence telling why you picked these places.

APPLYING GEOGRAPHY SKILLS

USING MAP SCALES

Answer the following questions to practice your skill of using map scales.

1. On the map scale at the right, one inch equals how many miles?

2. How many miles is Cincinnati from Uniontown?

3. What is the distance from St. Louis to Detroit?

4. Is Indianapolis closer to Louisville or to Rochester?

5. Why is it important to be able to read map scales?

INDIANA AND NEIGHBORING STATES

Summing Up the Chapter

Review the chapter before making a copy of the main idea pyramid below. The chapter theme is at the top of the pyramid. The main ideas are in the middle. Fill in the bottom with information that supports each main idea. Then describe how communities in both the United States and Mexico have changed in the past few years.

Communities are places where people live, work, and have fun together.

Communities are similar to each other.

Communities are different from each other.

CHAPTER
2

Communities and Geography

THINKING ABOUT GEOGRAPHY AND CITIZENSHIP

In Chapter 2, you will see scenes of our country's natural beauty. You will also see the many ways people use the land and water around them.

Land and water are important to all communities. By working together to protect the environment, people will always be able to enjoy the natural wonders of our planet.

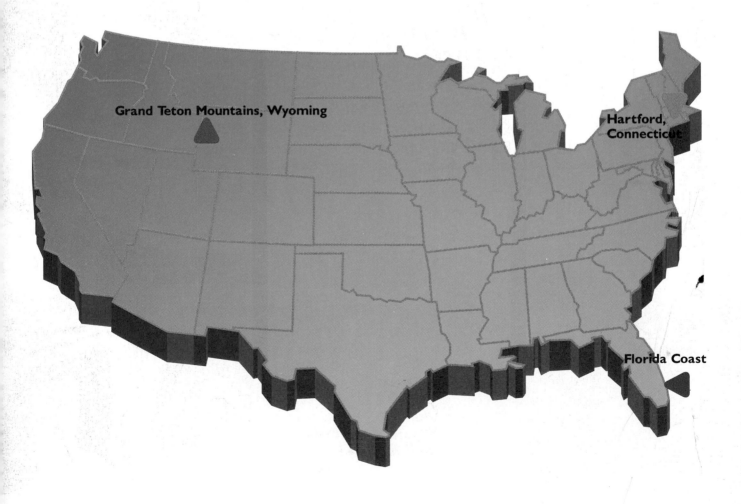

Grand Teton Mountains, Wyoming

Hartford, Connecticut

Florida Coast

People and animals enjoy the Atlantic Ocean along the coast of Florida.

In Hartford, Connecticut, and other communities, people recycle to help protect the environment.

The plains near the Grand Teton Mountains in Wyoming provide food for cows.

Our Country's Geography

Focus Activity

READ TO LEARN
What is geography?

VOCABULARY
geography
plain
landform
plateau
climate

PLACES
Atlantic Ocean
Pacific Ocean
Mississippi River
Rocky Mountains

READ ALOUD

It's a clear fall day. The mountain air is chilly. Inside her house, a woman puts on a jacket. She walks into the woods and hikes up the mountain. Along the way she picks up fallen branches. The leaves crunch under her feet. A squirrel runs away. The woman is cold and she thinks, "When I get home, I'll build a fire."

Geography Every Day

In this lesson you will see everyday events like the ones above in a new way. Events like these are part of the story of geography. Geography is the study of Earth's surface and the bodies of water that cover it. Geography is about how Earth is important to people's daily lives. It is also about how people change the land around them.

Take a look at the Infographic on pages 40–41. It shows some important features of our country's geography. You may find it helpful. You can refer to the Infographic as you read this lesson.

Splish, Splash, and Fish

What covers more of Earth than all the deserts, mountains, forests, cities, towns, and farms combined? The answer is water! How important is water? All plants, animals, and people need water to live.

Oceans are the largest bodies of water. The Atlantic Ocean and the Pacific Ocean are very large. They border the east and west sides of the United States. Oceans are made of salt water.

Rivers and lakes are also bodies of water. They are mostly made of fresh water. Sometimes they are very large. Use the Infographic to see which are the largest lakes in our country. Bodies of water can also be very small. A quiet pond or a wandering stream are smaller bodies of water.

People relate to bodies of water in many ways. Francis Akinsulie (ah kihn ZOO lee) is a student who lives in St. Louis, Missouri. Here's what he says about living along the mighty Mississippi River: "I like going to the river to see the boats going past carrying different things. I once saw someone catch a fish there and take it home in a bucket."

Compare the stream (above) with the Mississippi River at St. Louis (below), where Francis Akinsulie lives.

Skiing is one way people like Luis Garcia enjoy the Rocky Mountains.

Look at Those Landforms!

Did you ever notice that the land near your community may have different shapes? It can stretch out flat the way a plain does. A plain is a large area of flat land. Or land can also form a mountain, rising steeply to a point.

Mountains and plains are two kinds of landforms. A landform is the shape of the surface of the land. Two other landforms are hills and plateaus (pla TOHZ). A plateau is land that is raised above surrounding land. Plateaus are usually high and flat. Look at the Infographic. It shows a few of our country's many landforms. What kinds of landforms are near your community?

Luis Garcia lives in the community of Avon, Colorado. You can see from the Infographic that he lives in the Rocky Mountains. Luis says, "In the part of Mexico where I was born, it never snows. But here, with all the mountains, I get to go skiing and sledding. My whole class learned to ski together. Many people here have jobs that help people who come to ski."

Hot and Cold, Wet and Dry

Like the landforms in our country, the weather is also different in different communities. When we talk about the weather a place has over a long period of time, we are talking about climate.

How hot can it get? Take a July afternoon in Death Valley, California. Some people say you can cook an egg on the ground here before you can say "sunny side up." The climate here is hot and dry most of the year.

How cold can it get? Take a January day in Prospect Creek, Alaska. It's said that tears freeze here before they leave your eyes. Winters here are very cold.

How wet can it get? Take the island of Kauai (KOW i), Hawaii. It rains here about 460 inches every year. That's more rain than Death Valley gets in 400 years!

As you can see, our country has different kinds of climates. How would you describe the climate of your community?

In Death Valley (left) the climate is hot and dry. In Alaska (below) it is often very cold.

Infographic

Our Country's Landforms

You have just read that the United States has many different types of landforms. To learn more about them you can use a landform map like the one below. A landform map uses different colors to show different landforms. What type of landform is in the areas shaded green? What type of landform is in the areas shaded brown?

ALASKA

Prospect Creek

▲ Mt. McKinley 20,320 ft. (6,195 m)

PACIFIC OCEAN

0   500   1,000 Miles
0   500   1,000 Kilometers

WASHINGTON

COLUMBIA PLATEAU

Columbia R.

CASCADE RANGES

COAST RANGES

OREGON

SAWTOOTH RANGE

IDAHO

Snake River

MONTANA

ROCKY MOUNTAINS

NORTH DAKOTA

MINNESOTA

Mississippi River

SOUTH DAKOTA

BLACK HILLS

WYOMING

NEVADA

GREAT BASIN

SIERRA NEVADA

CENTRAL VALLEY

Great Salt Lake

UTAH

Avon

COLORADO

NEBRASKA

Platte River

IOWA

GREAT PLAINS

Missouri River

Death Valley

CALIFORNIA

PACIFIC OCEAN

Colorado River

ARIZONA

NEW MEXICO

KANSAS

Arkansas

MISSOURI

OZARK PLATEAU

OKLAHOMA

Arkansas River

ARKANSAS

LOUISIANA

Rio Grande

TEXAS

COASTAL

HAWAII

Kauai

PACIFIC OCEAN

0   100 Miles
0   100 Kilometers

0   100   200   300 Miles
0   100   200   300 Kilometers

N
W   E
S

THE UNITED STATES: LANDFORMS

Mountains
Hills
Plateaus
Plains

• City
■ Point of Interest

Sawtooth Mountains in Idaho

Hills in Virginia

Columbia Plateau in Oregon

Great Plains in Kansas

WISCONSIN

MICHIGAN

Lake Superior
Lake Michigan
Lake Huron
Lake St. Clair
Lake Ontario
Lake Erie

MAINE
VERMONT
NEW HAMPSHIRE
MASSACHUSETTS
NEW YORK
RHODE ISLAND
CONNECTICUT
NEW JERSEY
PENNSYLVANIA
DELAWARE
MARYLAND

OHIO
INDIANA
ILLINOIS
St. Louis

WEST VIRGINIA
Ohio River

KENTUCKY

VIRGINIA

TENNESSEE
Tennessee River

APPALACHIAN MOUNTAINS

PIEDMONT

NORTH CAROLINA

SOUTH CAROLINA

COASTAL PLAIN

ALABAMA
GEORGIA
MISSISSIPPI

PLAIN

ATLANTIC OCEAN

FLORIDA

Gulf of Mexico

41

A Poem Describes Geography

People live with landforms around them every day. Read the following poem. How many landforms can you find?

MANY VOICES
LITERATURE

OPEN RANGE

Prairie goes to the mountain,
　Mountain goes to the sky.
The sky sweeps across to the distant hills
And here, in the middle,
　Am I.

Hills crowd down to the river,
　River runs by the tree.
Tree throws its shadow on sunburnt grass
And here, in the shadow,
　Is me.

Shadows creep up the mountain,
　Mountain goes black on the sky,
The sky bursts out with a million stars
And here, by the campfire,
　Am I.

by Kathryn and Byron Jackson

range: open area of land
prairie: flat or rolling land covered with tall grasses

WHY IT MATTERS

What if someone told you that you would be studying geography this year? You might think you would be finding places on maps. But using maps is just one part of geography.

You have seen how geography is important to Francis Akinsulie, who lives near the Mississippi River. How else do you think geography makes a difference in people's lives? Luis Garcia's community is in the Rocky Mountains. Many people there rely on jobs that support skiing.

The location of a community has a lot to do with the jobs people do there. In forest areas many people work with wood from the trees. Where the climate is warm, people may work by providing help to sun-seeking visitors.

Geography makes a difference in people's lives. This difference can be seen every day in many communities throughout the world.

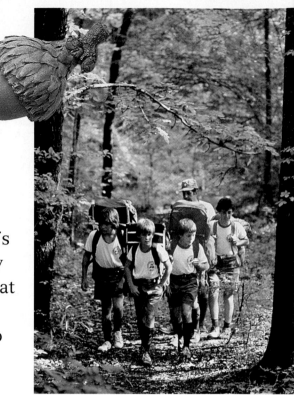

Geography is **important to the kinds of activities people enjoy in communities.**

✓✓ Reviewing Facts and Ideas

SUM IT UP

- Recognizing landforms is an important part of geography.
- Plains, mountains, hills, and plateaus are important landforms in our country.
- The climate in our country is very different in different areas.
- Geography is important to people's lives every day in different ways. It influences where people work and what they do for fun.

THINK ABOUT IT

1. What is a landform? Give three examples.
2. **FOCUS** What is geography?
3. **THINKING SKILL** If you lived near the water, what do you _predict_ you would do for fun?
4. **GEOGRAPHY** Look at the Infographic on pages 40–41. What plains are around the Arkansas River?

Fun with the Wind

People all over the world use the wind to fly kites. The first kites may have been flown in China more than 3,000 years ago.

Long ago kites were not only for fun. In some Asian countries they were used for fishing. More recently box kites have been used to carry weather instruments.

Today kites are used in many ways to explore the air and enjoy the wind.

Wherever you live, kites can be fun for you!

Pictured here are an old Polynesian fishing kite (left) and a modern box kite (above).

In 1752 Benjamin Franklin used a kite to show that lightning is one form of electricity.

Kites shaped like this come from the Asian country of Malaysia.

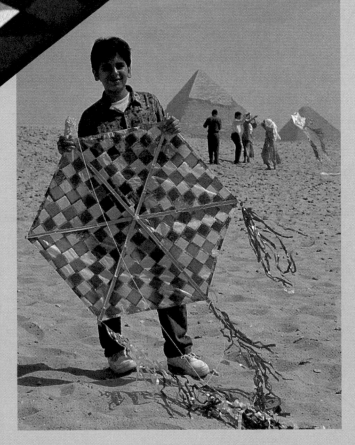

A boy in Egypt enjoys his kite. People all over the world have fun making and flying kites.

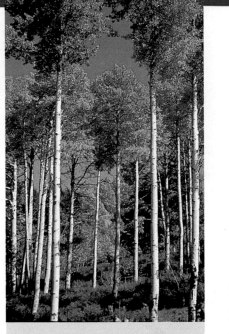

Caring for Our Natural Resources

READ ALOUD

The Oak is called the king of trees,
The Aspen quivers in the breeze,
The Poplar grows up straight and tall,
The Peach tree spreads along the wall,
The Sycamore gives pleasant shade,
The Willow droops in watery glade,
The Fir tree useful timber gives,
The Beech amid the forest lives.

A Wealth of Resources

This poem is called "Trees." It was written over 100 years ago by a poet named Sara Coleridge. She describes many different trees that grow on Earth. Do you have any of these trees in your community today?

Look around your classroom. Is there anything made from a tree? Perhaps your pencil or the paper in your book is made from trees. Trees are just one example of a natural resource. A natural resource is something found in nature that people use. In this lesson you will learn about other natural resources and why it is important to respect and care for them.

Focus Activity

READ TO LEARN
Why are natural resources important?

VOCABULARY
natural resource
mineral
environment
recycling

46

Land of Plenty

Look at the pictures on this page. They show some of our country's many natural resources. The United States is one of the richest countries in the world in natural resources.

Water is one of our most important natural resources. As you read in the previous lesson, the United States has many bodies of water, large and small. Plants need fresh water to grow. People and animals need fresh water to live. Boats travel on our oceans, rivers, and lakes. They carry people and goods.

Have you ever picked up a handful of soil? Did you know that you were holding another valuable resource? Soil is full of minerals to help plants grow. Minerals are things found in the earth that are not plants or animals. Iron, salt, and diamonds are all minerals.

You may live in the mountains, in the woods, near the ocean, or in the desert. But wherever you live, your community has many natural resources. Even the air you are breathing right now is a natural resource!

Natural resources include water and soil. People also use oil and metals from inside Earth.

Protecting the Environment

"Save the Whales." "Give a hoot . . . Don't pollute!" Have you ever noticed bumper stickers like these on a car? They show that people want to protect the **environment**. The environment is air, water, land, and the living things around us.

Protecting the environment and its resources takes a lot of work. Just putting a bumper sticker on a car is not enough. Every day you can take personal action to help protect the environment. Every time you use a bottle, can, or piece of paper, you can save it for **recycling**. Recycling is using something over again. Factories take used plastic, metal, and paper and recycle them.

There are other ways you can help protect the environment. A few years ago some eight-year-old girls in El Segundo, California, wanted to help their community fight air pollution. They knew that plants and trees improve the air. So they formed a group called the "Tree Musketeers." They then decided to plant trees and other plants around their community. Today their community is a more beautiful place to live. According to one Musketeer, Tara Church, "The trees help us keep the air in our community clean."

Tara Church, middle, and others plant trees (right). Recycling (above) helps protect the environment.

48

WHY IT MATTERS

Look around your classroom again. Now you may notice more natural resources than you did before. There is one more resource you may not have noticed: people! You, your teacher, your classmates, and everyone in your community are important resources. It is people who take the other resources around them and make them useful. It is people who will protect our natural resources for years to come.

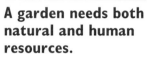

A garden needs both natural and human resources.

✓ Reviewing Facts and Ideas

SUM IT UP

- Our country is rich in natural resources including water, trees, soil, and the air we breathe.

- It is important to protect our environment. Everyone can take action to help make a difference.

- Recycling is one way to protect our environment.

- People are one of our most important resources.

THINK ABOUT IT

1. What are three examples of natural resources?

2. **FOCUS** Why are natural resources important?

3. **THINKING SKILL** How would you _sort_ materials from your home for recycling?

4. **WRITE** Write and design your own poster telling people to protect the environment. What will it say?

GEOGRAPHY SKILLS

Using Intermediate Directions

VOCABULARY

intermediate directions

WHY THE SKILL MATTERS

El Segundo, the hometown of the "Tree Musketeers," is located near Los Angeles. To find where Los Angeles is located, you can look at a map of California. What if you wanted to travel from Los Angeles to Sacramento? Could you use the map to explain which direction to go?

You could if you knew how to use intermediate directions. An intermediate direction is halfway between two cardinal directions.

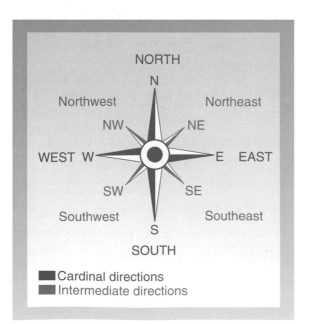

■ Cardinal directions
■ Intermediate directions

USING THE SKILL

You have already used a compass rose to find cardinal directions on a map. Look at the compass rose below. The cardinal directions are north, south, east, and west. North is shown by the letter **N**. What letters are used for east, south, and west?

Now look at the map on the next page. In which direction is Sacramento from Los Angeles? It is neither *exactly* north nor *exactly* west. Instead, it is northwest, which is between north and west. Northwest is an intermediate direction. Look again at the compass rose below and find northwest. It is shown by the letters **NW**. The other intermediate directions are northeast, southeast, and southwest. What letters does the compass rose show for them?

When you use intermediate directions, start by finding one place on the map. Then find the second place and describe the direction from the first place to the second. You may want to refer to the compass rose. If you start with Sacramento and go to Los Angeles, the direction is southeast.

TRYING THE SKILL

Now try describing directions between other places. Use the Helping Yourself box as you answer these questions.

Look at the map again. In which direction would you travel to go from Los Angeles to Denver, Colorado? In which direction would you go to get from Las Vegas, Nevada, to Los Angeles? How about Colorado Springs, Colorado, to Provo, Utah?

REVIEWING THE SKILL

1. What are intermediate directions?

2. If you were in Carson City, Nevada, in which direction would you travel to Tucson, Arizona? How can you tell?

3. In which direction is Salt Lake City, Utah, from Sacramento?

4. When is it helpful to know intermediate directions?

SOUTHWESTERN STATES

A Fishing Community in Peru

Focus Activity

READ TO LEARN
How are natural resources important to people in Paracas, Peru?

VOCABULARY
coast
peninsula
wildlife

PLACES
Paracas, Peru

READ ALOUD
"I live by the sea. My community is filled with beautiful beaches. There are hundreds of fish and other sea animals. I am lucky to live here. My family has been here for almost 100 years. I want to live here forever. The land and water provide us with so many things for life."

A Community by the Ocean

These are the words of a young boy. He lives with his family in the community of Paracas (puh RAH kus) in the country of Peru. Peru is located along the Pacific Ocean. That's the same ocean that borders the west coast of the United States. A coast is land next to an ocean. But Peru is thousands of miles away from the United States. It is on the continent of South America.

For communities like Paracas the ocean is important to people's lives. The ocean provides them with many natural resources. In this lesson you will learn about these resources. You will also see that people are concerned about protecting them.

52

Living in Paracas

Do you know all the people in your community? Well, most people know each other in Paracas. There are only about 100 houses in this community. Many families have lived there for many years.

Fishing is important to many ocean communities around the world. Fishing is also a very important part of the culture of Paracas. Almost everyone in the community makes a living from fishing.

Look at the map below to locate Paracas. Paracas is a **peninsula**. A peninsula is land that has water on all sides but one. An island also has water around it. How is a peninsula different from an island?

For people in Paracas, being near the water is a lot of fun. Many children in Paracas play soccer. But they play on the beach instead of on grass. They watch sea lions. But instead of going to a zoo, they go to a nearby beach. There they can see hundreds of sea lions!

The sea lion is one of many animals that live along the **coast** of Peru.

PERU

ECUADOR
COLOMBIA
Iquitos
Amazon River
Tarapoto
Chiclayo
BRAZIL
PERU
PACIFIC OCEAN
Lima
Paracas
Cusco
Arequipa
Lake Titicaca
BOLIVIA

★ National capital
• Other city

0   80   160 Miles
0   80   160 Kilometers

NORTH AMERICA
SOUTH AMERICA
PERU

MAP WORK

Paracas is located on the coast.

1. About how far is Paracas from Arequipa?
2. In which direction is Chiclayo from Paracas?
3. Why do you think many cities are located along the coast?

A Rich Peninsula

An important natural resource in Paracas is its wildlife. Wildlife are animals that live naturally in an area. Fish are a kind of wildlife.

In Paracas anchovies (AN choh veez) are the most important fish. That's because many fishers make their living from anchovies. Every year millions of small fish are caught and shipped all over the world. The ocean here also has many whales, turtles, and crabs.

Paracas is one of the most important stopping points for birds. Birds are also wildlife. Many birds migrate, or travel, south to Paracas. During the winter they come from faraway places in the north. Some birds fly all the way to Paracas from Canada! The sanderling is one of these long-distance fliers.

These natural resources are important to Paracas for another reason. Visitors come from all over the world to see the wildlife. Some people in Paracas have jobs helping these visitors.

Anchovies are an important resource for fishers in Paracas.

Infographic

Endangered Animals Around the World

In Paracas and other communities, wildlife is a valuable natural resource. But sometimes people don't take care to protect resources. Look at the Infographic on this page. Which endangered species have you heard of?

The California condor is the largest flying bird in the United States. Hunting, pollution, and the destruction of open land areas have threatened their existence.

The black rhinoceros lives in Africa. Their horns are used for medicines.

Giant pandas come from China. The bamboo trees they need for food are being destroyed.

Saltwater crocodiles live in places such as Australia and Asia. Their skins are used to make shoes, wallets, and other products.

The sperm whale was hunted for food, oil, and bone around the world. Other types of whales are also endangered.

Caring for Resources

People in Peru care about their natural resources. Like many communities in the United States, Paracas is becoming polluted. Waste from nearby businesses is dumped into the ocean. Some fish are unsafe to eat.

But the pollution problem in Paracas is improving. People are keeping their beaches clean. Businesses are being more careful not to dump dangerous wastes into the ocean.

By taking care of natural resources, people will be able to enjoy the beaches around Paracas for years to come.

WHY IT MATTERS

You have seen how important natural resources are to people in Paracas. You have also seen one way that people in communities all over the world are alike. They are all concerned about protecting these resources.

By working together, people will be able to protect Earth's natural resources for many years to come.

✓ Reviewing Facts and Ideas

SUM IT UP

- Paracas is an ocean community in the country of Peru.
- There are many natural resources in Paracas.
- Pollution is dangerous to people and wildlife in Paracas.
- People are working together to help fight pollution in Paracas and other places.

THINK ABOUT IT

1. What do people like about living in Paracas?
2. **FOCUS** How are natural resources important to people in Paracas, Peru?
3. **THINKING SKILL** How are the resources in your community *like* the wildlife in Paracas?
4. **GEOGRAPHY** Paracas is a peninsula. How is this important to life in the community of Paracas?

CITIZENSHIP
MAKING A DIFFERENCE

Keep Eustace Lake Clean!

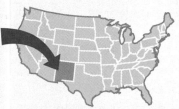

ZUNI, NEW MEXICO—
If you visit Eustace Lake in Zuni, New Mexico, you might see a sign that says, "Keep Eustace Lake Clean." It was made by sixth graders who took action to protect their environment.

It all started in the classroom of Jim Bizell, a teacher at Zuni Middle School. One of his students' favorite spots was Eustace Lake. The lake was once a great place to swim, boat, and fish. But it became unsafe to use. Kelton Kallestewa, one of Mr. Bizell's students, described the lake this way: "It was filled with tires, garbage, and bottles. The picnic tables were broken, and the bathroom walls were knocked down."

Mr. Bizell decided that the students could make a difference by cleaning the lake. Here's Kelton's description of what they did: "We began hauling weeds and removing glass. Four kids went out on a boat and took trash out of the lake. Other kids repaired the bathrooms and picnic tables."

Soon other members of the community were helping too. Some gave pipes to make swing sets. Others helped make pathways and put fish back in the lake.

Making a difference is "up to the kids," said Kelton. "We have the ability to do it. It makes me feel proud to have other people proud of me. When I see the lake now, I'm happy. I'll be able to fish!"

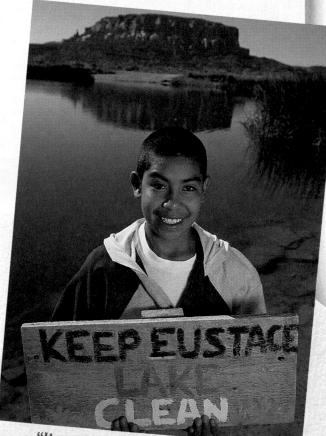

"It makes me feel proud . . ."

Kelton Kallestewa

57

GEOGRAPHYSKILLS

Understanding Hemispheres

VOCABULARY

hemisphere
equator

WHY THE SKILL MATTERS

You have read about the community of Paracas in Peru. To describe where Peru is, you can say it is on the continent of South America. By learning about hemispheres, you will also know another way to locate Peru. Use the Helping Yourself box on the next page as you study hemispheres.

USING THE SKILL

Earth is a sphere. A sphere is round like a ball or a globe. Look at Maps A and B. They show Earth divided into hemispheres. *Hemi* means "half," so a hemisphere is half of a sphere.

The Western and Eastern hemispheres are opposite halves of Earth. Peru is in South America, in the Western Hemisphere. Is Asia in the Eastern or Western Hemisphere?

Maps C and D on the next page show the Northern and Southern hemispheres. The equator, an imaginary line around the middle of Earth, divides these two hemispheres.

MAP A: Western Hemisphere

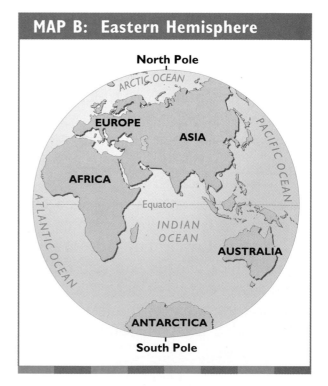

MAP B: Eastern Hemisphere

As you can see on Maps C and D, North America is in the Northern Hemisphere. What other hemisphere includes North America?

TRYING THE SKILL

Now try locating Europe and Africa on the hemisphere maps. Europe is in the Northern Hemisphere and what other hemisphere? Are Europe and North America in the same hemispheres? In which three hemispheres are parts of Africa?

HELPING Yourself

- The **equator divides Earth into Northern and Southern hemispheres.**
- **Earth can also be divided into Eastern and Western hemispheres.**

REVIEWING THE SKILL

1. Name the four hemispheres into which we divide Earth.

2. Which three hemispheres contain parts of South America? Which one contains all of South America? How did you find out?

3. Name all the continents found in the Northern Hemisphere.

4. What could you do to help a friend understand hemispheres?

MAP C: Northern Hemisphere

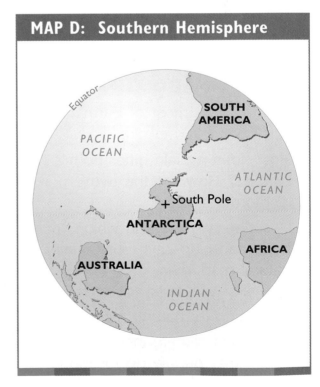

MAP D: Southern Hemisphere

CHAPTER 2 REVIEW

THINKING ABOUT VOCABULARY

Number a sheet of paper from 1 to 5. Beside each number write the word or term from the list below that best completes each sentence.

coast   recycling
minerals   wildlife
natural resources

1. Every Saturday my father and I bring bottles and newspapers to our community _____ center.

2. When I visit the _____, I love to walk along the sandy beach.

3. Today people are finding new ways to protect endangered _____ around the world.

4. Trees, water, and soil are three examples of our country's _____ .

5. Things found in the earth that are not plants or animals are known as _____ .

THINKING ABOUT FACTS

1. What covers most of Earth's surface?

2. How does a plain differ from a plateau? How are the two landforms similar?

3. Describe two ways in which your class can help save our country's natural resources.

4. Why are some people in Paracas protecting its natural resources?

5. How does climate influence the things that people do for fun in communities?

THINK AND WRITE

WRITING A JOURNAL ENTRY
Suppose that you are backpacking around the United States. Write an entry in your journal describing three kinds of natural resources that you observed on your trip.

WRITING A SPEECH
Write a speech explaining the importance of protecting endangered species around the world.

WRITING A LETTER
Suppose you were invited to spend a week in Paracas, Peru. Write a letter to your family describing everything you saw there. Remember to include a description of the kinds of natural resources found in Paracas as well as the kinds of things people do there for work and for play.

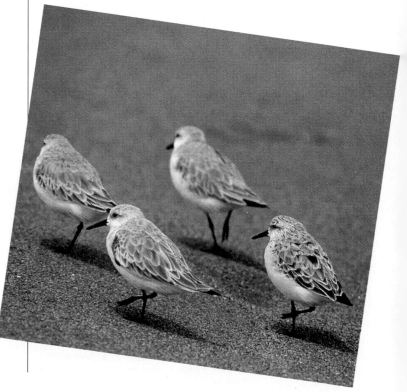

APPLYING GEOGRAPHY SKILLS

USING INTERMEDIATE DIRECTIONS

Answer the following questions about the map at the right to practice your skill at using intermediate directions.

1. What are the four intermediate directions?

2. Which city is southwest of Louisville?

3. Which community is southeast of Scotland?

4. In which direction is Cincinnati from Indianapolis?

5. Why is it important to understand intermediate directions?

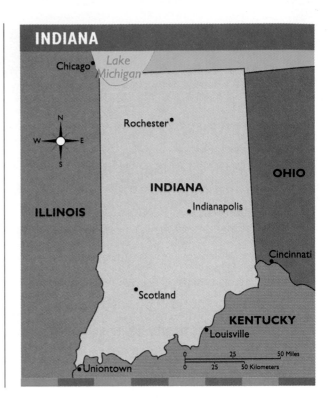

Summing Up the Chapter

Look at the word map below. Then review the chapter to find at least three items to list under the four headings. When you have filled in a copy of the map, use it to discuss how we depend on Earth and its natural resources.

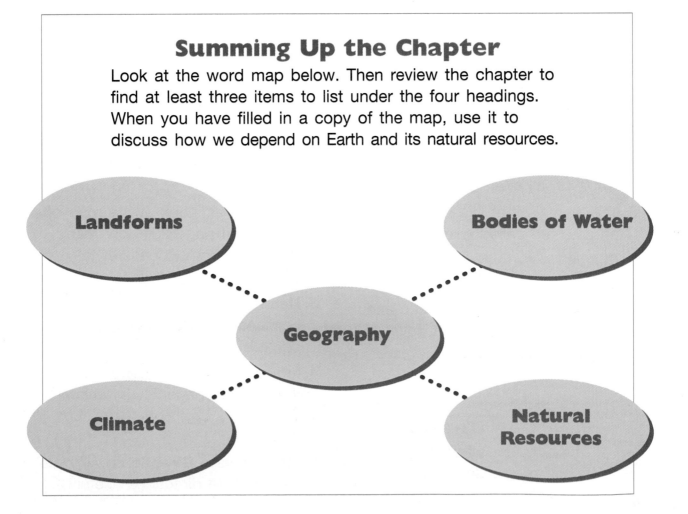

UNIT 1 REVIEW

THINKING ABOUT VOCABULARY

Number a sheet of paper from 1 to 10. Read the definition of each underlined word. Beside each number write **T** if the definition is true and **F** if it is false.

1. A <u>plain</u> is land that is raised above surrounding land.

2. A <u>rural</u> community is a place of farms or open country.

3. <u>Geography</u> is the study of the various plants and animals that live on Earth.

4. A <u>port</u> is a place where trains and buses pick up passengers.

5. A member of a community or a country is known as a <u>citizen</u>.

6. Land that stretches out flat is called a <u>plateau</u>.

7. A <u>peninsula</u> is land surrounded by water on all sides but one.

8. The animals that live naturally in an area are called <u>wildlife</u>.

9. <u>Climate</u> is the way it is outdoors each day.

10. The study of Earth's surface and the bodies of water that cover it is called <u>environment</u>.

THINK AND WRITE

WRITING ABOUT COMMUNITIES

Write a paragraph to convince someone to move to your community. In your writing include those qualities that make your hometown special.

WRITING A POEM

The United States has many different landforms. Read the poem on page 42. Then write a poem describing our country's landforms.

WRITING ABOUT PERSPECTIVES

What if you had just moved to Cuajimalpa, Mexico? Write a letter to a friend in the United States describing how life in Mexico might be different from life back home.

BUILDING SKILLS

1. **Map Scales** Why are map scales included on most maps in this book?

2. **Map Scales** Look at the map of Indiana on page 23. How many miles is it from Rochester to Uniontown?

3. **Hemispheres** Which two hemispheres are divided by the equator?

4. **Intermediate Directions** Look at the map on page 51. In which direction is Las Vegas from Los Angeles?

5. **Intermediate Directions** Why are intermediate directions useful?

YESTERDAY, TODAY & *TOMORROW*

In this unit you have read about the importance of natural resources. But in the past people were wasteful. Today, they are learning to care for resources. In the future, do you think people will continue to respect their environment?

READING ON YOUR OWN

Here are some books you might find at the library to help you learn more.

FAMILY PICTURES
by Carmen Lomas Garza
Learn what life is like for a Hispanic family living in Texas.

MY NEW YORK
by Kathy Jakobsen
Take a tour of New York City. See the sights. Wave to the Statue of Liberty.

TOWN AND COUNTRY
by Alice and Martin Provensen
Here's a look at life in the United States, on a farm and in a city.

UNIT PROJECT

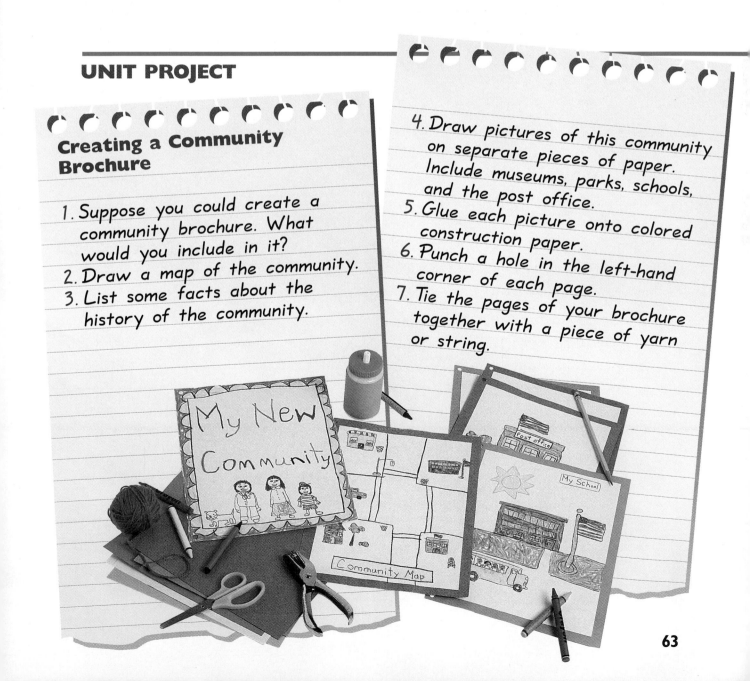

Creating a Community Brochure

1. Suppose you could create a community brochure. What would you include in it?
2. Draw a map of the community.
3. List some facts about the history of the community.
4. Draw pictures of this community on separate pieces of paper. Include museums, parks, schools, and the post office.
5. Glue each picture onto colored construction paper.
6. Punch a hole in the left-hand corner of each page.
7. Tie the pages of your brochure together with a piece of yarn or string.

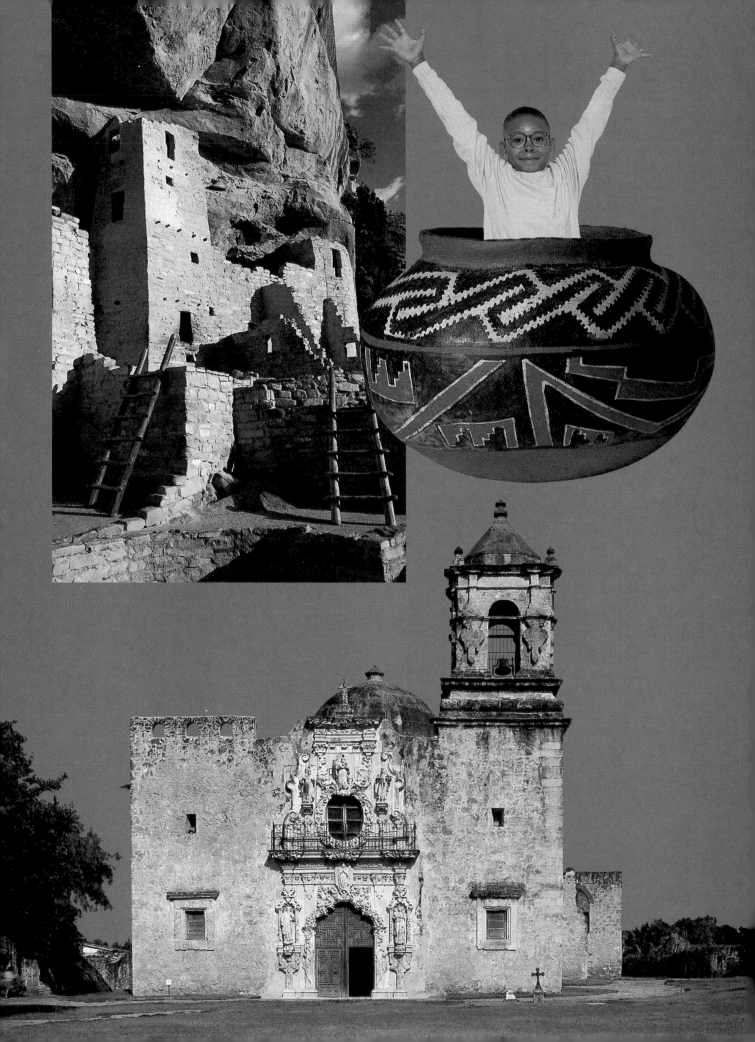

Looking Back to the Past

WHY DOES IT MATTER?

Who first lived in your community? Why do you think they decided to live there?

In this unit you will learn about three very different communities where people lived long ago. These communities were built in different places by different groups of people. Learning about them helps us to discover our country's past and to understand the story of our earliest communities.

As you explore these communities, think about how the past is still part of our lives today.

LIVING HISTORY

It's morning at Plimoth Plantation, in Massachusetts. Time to gather firewood and feed the chickens. Later, the floor needs to be swept. It's hard work—especially when you're wearing Pilgrim-style clothes. Young people sometimes work at Plimoth Plantation. This village was built to look just like the one the Pilgrims built after they sailed across the Atlantic Ocean from England. These kids find out for themselves what daily life was like in the 1620s.

GEO JOURNAL

Write a letter to a friend telling about a job you'd like to have at Plimoth Plantation.

CHAPTER 3

A Native American Community at Mesa Verde

THINKING ABOUT GEOGRAPHY AND HISTORY

The first American communities were started by Native Americans. They lived all across the land we now call the United States. People in these communities made their clothing, homes, and food from the natural resources they found where they lived.

In Chapter 3 you will learn about the Native Americans. You will also visit Mesa Verde, a Native American community built long ago high on the side of a cliff. The map shows you where Mesa Verde is located. The time line shows you when important events ocurred.

1100s-1300s
The Anasazi build communities in cliffs

1300s-1450s
The Anasazi leave Mesa Verde

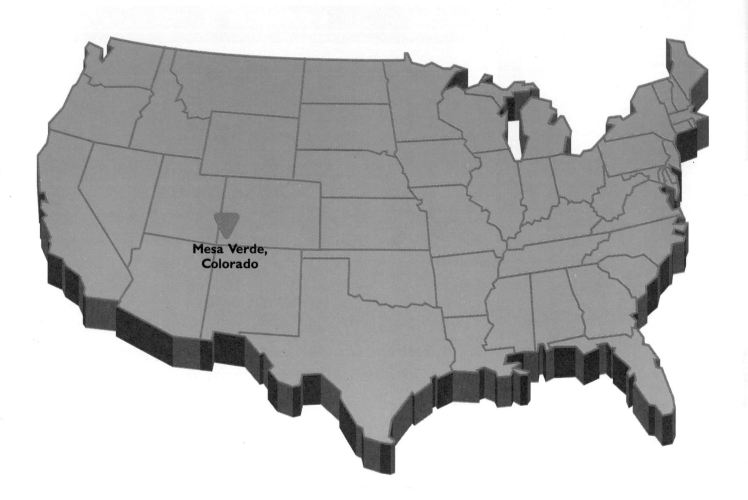

Mesa Verde,
Colorado

TODAY

**People visit Mesa Verde
National Park**

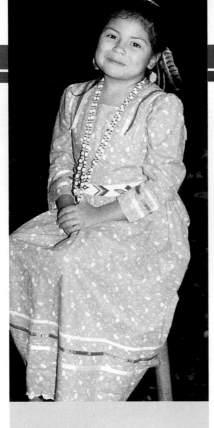

Focus Activity

READ TO LEARN
Who lived in the first American communities?

VOCABULARY
history

Native American Communities

READ ALOUD

"All the time I learn things about my Cherokee culture. Sometimes when I'm doing chores for my mom like pulling up weeds in the backyard, I make little woven baskets out of grass like our people used to make long ago. I am happy to be Cherokee. I am proud of it."

The First Communities

These are the words of Stormi Welch. She is a nine-year-old Cherokee who lives in the state of North Carolina. She is very proud of her Cherokee culture and her past. The Cherokee are just one of many Native American groups who live in the United States today.

"Native American" or "Indian" are names for the first people to live in the land that became the United States of America. It is important to understand how Native Americans lived long ago. Native Americans are part of our country's history. History is the story of the past. In this lesson we'll look back at our country's first communities.

Native American Storytelling

Many different groups of Native Americans lived in this land long ago. Each group had its own culture. But one thing most Native Americans shared is a love of storytelling. They still do today. The following story was written by Tina Naiche (NAH chee), a young Apache. The Apache are a group of Native Americans who live in the southwest part of our country.

MANY VOICES LITERATURE

Story by Tina Naiche, written in 1976.

Coyote Gets Turkey Up a Tree

Coyote is a great figure for the Apaches. He is good at tricking other animals but he is always getting fooled himself. Coyote stories show our pleasure in outwitting our enemies— and they also show how easy it is to be fooled.

Here's one way Coyote was fooled.

Coyote found Turkey up in a tree.

He knew it would be easy to catch him. All he had to do was chop down the tree.

Coyote chopped and chopped. Just as the tree was about to fall, Turkey flew to another tree.

Coyote knew what to do. He got busy chopping that tree down too. He chopped and chopped. Then just as the tree was falling, Turkey flew again.

That went on all day. By evening Coyote was lying on the ground panting. Turkey just flew away home.

Many Cultures

What does the story tell you about the Apache? Like most Native American groups, they believed people could learn from animals.

Long ago, Native Americans shared some beliefs, such as learning from animals. But they also had many differences. Some groups were as unlike each other as people from different countries are today. Each group of people had its own special culture. Each had its own language and its own religion.

Native American cultures were partly shaped by the natural resources around them. Look at the map on the next page. You can see that buffalo roamed the Great Plains in the middle of what is now the United States. The Plains Indians skillfully used the buffalo for food, clothing, and shelter. Look at the map again. What can you tell about the cultures of other Native American groups?

National Museum of the American Indian

The Plains Indians decorated buffalo hide and used it to make robes and moccasins.

National Museum of the American Indian

Joslyn Art Museum

NATIVE AMERICAN CULTURAL AREAS

MAKAH
CHINOOK
BLACKFOOT
LAKOTA
CROW
CHEYENNE
MENOMINEE
Lake Superior
Lake Michigan
Lake Huron
L. Ontario
Lake Erie
IROQUOIS
WAMPANOAG
DELAWARE
POMO
UTE
ILLINOIS
POWHATAN
HOPI   ANASAZI
NAVAJO
ZUNI
APACHE
COMANCHE
CHEROKEE
CHICKASAW
ATLANTIC
OCEAN
PACIFIC
OCEAN
CADDO
COAHUILTECAN
TIMUCUA
SEMINOLE
Gulf of Mexico

Northwest Coast		Plains
California-Intermountain		Eastern Woodlands
Southwest		Southeast

0   200   400 Miles
0   200   400 Kilometers

MAP WORK

Native American groups living in the same area shared similar cultures.

1. In which area did the Pomo live? What did people of that area make?

2. Which Native American group lived by Lake Michigan?

3. How might the Timucua and the Zuni have been alike and different?

From this map you can see where different groups of Native Americans lived long ago. Each color stands for a different cultural area. Groups in the same area shared a similar culture. Find the Native American group called the Anasazi (ah nuh SAH zee) on the map. How did they probably get food? How can you tell?

Living Off the Land

Natural resources helped shape the way Native Americans lived in communities. Look again at the map on page 73. In the Eastern Woodland culture group, find the Iroquois. The land they once lived on is now part of New York State. It was mostly forests. On the rich land they grew corn, beans, and squash. The Iroquois lived in shelters covered with bark called longhouses. These houses held many families. Water came from the lakes and rivers in the Northeast. Today many Iroquois still live in this area.

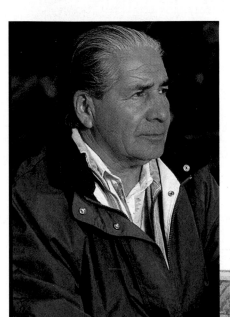

Dr. Oren Lyons is a leader of the Iroquois people today (left). Long ago Iroquois families shared a longhouse made of wood and bark (below).

From the map on page 73, locate the Makah (mah KAH). How do you think their environment influenced the way they lived? They lived along the West Coast. The Pacific Ocean and the rivers were valuable resources. The Makah were skilled fishers. Today some Makah still live and fish in this area.

WHY IT MATTERS

Native Americans are an important part of our country today. Stormi Welch's Cherokee people live in North Carolina and Oklahoma. As with many Native American groups, their culture continues to be an important part of Cherokee life today.

In learning about the history of the United States, it is important to study how Native Americans lived long ago. In the next lesson we will read about the Anasazi. We will learn about their land, resources, and culture. We will also see how part of their culture lives on today.

To hunt seals and whales, the Makah used canoes carved from logs.

Reviewing Facts and Ideas

SUM IT UP

- History is the story of the past.
- Native Americans were the first people to live in the land that is now the United States.
- There are many different Native American groups in our country today. Each has its own special culture.

THINK ABOUT IT

1. What is history?
2. **FOCUS** Who lived in the first American communities?
3. **THINKING SKILL** How was the Iroquois community *like* your community? How was it *different*? How can you tell?
4. **GEOGRAPHY** Look at the map on page 73. How do you think geography influenced the Seminole?

COMING TOGETHER AT A
POWWOW

Native Americans of yesterday and today have many different cultures. Yet one thing most share is a legacy of music and dance.

Today the powwow is one way Native Americans celebrate their culture and their past. Long ago, powwows were used to give good luck to hunters and farmers.

If you were part of a powwow today, you would watch and perform dances and songs from long ago. You might also make new friends. Let's see what it's like to join in at a powwow.

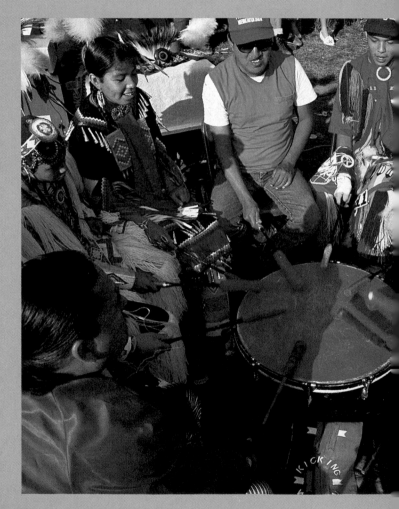

The players and singers around the drum are part of a group called "The Drum" (above). It provides the "heartbeat" for singing and dancing. Young people often make their own costumes (right).

Native Americans in the past also enjoyed visiting with each other. The woman and girls are doing beadwork.

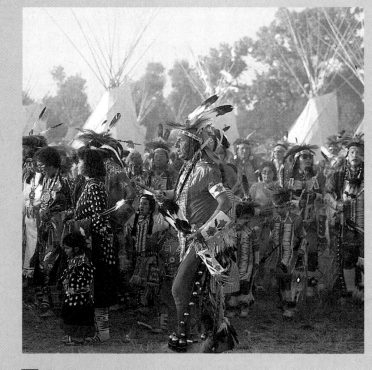

Powwows bring together old and young, boys and girls, and men and women. Some people dress in everyday clothing. Others wear traditional Native American clothing.

The Geography of Mesa Verde

Focus Activity

READ TO LEARN
What is the geography of Mesa Verde like?

VOCABULARY
desert
canyon
cliff
mesa
technology

PLACE
Four Corners
Mesa Verde

READ ALOUD

Here the land is dotted with table-flat landforms that rise to the hot sun.

Here dramatic cliffs drop suddenly into deep canyons.

Life in the Desert

Have you ever seen a place like the one just described? It is an area in the southwestern part of our country called a desert. A desert is a very dry environment where little rain falls. On a summer's day, the temperature in the desert can get extremely hot. But at night, the temperature drops and it's much cooler.

Look at the map on the next page. It shows part of the states of Colorado, New Mexico, Utah, and Arizona. This desert area is often called the Four Corners. Can you see why? The four states all meet in one place. Long ago no states were there. But there were communities. And the people who lived in these communities were called the Anasazi.

A Difficult Environment

As you learned in the last lesson, Native Americans made good use of natural resources. The Iroquois lived in the northeastern part of our country. They used trees to make houses. The Plains Indians of the West hunted buffalo to use the skins for clothing and shelter. You read that the Makah lived in the northwestern part of the United States. They skillfully used trees to build their homes and boats.

The Anasazi also made the best of their very dry environment. The Anasazi were mostly farmers. They grew corn, beans, and squash. They also raised turkeys, which need little water.

The Anasazi used the resources of the desert to meet their other needs too. They used plants to make shoes and clothes. They also made pottery from the clay of the dry ground.

The Anasazi made sandals from the yucca (YUK uh) plant of the desert.

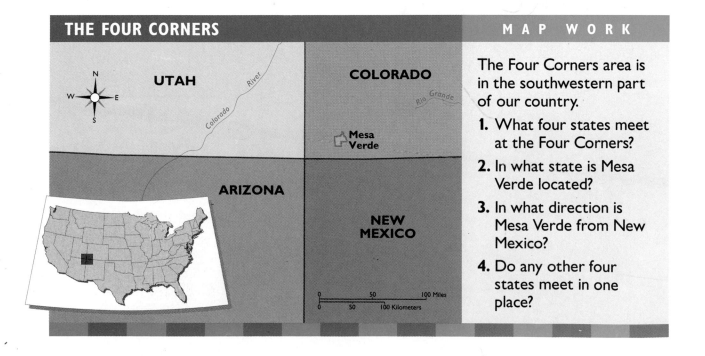

THE FOUR CORNERS

UTAH
COLORADO
Colorado River
Rio Grande
Mesa Verde
ARIZONA
NEW MEXICO

0   50   100 Miles
0   50   100 Kilometers

MAP WORK

The Four Corners area is in the southwestern part of our country.

1. What four states meet at the Four Corners?
2. In what state is Mesa Verde located?
3. In what direction is Mesa Verde from New Mexico?
4. Do any other four states meet in one place?

Mesas, Cliffs, and Canyons

The land of the Southwest is not all flat. As you can see in these pictures, there are many different landforms. To the Anasazi these shapes were not just beautiful. They were also great natural resources.

Deep canyons were carved into the land by mighty rivers. A canyon is a deep river valley with steep sides. Many communities were built along the walls of these canyons. Some Anasazi even made buildings and homes in the cliffs! A cliff is the steep face of a rock.

From the pictures here, find the landform that looks like a high, flat table. The name for that landform is mesa (MAY suh). In fact, *mesa* is the Spanish word for "table." Sometimes the Anasazi built their homes in the steep sides of mesas. Like canyons and cliffs, mesas protected them from enemies and the environment.

One Anasazi community in this area was Mesa Verde (VUR dee). The Spanish word for "green" is *verde*. You already know what *mesa* means. Can you guess why this area is called Mesa Verde?

Mesas and cliffs are two southwestern landforms. Desert wildlife includes lizards.

Using Technology

The Anasazi made use of technology (tek NAHL uh jee) to help them in different ways. Technology is the use of tools and materials to serve people's needs. Pointed sticks were made to dig ditches for collecting the little rain that fell at Mesa Verde. The water was then used to grow crops.

WHY IT MATTERS

Suppose it is a time long ago, before your community was built. There were no highways or telephones. The Native Americans have already built many communities. Like people today, they used the land around them for all of their resources.

In the next lesson you will learn how the Anasazi worked with the land around them. You will see how they lived in a special community in the land of mesas and canyons.

The Anasazi made stone axes to clear fields for farming.

Reviewing Facts and Ideas

SUM IT UP

- The environment of a desert is very dry.
- The landforms of the area now called the Four Corners include canyons, cliffs, and mesas.
- The Anasazi were one group who lived in this desert area. They worked as farmers to meet their needs.
- Technology improved the life of the Anasazi.

THINK ABOUT IT

1. What is the climate of Mesa Verde?

2. **FOCUS** What is the geography of Mesa Verde like?

3. **THINKING SKILL** What do you _predict_ would happen to the plants at Mesa Verde if it did not rain there for a long time? Explain your answer.

4. **WRITE** Look again at the pictures in this lesson. In your own words, describe the landforms you see.

Mesa Verde Long Ago

READ ALOUD

A chickadee chirps in the distance. It is early morning, and an eight-year-old boy stirs in his bed. He has a busy day ahead of him.

Morning at Mesa Verde

The description you have just read does not sound very unusual, does it? But let's take a closer look. The boy's bed is actually a mat made from the leaves of the yucca plant. His blanket is made from turkey feathers. His "pajamas" are woven from plants.

He lives with his family in a house with many rooms. It is built into the side of a mesa. It is called a cliff house. As he starts his day, the people in his community are already busy. Some men and women are making pots out of clay. Others are sharpening stones to use as knives. The young boy is eager to join them.

The boy's name is Little Rabbit. He is an eight-year-old Anasazi who lives at Mesa Verde. The time is 1,000 years ago. Let's see what Little Rabbit's day is like.

Focus Activity

READ TO LEARN
How did the Anasazi live?

VOCABULARY
kiva
artifact

Community Life

To start the day, Little Rabbit finds his father, Strong Deer. He is outside sharpening an arrow. The Anasazi men sometimes hunt with spears and bows and arrows. They also farm and weave blankets. Little Rabbit is eager for the day he will be old enough to hunt and weave. "Not today," says his father. "Today you will help your mother."

Little Rabbit's mother is Swift Raven. Like many women, she takes care of the children and the home. She also cooks, makes pottery, and weaves baskets. Little Rabbit's new little sister, Bright Owl, is strapped to a board on her mother's back. "Good morning, Little Rabbit," his mother says. "Will you get me some water for the turkeys?" Little Rabbit takes a basket to the well. The baskets are woven so tightly that no water can spill. That is a good thing. Little Rabbit knows that water can be hard to find.

Soon all the women and children will go to the nearby field to gather beans and corn. All of the families work together and share their food. From the Infographic on the next pages, you can see different ways the Anasazi worked together.

Infographic

A Day with the Anasazi

Pretend you are standing across from the cliff house where Little Rabbit and his family lived long ago. What might you see?

Older women help care for the young children.

Older men are sitting in the sun, telling stories.

The hole in the ground is the entrance to a special room used for religious purposes called a kiva.

Little Rabbit is carrying a basket filled with water.

Many storage rooms
are used to hold
crops and grain.

Women and children are
grinding corn.

Swift Raven is making
clay pots for cooking
and storage.

Strong Deer is sharpening
an arrow for hunting.

85

The Anasazi Culture

Religion was an important part of Anasazi culture. In the Infographic you learned that the kiva was used for religious purposes. Sometimes it was also used as a workplace.

The drawing below gives you a close-up view of a kiva in Little Rabbit's community. It was used mostly by men. At times women used the kivas as well. The Anasazi believed that people came to Earth from special holes in the ground. A kiva had a hole for this reason.

The walls of the kiva have colorful paintings. Stone benches are built into the walls. A fire in the center of the floor provides warmth.

Not all religious ceremonies take place in the kiva. For Little Rabbit tomorrow will be an exciting day. There will be a dance held in a field. Dancers will give thanks for the ripe food from the fields. They will wear colorful outfits and masks. One day Little Rabbit will take part in the dance. It too is a part of Anasazi culture.

The Anasazi used a ladder to enter a kiva.

WHY IT MATTERS

How do we know what Little Rabbit's day might have been like 1,000 years ago? We do not know for sure. People did not write or take photographs back then. Scientists have tried to piece together the clues by looking at artifacts. Artifacts are objects left behind by a group of people. Pottery, tools, pieces of clothing, and buildings are all artifacts.

Today, Native Americans like this Pueblo woman still make pottery similar to the Anasazi pottery of long ago.

The Anasazi left Mesa Verde and other communities about 700 years ago. Scientists are not sure why. Some say that perhaps there was no rain for a long time. Or perhaps they were forced out by another Native American group.

Although the Anasazi have disappeared, parts of their culture remain. Today Pueblo (PWEB loh) villages have kivas. The kivas are just like the ones the Anasazi had long ago. In the next lesson you will learn another way the culture of the Anasazi continues today.

✔/// Reviewing Facts and Ideas

SUM IT UP

- The Anasazi lived in communities built into the sides of mesas.
- Children helped with many tasks.
- Men hunted, farmed, and weaved.
- Women worked in the fields, made pottery, and took care of the younger children.
- Religion was an important part of Anasazi culture.

THINK ABOUT IT

1. What are two ways the Anasazi worked together in their community?

2. **FOCUS** How did the Anasazi live?

3. **THINKING SKILL** _Sort_ activities people did at Mesa Verde into fun activities and work activities.

4. **GEOGRAPHY** What landforms are in Little Rabbit's community?

Mesa Verde Today

READ ALOUD

"Welcome to Mesa Verde National Park. My name is Maxwell Rudolph. Only people who work for the park can live here. My father is a Park Ranger."

Mesa Verde National Park

You have just been welcomed to Mesa Verde National Park by Maxwell Rudolph. Maxwell is a nine-year-old boy who lives in the park with his family. Only a few people live in the park today. But long ago many Anasazi lived here in a big community.

As you have read, the Anasazi mysteriously left Mesa Verde long ago. No group of people has lived in the cliff houses since. Today visitors can see the place much as it used to be.

Over many years much of the land in our country has changed. Paved highways have been laid down. Skyscrapers and shopping malls have been built. But as a national park, Mesa Verde has been protected from change. Let's join Maxwell and his father for a tour to see how the Anasazi lived over 700 years ago.

Focus Activity

READ TO LEARN
What can be learned by visiting Mesa Verde National Park today?

VOCABULARY
museum

PLACE
Mesa Verde
   National Park

Welcome to Mesa Verde!

From the entrance to the park, it takes a half-hour drive just to reach the Far View Visitor Center. That gives you an idea of how big the park is! At the Visitor Center, Maxwell's father greets thousands of visitors every year. Look at the map of Mesa Verde National Park below. It shows you where places to visit are located.

"The best place to start our tour is at the museum," says Mr. Rudolph. A museum is a place where people can look at objects of art, science, or history.

"From here, there are many places to go," says Mr. Rudolph. "Of these places, you can walk by homes from about 1,000 years ago."

By visiting Mesa Verde or looking at jewelry and other objects, people can learn about the Anasazi culture.

MESA VERDE NATIONAL PARK

Cortez

COLORADO

- Place of Interest
- Road
- Park Boundary
- // Park Entrance

Far View Visitor Center

Mancos River

Spruce Tree House
Long House
Museum
Cliff Palace
Balcony House

0 2 4 Miles
0 2 4 Kilometers

MAP WORK

Mesa Verde National Park was created in 1906.

1. What are some places of interest in the park?
2. How far is the museum from the Visitor Center?
3. What happens to the road before it reaches the Visitor Center?

Respecting the Past

Mr. Rudolph takes visitors to sites where the Anasazi lived long ago. On the paths, they hike past yucca plants like the ones used every day by the Anasazi. Visitors climb ladders to reach the old rooms. They also climb down ladders to see the kivas. There are many different things Mr. Rudolph hopes the visitors will learn.

"Of course, I want people to learn what life might have been like long ago," he says. "But that is not the most important thing. I want them to respect the past. I tell them to act as if they are walking through someone's home—because they are!"

Mr. Rudolph also tells visitors to Mesa Verde not to touch or remove any artifacts. He then reminds them that the kivas are still very important to some Native Americans today. Pueblo, Zuni, and Hopi people still live in nearby areas. Many of their beliefs and customs are similar to those of the Anasazi long ago.

Visitors climb a ladder to reach rooms at Long House (left) and see Anasazi homes at Cliff Palace (right).

As the tour ends Mr. Rudolph leaves visitors with an important reminder: "We study the past to learn something we can use today. One of the most important things we can learn from the Anasazi is to work well together in our communities. Another important lesson is to respect nature and think about the long-term effects of our actions."

WHY IT MATTERS

By studying the past we learn how people lived in communities. One way to study and learn about the past is to visit a museum or a place like Mesa Verde National Park.

Look around your own community. Ancient artifacts may not be in your backyard. But your community does have a history that goes back a long time. And chances are, if you study that history, you'll learn something about your community today.

Mr. Rudolph teaches children about the Anasazi at Mesa Verde.

✓ Reviewing Facts and Ideas

SUM IT UP

- Visitors to Mesa Verde National Park can learn about the past by seeing artifacts.
- Visitors can see what life was like long ago.
- Visitors must be respectful of the sites they see.
- By learning about the past, we can learn about our communities today.

THINK ABOUT IT

1. Why is the museum a good place to start the park tour?

2. **FOCUS** What can be learned by visiting Mesa Verde National Park today?

3. **THINKING SKILL** What do you _predict_ might happen to Mesa Verde if it were not a national park?

4. **GEOGRAPHY** Look at the map on page 89. Use the scale to find the distance from the Balcony House to the museum.

THINKINGSKILLS

Making Decisions

VOCABULARY

decision

WHY THE SKILL MATTERS

Every day in your life you make decisions. A decision is a choice that is made. When you choose what clothes to wear in the morning, you are making a decision.

Sometimes making a decision is very easy. You might know that one choice would be a big mistake and the other would be exactly right. But sometimes, making decisions can be hard. Use the Helping Yourself box on the next page to guide you in making decisions.

USING THE SKILL

Suppose that you and your family are visiting Mesa Verde National Park. You have only one day to spend there. After you have visited the museum, your mother says it's up to you to decide where to go next. How would you decide what sites to see?

In making a decision, it is important to set a goal. Your goal could be to see and learn as much as possible at Mesa Verde in only one day.

You could then gather information to learn what your choices are. Pictured above is a visitor's guide to Mesa Verde National Park. It provides important facts about different sites.

Each choice from the guide has advantages and disadvantages. Cliff Palace is the biggest place. Spruce Tree House is not quite as large. Both are near each other.

Long House is the second largest place. It has a beautiful view. But it is far from both Spruce Tree House and Cliff Palace.

You decide that too much time would be spent traveling to Long House. Your decision could be to visit Cliff Palace. Then, if there were time, you could also visit Spruce Tree House. After all, you have only one day to spend at the park!

TRYING THE SKILL

Now suppose you are at the gift shop near the museum. Your mother has given you $5 to spend. From the picture below, you can see what things you can buy for $5. What will you decide to buy? What should you do first to make your decision? If your goal is to learn what Mesa Verde is like today, what would you choose to buy?

REVIEWING THE SKILL

1. What does it mean to make a decision?

2. What is one decision you made today?

3. How did you make your decision?

4. Why is it important to learn how to make good decisions?

PRICE LIST

History Book	$5.00	Photo Book	$5.00
Hat	$5.00	Patch and Pin	$5.00
Tour Guide	$5.00	Key Chains	2 for $5.00
Coloring Book	$5.00		

CHAPTER 3 REVIEW

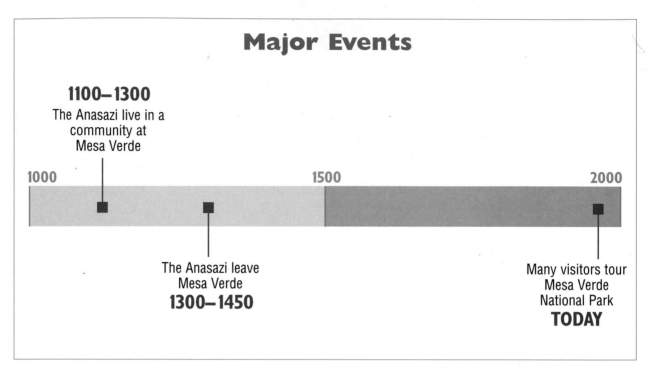

Major Events

1100–1300
The Anasazi live in a community at Mesa Verde

1000   1500   2000

The Anasazi leave Mesa Verde
1300–1450

Many visitors tour Mesa Verde National Park
TODAY

THINKING ABOUT VOCABULARY

Number a piece of paper from 1 to 10. Read the definition of each underlined word. Write **T** if the definition is true and **F** if it is false. If it is false, write a sentence correctly defining the word.

1. A <u>desert</u> is a very dry environment with little rainfall.

2. <u>Technology</u> is the study of how animals live on a farm.

3. <u>Artifacts</u> are tools used to dig up objects left by a group of people.

4. The landform that looks like a high, flat table is a <u>cliff</u>.

5. A <u>canyon</u> is a deep river valley with steep sides.

6. The story of our past is our <u>history</u>.

7. A <u>museum</u> is a place where people can look at objects of art, science, or history.

8. A <u>mesa</u> is a steep face of a rock.

9. A <u>kiva</u> is a large farming tool.

10. A <u>decision</u> is making a choice.

THINKING ABOUT FACTS

1. How did the natural resources in an area matter to the people living there? Give an example.

2. In what area of our country did the Anasazi live long ago?

3. Why did the Anasazi build their homes in cliffs and in the sides of mesas?

4. How do we know what life was probably like for Native Americans long ago?

5. Why do we study the past?

THINK AND WRITE

WRITING A JOURNAL ENTRY
Suppose you lived at Mesa Verde long ago. Write a journal entry about a day in your life. Describe what you eat, what you wear, and what you do during the day.

WRITING A COMPARISON
Write a paragraph comparing the life of the Anasazi and the Makah. You may want to compare the area they lived in and what they ate.

WRITING A POSTER
Write a poster encouraging people to visit Mesa Verde National Park. What would you describe about the park? What places would you want to tell people about?

APPLYING THINKING SKILLS

MAKING DECISIONS
Answer the following questions to practice the skill of decision making.

1. What are the steps to follow in making a decision?

2. How do you decide what homework to do first? What do you think about before deciding?

3. Suppose you are invited to play by two different friends. One you play with often. The other you have wanted to play with for a long time. Identify the steps you would take in deciding. What are the possible results of each choice?

4. How do you decide what to do for fun on a rainy day?

5. Why is it important to consider all choices when making a decision?

Summing Up the Chapter

Review the chapter and complete a copy of the main idea table below. In the table legs, list how the Anasazi met the basic needs shown in the table feet. Then write an answer to the question: In what ways did the natural resources of the area help shape the way the Anasazi lived?

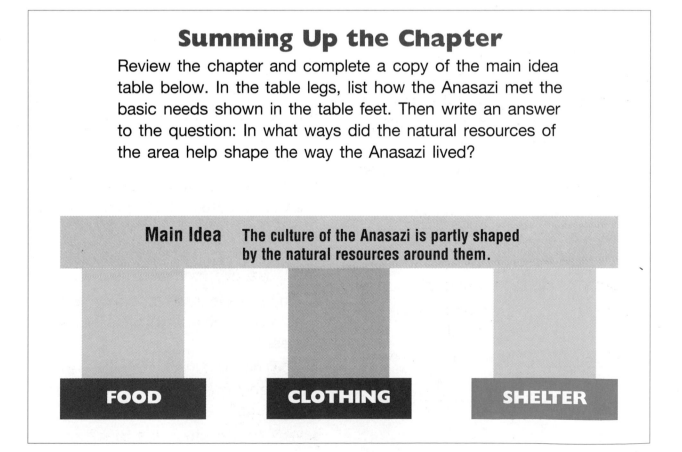

Main Idea The culture of the Anasazi is partly shaped by the natural resources around them.

FOOD   CLOTHING   SHELTER

An English Colony at Jamestown

THINKING ABOUT GEOGRAPHY AND HISTORY

About four hundred years ago, a group of people set sail from England to North America. They built a village called Jamestown.

The land where the English settled was home to a group of Native Americans called the Powhatan. It was a place rich in forests and rivers. As you read Chapter 4, see how both groups of people used the land's resources. Start by studying the map and time line here.

1607

Colonists arrive at Jamestown

1614

Marriage of Pocahontas and John Rolfe

Jamestown,
Virginia

TODAY

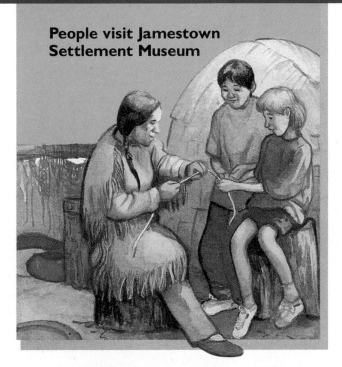

People visit Jamestown
Settlement Museum

The Geography of Jamestown

READ ALOUD

"There are fair meadows and goodly tall trees . . . beautiful strawberries and excellent good timber."

Focus Activity

READ TO LEARN
What is the geography of Jamestown like?

VOCABULARY
bay
coastal plain

PLACES
Jamestown
Virginia
Chesapeake Bay

Land of Many Resources

These words were written a long time ago by George Percy. He was a passenger on a small ship that sailed from England to North America in 1607. Percy and other Englishmen on the ship dreamed of gold and other riches in the land that is now the United States.

Look at the map on the next page. The area where the Englishmen started their community is called Jamestown. It was named for the King of England, James I. Today it is in the state of Virginia.

As you can tell from George Percy's words, the environment of Jamestown seemed good. There were trees for building houses and food to eat. It looked like a fine place to build a community. In this lesson let's take a closer look at the geography of Jamestown.

Using Natural Resources

The English were not the first people to build communities in Virginia. Native Americans had lived in the area for thousands of years. They had learned over time how to make good use of natural resources. Tall pine trees were used for building houses and for making bows and arrows. They also carved out trees and used them as canoes.

Look at the map shown below. In 1607 a Native American people called the Powhatan (pow uh TAN) lived in what is now eastern Virginia. They fished in the James River and Chesapeake Bay. A bay is a body of water partly surrounded by land. Can you find where Chesapeake Bay meets the James River?

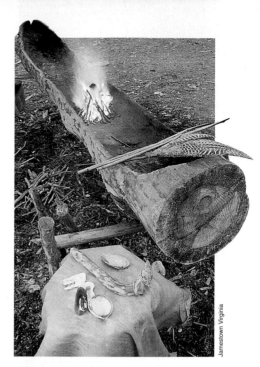

Native Americans used resources like trees to build canoes and other important items.

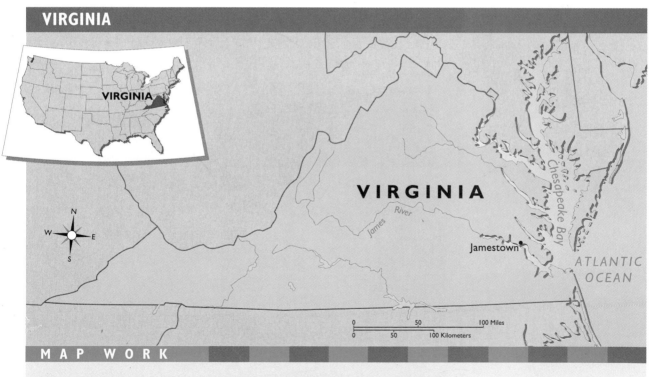

VIRGINIA

MAP WORK

English colonists built a community at Jamestown in 1607.

1. How far is Jamestown from the Atlantic Ocean?
2. What body of water is between the Atlantic Ocean and the James River?
3. Why do you think canoes were important to the Powhatan people?

99

Living with the Environment

In the last chapter you read about how the Anasazi used natural resources to survive in the dry environment of Mesa Verde. But the Powhatan's environment around Jamestown was different. There was plenty of rain for plants and trees. The area around Jamestown is a coastal plain. A coastal plain is flat land along the coast. It was good for farming. The Powhatan grew corn, beans, and squash. They also hunted deer and other animals.

The English also liked Jamestown's environment. They saw the location as a good place to build a community. Their boats had a good port in the deep waters of Chesapeake Bay. The waters, which surrounded the English on three sides, helped to protect the English against attack. The Native Americans and the Spanish often used land routes for attack.

Links to
CURRENT EVENTS

Catch of the Day!

What are new ways people use natural resources?

Virginia's waters have long provided people with food. Today fish and shellfish are not only found in the water, but also on land! They are now raised in tanks on fish farms in Virginia.

Where do the foods you eat come from? Keep a list. Then compare your list with others from your class.

This artwork from the 1800s shows the English using resources of the forest to build Jamestown.

The Granger Collection

WHY IT MATTERS

Environment makes a difference to communities. People need resources from the environment to live. This fact was true in our country's past too.

For the Powhatan long ago, the environment provided resources for farming and fishing. For the English, Jamestown provided a good port for ships. The port was also useful in protecting against attacks by their enemies. The land around Jamestown also provided wood for building houses.

For both the Powhatan and the English, survival meant living with the environment around them.

Corn, squash, and beans were among the foods that the Powhatan grew.

✔️ Reviewing Facts and Ideas

SUM IT UP

- Hundreds of years ago, people sailed from England to build a community in the area they named Jamestown.

- Native Americans were already living in communities in the area around Jamestown.

- Jamestown's environment was good for farming.

- The land around Jamestown was called a coastal plain.

- Chesapeake Bay provided a good port for the English ships. It also provided food for the Powhatan.

THINK ABOUT IT

1. How did the English and the Powhatan use the natural resources at Jamestown?

2. **FOCUS** What is the geography of Jamestown like?

3. **THINKING SKILL** Suppose you wanted to build a community. How would you _decide_ on a place? State your goals.

4. **GEOGRAPHY** Name two bodies of water near Jamestown. You can use the map on page 99.

NOVA BRITANNIA.
OFFERING MOST
Excellent fruites by Planting in
VIRGINIA.

Exciting all such as be well affected
to further the same.

LONDON
Printed for SAMVEL MACHAM, and are to be sold at
his Shop in Pauls Church-yard, at the
Signe of the Bul-head.
1609.

Bettmann

Focus Activity

READ TO LEARN
What was life like for the colonists?

VOCABULARY
colony
colonist
slavery

PEOPLE
Powhatan
John Smith
John Rolfe
Pocahontas

Jamestown Long Ago

READ ALOUD

"I insist that the guns and swords, the cause of all our jealousy and uneasiness, be removed and sent away."

Powhatan and the English Meet

These words were said by Powhatan, the leader of the Powhatan people in 1609. He was speaking to John Smith, the leader of the English at Jamestown. Powhatan was hoping for peace between his people and the English.

The Powhatan and the English met in 1607. That was the year the English first arrived at Jamestown. It was a very long time ago— almost 400 years!

The meeting between the Powhatan and the English is one of the early stories in the history of our country. It is a story of good times. It is also the story of hard times. The English struggled to build a community at Jamestown. The Powhatan struggled to find a way to live peacefully with the English. In this lesson you will meet some of the important people who helped the new community survive.

The English at Jamestown

Men like John Smith were sent by England to start a colony at Jamestown. A colony is a place that is ruled by another country. The English hoped that the colony would provide resources and riches like gold for people back in England.

The people sent to Jamestown were called colonists. A colonist is someone who lives in a colony. Colonists did not only want to build a new community. They also hoped that they, too, would get rich from Jamestown's resources.

Powhatan (below left) and his people were already living around Jamestown when John Smith (in frame) and other English colonists arrived.

The Granger Collection

103

Difficult Times

Soon after arriving at Jamestown, the colonists found life hard. They had problems growing food. Many of them were not farmers. They did not realize how hard they needed to work. Some colonists even refused to work.

A strong leader was needed to help the English. They found one in John Smith. He made a new rule. He said, "He that will not work, shall not eat."

Smith made another important decision. He asked the Powhatan for help. The colonists learned how to grow corn and other food from the Powhatan.

Even with the help of Powhatan and his people, the colonists struggled. The winter of 1609 was called a "starving time." There was little food. Colonists were dying from diseases. Read once again the words of colonist George Percy. What does he say about life in Jamestown?

Colonists had to learn how to farm for food in order to survive.

MANY VOICES
PRIMARY SOURCE

Written by George Percy, about 1609.

Our men were destroyed with cruel diseases and swellings and burning fevers and by wars. Some departed suddenly, but for the most part they died of famine. There were never Englishmen left in such misery as we were. The settlers began to feel the sharp hunger which no man can truly describe.

departed: died
famine: starving, hunger

The Colony Survives

Life continued to be hard for the colonists. Their dreams of finding gold never came true. But in 1612 some changes turned the colony around. A colonist named John Rolfe began growing a new kind of tobacco and sending it back to England. The tobacco was sold for a lot of money. It helped make the colony and England richer.

Until this time the English sometimes fought with the Powhatan. But in 1614 John Rolfe married Pocahontas. She was the daughter of Powhatan. Their marriage led to a long time of peace between the Powhatan and the English. The colony began to grow.

By 1624 other English colonies were also growing along the coast of the Atlantic Ocean. To learn more about the early years of these colonies turn the page.

The marriage of Pocahontas and John Rolfe brought peace to Jamestown. A statue of Pocahontas stands in Jamestown today.

The Granger Collection

Infographic

The Thirteen Colonies

Virginia was not the only English colony in North America. Soon there were 13 English colonies along the Atlantic coast. These colonies later became the first thirteen states of our country.

PLYMOUTH, MASSACHUSETTS

The Pilgrims started Plymouth, Massachusetts, in 1620 to practice their own religion. The Wampanoag (wahm puh NOH ahg) people helped the Pilgrims fish and farm. To thank God for their harvest the Pilgrims had a Thanksgiving meal with the Wampanoag.

Maine (part of Massachusetts)

New York

New Hampshire

Massachusetts

Rhode Island

Connecticut

Pennsylvania

New Jersey

Delaware

Virginia

Maryland

North Carolina

South Carolina

Georgia

PHILADELPHIA, PENNSYLVANIA

William Penn followed the Quaker religion. In 1682 in Pennsylvania he started a community called Philadelphia. Penn became friends with the Delaware people. They signed a peace agreement that lasted many years.

SAVANNAH, GEORGIA

Savannah became the first colonial community in Georgia in 1733. Some of the colonists here were people who owed money in England. They repaid the money they owed by farming land.

Africans Arrive

Many different people came to the colonies. Some came to build new lives. Some came to seek riches. Others were looking for religious freedom. Some who came had been forced into slavery. Slavery is the practice of one person owning another.

People forced into slavery in the colonies came from Africa. They were captured and taken across the Atlantic Ocean in slave ships. They were then sold into slavery.

WHY IT MATTERS

Starting a community was hard for the colonists. But after years of struggle, the little community of Jamestown grew larger. It was joined by other colonies. Later, these colonies—13 in all—came together as a new country, the United States of America.

Bettmann

African people were sold into slavery in the colonies.

✓ Reviewing Facts and Ideas

SUM IT UP

- The English colonists began Jamestown in 1607.

- The winter of 1609 was called a "starving time." Many colonists died.

- In 1612 John Rolfe introduced a new kind of tobacco. It made the colony richer.

- There were 13 English colonies, which later became the United States of America.

THINK ABOUT IT

1. Why did the English set sail for Jamestown?

2. **FOCUS** What was life like for the colonists?

3. **THINKING SKILL** Look at the Infographic on page 106. Put Plymouth, Philadelphia, and Savannah in *order* by the dates they were started.

4. **WRITE** Imagine you are a colonist living in Jamestown. Write a letter describing your new life to your family back in England.

Jamestown Today

"We do many of the things that the Powhatan and the English did long ago. We have cooking fires burning. We tan deer hides. We even show kids making rope."

A Step Back in Time

These are the words of Erik Holland. He is a guide at Jamestown Settlement. The settlement is a living history museum. A living history museum takes you back in time. It is a place where people dress, talk, and do things as they did long ago. Erik's job is to show people how English colonists and the Powhatan lived here in the 1600s.

Let's visit Jamestown Settlement. The first thing you notice is people's clothing. Guides like Erik are dressed in clothes like those worn by Native Americans or colonists hundreds of years ago. While they may look different at first, Erik tells visitors: "My moccasins are almost like the tennis shoes kids wear today. Tennis shoes are made from animal skins. So are my moccasins."

Focus Activity

READ TO LEARN
What do visitors see at Jamestown Settlement?

VOCABULARY
living history museum

PLACES
Jamestown Settlement

English Village

Like Erik's moccasins, most of the things you see at Jamestown Settlement are not the actual artifacts from long ago. Instead, they are copies. People have studied Jamestown's history very carefully to create copies that look real.

Jamestown/Yorktown Foundation

Look at the pictures on this page. The English houses are built from plaster and grass. The clothes people are wearing are made from wool and cotton. The ship instruments they are using are made from iron and wood.

Near the houses are three ships docked in the James River. They are named *Susan Constant, Godspeed,* and *Discovery.* They are copies of the original boats colonists like Captain John Smith sailed on many years ago. Climb aboard! You will see how small the spaces are. You can imagine how crowded it must have been. After all, the colonists also had to bring pigs, chickens, goats, and lots of supplies.

Fun at Jamestown Settlement includes visiting ships and seeing how people lived in the 1600s.

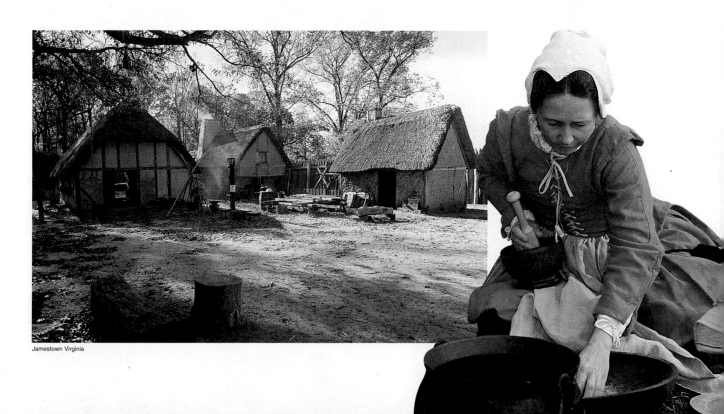

Jamestown Virginia

Powhatan Village

In talking about visiting Jamestown Settlement today, Erik tells visitors, "It's fun to see different cultures from the past. You have seen how the English lived. Now let's see how the Powhatan lived."

In the Powhatan village you can see Native Americans grinding corn. You can see how they cooked their meals. You can even smell fish and meat cooking. But stand back. The fire is hot!

You can actually make rope like the Powhatan did long ago. You will even get to play games that children played long ago. The Powhatan houses were made from wood frames covered with grass. How are they different from the ones the colonists lived in?

At the Powhatan village visitors learn to make rope the way people did long ago.

Learning History

When you visit Jamestown Settlement, something may occur to you. In some ways the lives of these two groups were so different. But in other ways their lives were similar. They both needed to make homes, clothes, and food. They both took care of their communities. As he closes his tour, Erik tells visitors, "By visiting us here you see and do things that people in the past did every day. It's a great way to learn history."

WHY IT MATTERS

Visiting a place like Jamestown Settlement is a fun and interesting way to learn about the history of people and their communities. Reading books, watching movies, and talking to people can also teach you about history.

In our country today, we live with our history all around us. In the next chapter you will learn about another community with a history that is important to its people today.

The Powhatan made needles from bone and used them to sew clothing made from animal skins.

✓ Reviewing Facts and Ideas

SUM IT UP

- Jamestown Settlement was created to show people what life was like long ago.

- Visitors can see and do many things. They can climb aboard ships, smell food cooking, and visit a Powhatan village and an English village. They can even make things like people did long ago!

THINK ABOUT IT

1. What is a living history museum?

2. **FOCUS** What do visitors see at Jamestown Settlement?

3. **THINKING SKILL** How was life in the Powhatan village *like* life for the colonists? How was it *different*?

4. **WRITE** Write a brief travel guide for Jamestown Settlement. Describe what people can visit.

STUDYSKILLS

Reading Time Lines

VOCABULARY
time line

WHY THE SKILL MATTERS
The events you have read about in Jamestown happened hundreds of years ago. Sometimes reading about the past can be confusing. What happened first? What happened next? A time line can tell you the order in which events happened. Reading time lines will help you to understand history.

USING THE SKILL
You have read about how Jamestown grew as a community. How do you think a new community would grow today? Suppose that a group of people call their community "Newtown." Look at the time line below to see how this community might grow.

Read the time line from left to right. The dates tell you that the earliest event is the building of roads and houses. The last event is the opening of the shopping center. What happened the year before the Fire Department started?

Newtown's Early History

1990
Roads are paved and first houses are built

1991
People move into houses

1992
Community leaders are chosen

1993
Fire department is started and hospital opens

1994
Main Street shopping center opens

TRYING THE SKILL

When you read about Jamestown, you saw words such as "long ago" and "starving time." These words told you something about time and let you know when things happened at Jamestown.

There were many important events in Jamestown's early history. The time line below will help you understand the order in which some of these events happened.

This time line shows events between 1600–1615. How many events does it show? Read the time line. What is first on the time line? In what year did the next event happen? What was it?

HELPING Yourself

- **Time lines** show the order in which things happen.
- Read time lines from left to right.
- Note the date of each event.

REVIEWING THE SKILL

1. What do time lines show?

2. Which did the people of Newtown build first—a shopping center or a hospital? How do you know?

3. In what year did John Rolfe and Pocahontas get married?

4. How do time lines help you to understand history?

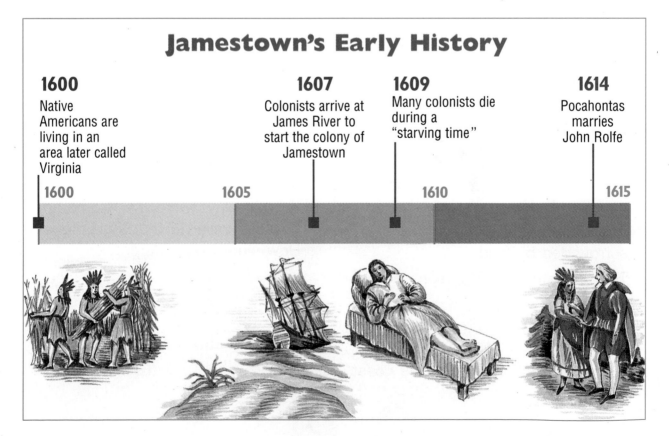

Jamestown's Early History

1600
Native Americans are living in an area later called Virginia

1607
Colonists arrive at James River to start the colony of Jamestown

1609
Many colonists die during a "starving time"

1614
Pocahontas marries John Rolfe

1600   1605   1610   1615

CHAPTER 4 REVIEW

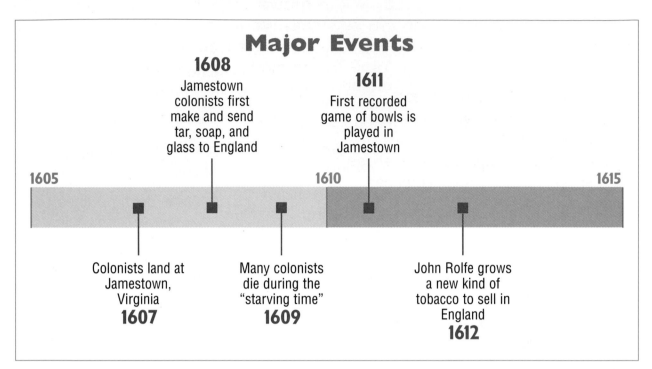

Major Events

1608
Jamestown colonists first make and send tar, soap, and glass to England

1611
First recorded game of bowls is played in Jamestown

1605 · · · · · 1610 · · · · · 1615

Colonists land at Jamestown, Virginia
1607

Many colonists die during the "starving time"
1609

John Rolfe grows a new kind of tobacco to sell in England
1612

THINKING ABOUT VOCABULARY

Number a piece of paper from 1 to 5. Beside each number write the word or term from the list below that matches the statement.

bay   colony
coastal plain   slavery
living history museum

1. A place that is ruled by another country
2. A body of water that is partly surrounded by land
3. The practice of one person owning another
4. A place where people dress, talk, and do things as they did long ago
5. An area of flat land along the coast

THINKING ABOUT FACTS

1. Why was Jamestown a good spot to start a colony?
2. Why did England begin colonies in North America? Why did people come to the colonies?
3. What problems did the first colonists of Jamestown have?
4. Why do people visit Jamestown Settlement today?
5. In what ways were the Powhatan houses similar to the English ones? How were they different?

THINK AND WRITE ◀▤▶

WRITING A COMPARISON
Write a paragraph comparing the geography of Mesa Verde with that of Jamestown.

WRITING A LETTER
Suppose you are a colonist at Jamestown in 1607. Write a letter to somebody in England about your life in North America. Include experiences such as meeting a Native American, building a home, and surviving a hard winter.

WRITING A CONVERSATION
Write a made-up dialogue between a Native American and a colonist at Jamestown.

APPLYING STUDY SKILLS

READING TIME LINES
Answer the following questions to practice the skill of reading time lines. Use the Major Events time line shown on the previous page.

1. What is a time line?
2. What happened in 1609?
3. Which event happened first, the first shipment of goods to England or the development of a new kind of tobacco? In what year did each take place?
4. What is one thing colonists did for fun at Jamestown?
5. When are time lines useful?

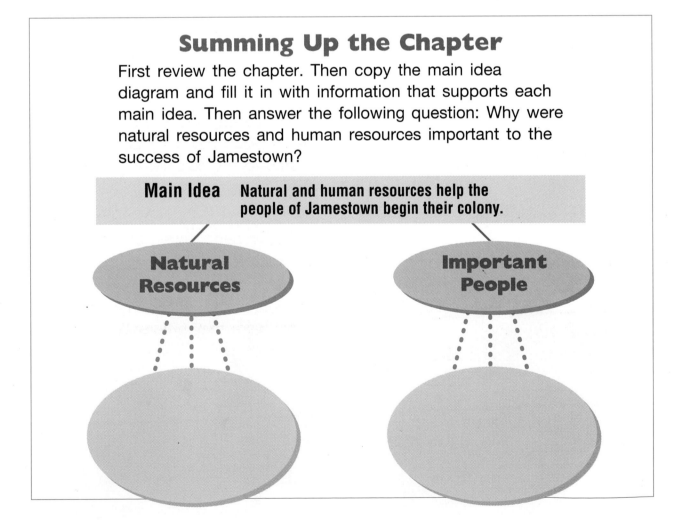

Summing Up the Chapter

First review the chapter. Then copy the main idea diagram and fill it in with information that supports each main idea. Then answer the following question: Why were natural resources and human resources important to the success of Jamestown?

Main Idea Natural and human resources help the people of Jamestown begin their colony.

Natural Resources

Important People

CHAPTER 5

A Spanish Mission in San Antonio

THINKING ABOUT GEOGRAPHY AND HISTORY

Today San Antonio is a busy city on a river in Texas. Long ago Native Americans lived along the same river. Their lives changed when Spanish people came and started a new kind of community.

In Chapter 5 you will learn about these new communities and the growth of San Antonio. You will also see how Spanish culture is still a celebrated part of life in San Antonio today.

1700s

Missions are built

1836

Texas wins freedom from Mexico

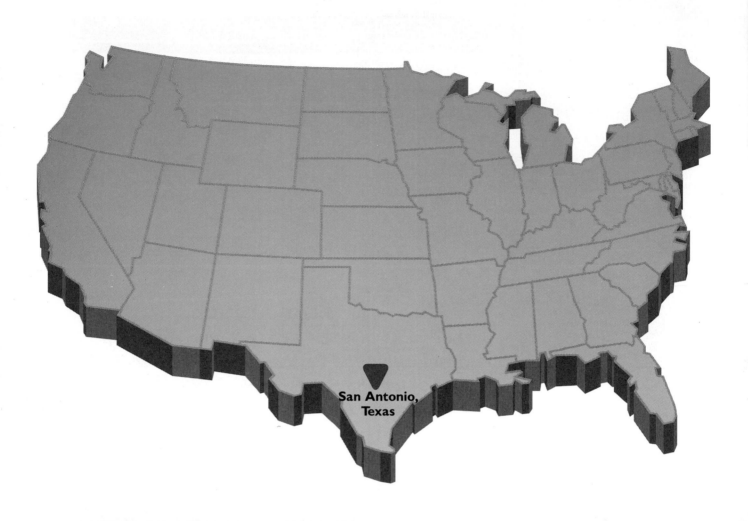

San Antonio,
Texas

TODAY

People enjoy the River Walk
in San Antonio

The Geography of San Antonio

READ ALOUD

Thousands of years ago a Native American group called the Payaya (PĪ yah yah) Indians lived along the San Antonio River. They called it Yanaguana (YAH nah GWAH nah), which means "refreshing waters" in their language. Let's take a walk along the river to see how it is important to people today.

Focus Activity

READ TO LEARN
How is the San Antonio River important?

PLACES
San Antonio, Texas
River Walk
San Antonio River

The River Walk

Pretend it is a hot summer day in San Antonio, Texas. The thermometer reads 93°F. You decide to head for the River Walk.

What is the River Walk? In the 1920s citizens of San Antonio had different ideas about what to build along the San Antonio River. But one idea by a man named Robert Hugman drew a lot of attention. He came up with a plan to build the River Walk. He hoped it would help business and protect the beauty of the river. Today it is an area with sidewalks, trees, restaurants, and shops. It also provides jobs for many people.

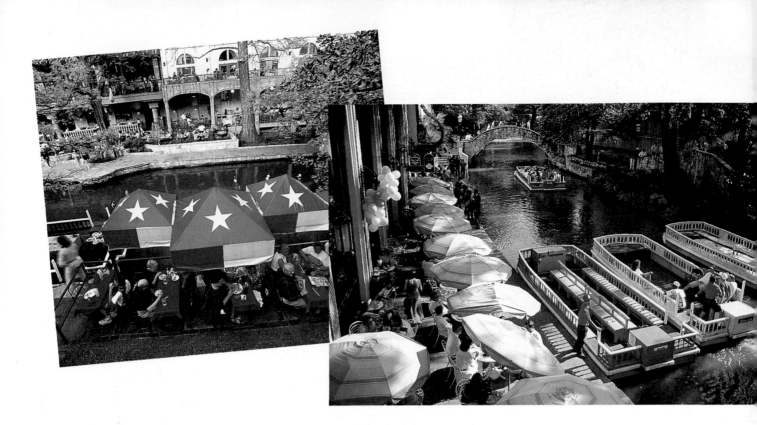

The San Antonio River

On days like today it may seem that half the people in San Antonio can be found along the San Antonio River. The breeze off the river cools the air.

The sounds of people and music lead you right to the heart of the River Walk. People are speaking English and Spanish. Other languages can be heard, too. People from all over the world come to visit this community. They can learn a lot about the geography and culture of San Antonio.

You're not here just to see people, though. You want to see the San Antonio River. You enjoy watching the water flow by. You also like seeing the many trees and flowers.

Babbling Waters

You stroll along the River Walk for a while. Then you come to your favorite spot by the river. There are no more shops and sidewalks, no more music and laughing. You see beautiful flowers and tall cypress and pecan trees.

You sit down on the grass along the river. You can hear leaves rustling in the trees. You can also hear the babbling waters of the river.

You may wonder where the river begins. Look carefully at the map below. About where does the river start?

SAN ANTONIO, TEXAS

TEXAS

San Antonio

Mc Nay Art Museum
Northwest Expressway
Olmos Basin Park
San Antonio Zoo
San Pedro Playhouse
Mc Allister Freeway
Pan Am Expressway
0   2   4 Miles
0   2   4 Kilometers
Interstate 10
Loop 410
Museum of Art
Coliseum
River Walk
The Alamo
La Villita
Loop 410
U.S. Route 90
Interstate 10
Interstate 37
Salado Creek
Mission Concepción
San Antonio River
Loop 410
Military Drive
Mission San José
N
W   E
S
Pan Am Expressway
Mission San Juan
Loop 410
Mission Espada

Central business district
Park
Mission
Point of interest
Beginning of river

M A P   W O R K

San Antonio is a growing city in Texas.

1. What points of interest are located within the central business district?
2. In which direction does the river run below the business district?
3. How does the map show that the river is important to San Antonio?

120

Living with the River

You hear some noises from the busy shops at the River Walk. You smile at the sound of people enjoying the river. The city of San Antonio grew because of the river.

Until the 1950s much of the land around the San Antonio River was used for growing crops. Water from the river made the soil moist and full of minerals. The climate was good for farming.

But today most of the land is used in a different way. Buildings and roads are being built on the land once used for farming.

Long ago the land near the San Antonio River was used mostly for farming.

WHY IT MATTERS

The San Antonio River is just one part of the geography of San Antonio. It is important to the growth of the city. But San Antonio has grown for other reasons as well. In the next lesson you will learn more about the history of this city.

✓ Reviewing Facts and Ideas

SUM IT UP

- The San Antonio River has been important to life in the area for thousands of years.
- The River Walk is an area of shops and restaurants along the San Antonio River today. It provides jobs for many people.
- The river made it possible to farm for food.

THINK ABOUT IT

1. What is the River Walk?
2. **FOCUS** How is the San Antonio River important?
3. **THINKING SKILL** What would you _decide_ to do if you visited the San Antonio River?
4. **GEOGRAPHY** Look at the map on page 120. How far is the River Walk from the beginning of the San Antonio River?

San Antonio Long Ago

READ ALOUD

Do you know where the name Texas comes from? One Native American people, the Caddo, called each other Tejas (TAY hahs). That meant "friends." When the Spanish people arrived, they called the area Texas.

Early People in Texas

Long ago there were many groups of Native Americans, such as the Caddo, living in what is now the state of Texas. In the last lesson you read about the Payaya. They were part of another group of Native Americans called the Coahuiltecan (kwah weel TEH kan). The Coahuiltecan lived for many years throughout a large part of what is now Texas and Mexico.

Like the Anasazi, the Coahuiltecan used the natural resources around them. Their homes were made from grass and branches. They ate roots, nuts, and fruit. In hot, dry areas the Coahuiltecan ate the fruit of cactus plants. A cactus is a type of plant with sharp spines. It grows in dry environments. In some areas there were few large animals. As a result, the Coahuiltecan had to hunt for smaller animals like lizards and deer.

Focus Activity

READ TO LEARN
What was life like in a mission in San Antonio?

VOCABULARY
cactus
mission
missionary
independence

122

The Spanish Begin Missions

In the 1700s life changed for the Coahuiltecan. Spanish-speaking people came north from Mexico and set up missions. Missions were communities set up by Roman Catholic priests to teach their religion to others. The priests who set up the missions were called missionaries.

Missions offered Native Americans food and a safe place to live. The Native Americans were expected to work for their food. They also had to learn more about the Catholic religion.

In the 1700s there were five missions in what is now the city of San Antonio. To learn about life in a mission, turn the page.

The Coahuiltecan used natural resources like the cactus for food. They used trees and stones to build missions.

Infographic

Living at a Mission

This Infographic shows mission life long ago. What were some of the tasks people did to support their community?

Men make wood and metal tools and other things needed at the mission.

The church is the center of the community. Missionaries live in rooms behind the church.

Women spin cotton, weave, and make pottery and baskets. They also fish, care for the children, and prepare food. Corn is an important crop.

Native Americans live in rooms built within the thick stone mission walls.

Missionaries teach Native American children to read and write in Spanish.

Every day starts with prayer. At noon and in the evening the whole community gathers to pray again.

Texas Joins the United States

Mission life continued over one hundred years. Over that time some Native American groups kept their culture. But many groups like the Coahuiltecan lost their old way of life. They began to speak Spanish. They became Catholic. Over time the Coahuiltecan's own culture disappeared.

In 1821 another important change came to Texas. The people of Mexico won their independence from Spain. Independence is freedom from others. The new country of Mexico now included Texas. But many people in Texas did not want to be part of Mexico.

A war began in 1836 between Texas and Mexico. One battle took place at the mission called The Alamo. During this battle a large Mexican army defeated a small group of Texans. But after more battles that same year, Texas finally defeated Mexico and won its independence. Several years later, in 1845, Texas joined the United States of America.

Today people in Texas are proud of their state flag.

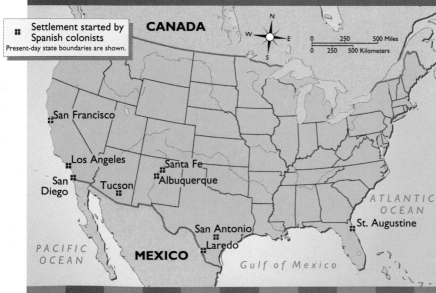

SPANISH COLONIAL SETTLEMENTS

MAP WORK

Settlement started by Spanish colonists
Present-day state boundaries are shown.

CANADA

W · N · E · S

0   250   500 Miles
0   250   500 Kilometers

San Francisco

Los Angeles

Santa Fe

San Diego   Tucson   Albuquerque

PACIFIC OCEAN

San Antonio

Laredo

MEXICO

Gulf of Mexico

ATLANTIC OCEAN

St. Augustine

Many Spanish missionaries and colonists came north from Mexico to settle in Texas and other places.

1. Which settlements are located on an ocean?

2. About how many miles is it from San Antonio to San Diego?

3. What could you predict about the culture of the communities shown?

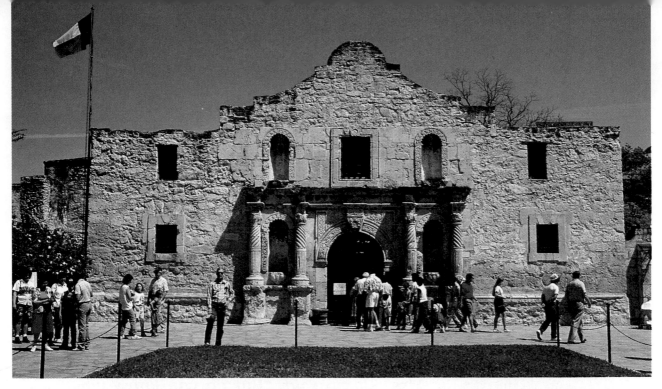

WHY IT MATTERS

Look at the map on the previous page. As you can see, there were many settlements started by Spanish colonists in what are now cities in the United States. Today Spanish culture is still an important part of life in San Antonio as well as other cities in our country.

Each year many people visit The Alamo. It is now a museum.

Reviewing Facts and Ideas

SUM IT UP

- The Coahuiltecan lived in what is now Texas and Mexico.
- Spanish missionaries set up missions to teach Native Americans the Catholic religion.
- Many Native Americans lost their own culture because of mission life.
- In 1821 Mexico won its freedom from Spain.
- Texas joined the United States of America in 1845.

THINK ABOUT IT

1. How did the Coahuiltecan use their resources?
2. What did the missionaries offer the Native Americans?
3. **FOCUS** What was life like in a mission in San Antonio?
4. **THINKING SKILL** How was life for men in the mission _different_ from life for women? How was it _alike_?
5. **GEOGRAPHY** Look at the map on page 126. In what direction is Laredo from Santa Fe?

Focus Activity

READ TO LEARN
How do people celebrate San Antonio's culture?

VOCABULARY
Fiesta
volunteer

San Antonio Today

READ ALOUD

Barbara Shupp has lived in San Antonio for over 60 years. "I went to many famous cities," Mrs. Shupp said. "But do you know what? When I came back to San Antonio, I decided it was the prettiest city in the world. No other city compares!" In this lesson you will see why many people proudly call San Antonio home.

A Growing City

You just read about mission life in San Antonio. Today San Antonio is very different. It has grown from the days of the missions. San Antonio is the tenth largest city in the United States. It was also the first major city to have a mayor of Hispanic descent, Henry Cisneros.

Mrs. Shupp has seen a lot of changes take place in San Antonio. She likes to watch her nine-year-old granddaughter, Susann Speer, grow up in the same city she did. "But in some ways," Mrs. Shupp laughs, "San Antonio is not the same city at all! When I was a young girl like my granddaughter, San Antonio was like a small town. River Walk was not built up. There were no shopping malls. Instead, there were many small shops. We could even rollerskate in the streets because there were very few cars!"

The Past Lives On

San Antonio is a city that combines its history with its life today. Every year thousands of people visit the missions. They learn about how the Spanish and Native Americans lived long ago. Some of the missions are still used as churches. The Alamo is now a museum honoring Texas's past.

The past continues in other ways as well. San Antonio's Spanish and Mexican roots can be seen and heard everywhere. Many people are Mexican American. They speak Spanish as well as English. Susann likes the mix of people. "Sometimes my friends and I sing Christmas carols for people in a nursing home," she says. "We sing the songs in Spanish and English. I'd like to learn more Spanish."

Susann Speer (above) likes the mixture of the past and present in San Antonio. Mission San José is still an active church (below). People celebrate their culture in festive costumes (below right).

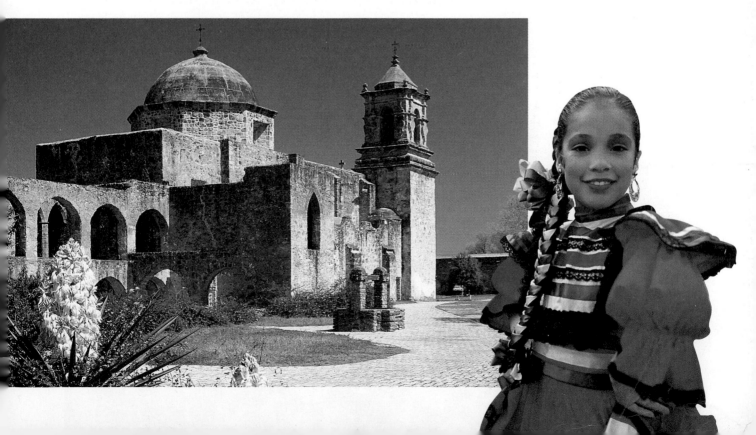

Fiesta in San Antonio

You can learn a lot about a community by watching its celebrations. San Antonio has many celebrations, festivals, and events all year long. The celebrations show the many different cultures that make up this city. "That's one thing I like about San Antonio," says Susann. "There's always something special going on."

For Susann and her grandmother, there is one festival they like most of all. It is a weeklong event called Fiesta. *Fiesta* means "festival" in Spanish. Fiesta includes San Jacinto Day. It celebrates the day Texas won freedom from Mexico on April 21, 1836.

Fiesta is the biggest celebration of the year. Many volunteers help to make it a success. A volunteer is someone who does something by choice, without pay. Volunteers help organize parades and many other activities. For ten days the city becomes a big party. There are over 150 different events to see.

How *much candy did you get?*

Many Mexican games are popular in San Antonio. A favorite one involves a piñata. A piñata is a hanging paper animal filled with candy. It is used to celebrate special events. Children are blindfolded and take turns hitting the piñata with a stick. When it breaks open, the candy falls to the ground. Children then pick up the candy.

San Antonio's Fiesta Parade includes floats covered with flowers. In the past people threw flowers in a playful battle.

Memories of San Antonio

A few years ago there was a writing contest during Fiesta. People were asked to write about their memories of San Antonio's past. Mrs. Shupp was so excited about this, she entered the contest. Here is what she said about her memories of the Fiesta Parade. What do you remember most about celebrations in your community?

Story by Barbara Shupp written in 1985.

To our family the Fiesta Parade was the **consolidation** of all the events of the year. Neither rain nor shine could keep us away. My love for the parade was probably why I went to work that morning even though I didn't feel well. It was the big day of the parade and I wouldn't let a sore throat stop me from going! As I stood waiting for the parade, I began to shake. The weather was warm, but I was freezing. What should I do? I didn't want to miss the parade, but I felt too sick to stay outside. Then it came to me—I would go sit inside the nearby movie house. As I sat watching a movie, I could hear the marching band come down the street. Even though I couldn't see the flag, I had a lump in my throat when it went by. Who would have thought that the parade's number one fan would be watching a movie as it went by!

---

consolidation: coming together

The Livestock and Rodeo show is one way people celebrate in San Antonio.

Living Together

Mrs. Shupp likes to talk about things she remembers from growing up in San Antonio. "One thing hasn't changed," Mrs. Shupp notes. "You still meet interesting people. San Antonio has always been a place where different people live together. I am glad that Susann is growing up in San Antonio today."

WHY IT MATTERS

You have learned about San Antonio's rich past. You have also seen how people in San Antonio celebrate their culture.

Every community has its own special past. People enjoy remembering their past and joining in celebrations. These are some of the reasons that people like living in communities.

✔ Reviewing Facts and Ideas

SUM IT UP

- San Antonio has grown into a large, busy city.
- San Antonio celebrates its cultures with many festivals and events like Fiesta.
- One way to learn about the past is to listen to people who remember it.
- San Jacinto Day celebrates Texas's independence from Mexico on April 21, 1836.

THINK ABOUT IT

1. What signs of San Antonio's past can still be seen today?
2. What is one thing Mrs. Shupp likes about living in San Antonio?
3. **FOCUS** How do people celebrate San Antonio's culture?
4. **THINKING SKILL** How is San Antonio *like* your community today? How is it *different*?
5. **WRITE** Think about something you want to remember about your community. Write about that memory.

From the Community Garden

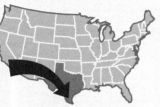

SAN ANTONIO, TEXAS— Tiffany Rogers started volunteering at the Children's East Community Garden in San Antonio just a few years ago. Back then she could not tell a cucumber plant from a tomato plant. Now she raises her own vegetables such as carrots and spinach. She even brings them home for dinner!

For Tiffany the garden is very special. It is a place where she helps the community by growing plants and vegetables for herself and others.

Volunteers are given a small piece of land by community leaders. Local businesses help with seeds and tools. About 20 children and 40 adults work in the garden.

People like Vernon Mullins teach Tiffany and others about planting, weeding, and watering. Mr. Mullins likes his job because he, too, is making a difference in his community.

"Working in the community garden, we all become friends," he said. "If one person sees another person needs help, they pitch in. We also give the food we grow to needy people in the community."

Working in the community garden has taught Tiffany how to make a difference in her community. It has also taught her a lot about plants. And it sure keeps Tiffany busy. "You get lots of exercise and you don't waste time sitting home," she said.

"You get lots of exercise . . . "

Tiffany Rochelle Rogers

STUDYSKILLS

Reading Bar and Line Graphs

VOCABULARY

bar graph   line graph

WHY THE SKILL MATTERS

In the last lesson you learned about San Antonio today. In studying San Antonio it is helpful to compare its population with those of other large cities in Texas. It is also useful to see how San Antonio's population has changed over time. One way to view this information is to use graphs.

READING A BAR GRAPH

Suppose you want to compare the populations of San Antonio and other Texas cities. Look at the bar graph at right. A bar graph uses bars of different heights to show amounts. This bar graph shows the populations of three of the largest cities in Texas.

Look at the bottom of this bar graph. Which cities does it name? Look at the numbers on the left side of the graph. The numbers stand for populations.

Now "read" the graph. First find the bar for San Antonio. Slide your finger to the top of the bar. Now slide your finger across to the number at the left. The number is just below one million. The population of San Antonio is about one million people.

Now find the bar for Houston. About how many people live in Houston?

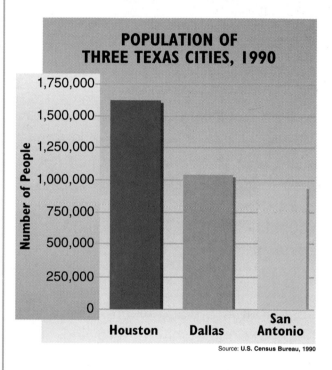

Source: **U.S. Census Bureau, 1990**

READING A LINE GRAPH

Another kind of graph is a line graph. A line graph shows how something changes over time. Look at the line graph on the next page. It shows how the population of San Antonio has changed over time.

The dots for each year are connected by a line. The line shows you a picture of what happened to San Antonio's population.

134

Run your finger along the line. Note the dates at the bottom and the numbers at the left. How has the city's population changed between 1850 and 1990?

TRYING THE SKILL

You may find it useful to refer to the Helping Yourself box as you continue to study the graphs. Which graph would you use to find the population of Dallas in 1990? Which would you use to compare San Antonio's population in 1900 with its population in 1990?

What happened during this time?

REVIEWING THE SKILL

1. Which city on the bar graph has the largest population? Tell how you know.

2. What is the earliest year shown on the line graph? How can you tell?

3. About how many people lived in San Antonio in 1950?

4. What would you tell someone to do to make it easier to read a graph?

POPULATION OF SAN ANTONIO, 1850 TO 1990

Number of People / Year

Source: **U.S. Census Bureau, 1990**

CHAPTER 5 REVIEW

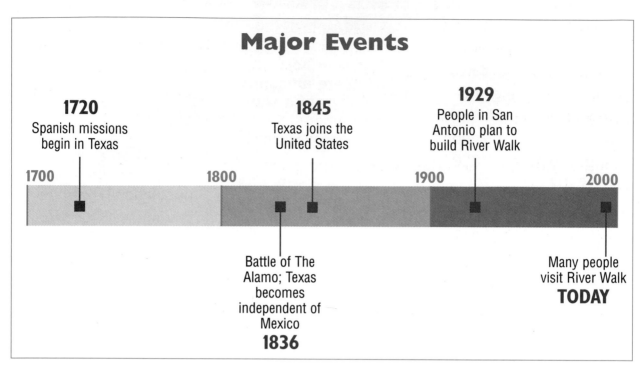

Major Events

1720
Spanish missions begin in Texas

1845
Texas joins the United States

1929
People in San Antonio plan to build River Walk

1700   1800   1900   2000

Battle of The Alamo; Texas becomes independent of Mexico
1836

Many people visit River Walk
TODAY

THINKING ABOUT VOCABULARY

Number a piece of paper from 1 to 5. Beside each number write the word that best completes each sentence.

cactus   missions
Fiesta   volunteers
independence

1. Texas won its _____ from Mexico in 1836.

2. To teach Native Americans about Spanish culture and religion, the missionaries set up _____ .

3. Thanks to the unpaid work done by _____, the party went well.

4. The dry desert is home to many types of _____ plants.

5. _____ is a celebration of Texas's independence from Mexico.

THINKING ABOUT FACTS

1. How did the missionaries change the lives of the Coahuiltecan people? What happened to the Coahuiltecan culture?

2. In what year did Texas join the United States? What events took place before this happened?

3. How has the area around the San Antonio River changed since the 1950s? Why is it good for farming?

4. Why is Spanish a common language in San Antonio today?

5. How do people in San Antonio celebrate their culture? What cultural celebrations take place in your community or one nearby?

THINK AND WRITE

WRITING A STORY
Write a brief story about a typical day of a child living at a mission long ago.

WRITING A THEME SONG
Write a theme song to be performed at Fiesta. In it describe San Antonio's past and present.

WRITING AN ADVERTISEMENT
Suppose you work for an advertising company and have been asked to create a magazine advertisement about San Antonio. Write an advertisement to tell people what is special about San Antonio.

APPLYING STUDY SKILLS

READING BAR AND LINE GRAPHS
Answer the following questions to practice the skill of reading bar and line graphs. Use the graphs on pages 134–135.

1. What is the difference between a bar graph and a line graph?

2. Which city has the larger population, Houston or Dallas? Which graph tells you this?

3. Did more people live in San Antonio in 1850 or in 1950?

4. Which graph tells you about changes over time?

5. What information about yourself could you show on a line graph?

Summing Up the Chapter

Fill in a copy of the Venn Diagram below. In the circle on the left, write the words that describe San Antonio in the 1700s. In the circle on the right, write the words that describe San Antonio today. Where the circles meet, write the words that describe both time periods. How has San Antonio changed since the 1700s? How is it still the same?

1700s   **BOTH**   **TODAY**

UNIT 2 REVIEW

THINKING ABOUT VOCABULARY

Number a sheet of paper from 1 to 10. Beside each number write the word from the list that best completes each sentence.

artifacts	kiva	technology
Bay	mesa	volunteers
decision	mission	
desert	museum	

1. _____ is the use of tools and materials to serve people's needs.

2. Ships heading into Jamestown sailed on the Chesapeake _____ .

3. A _____ was a community where Native Americans lived and practiced the Catholic religion.

4. Scientists often use _____ to learn about how a group of people lived long ago.

5. The tour book listed many places to visit. We had to make a _____ about where to go first.

6. A _____ was a room used by the Anasazi for religious purposes.

7. The climate is usually hot and dry in a _____ .

8. _____ work for free in different places within communities.

9. A _____ is a landform that looks like a high, flat table.

10. At a _____ people can look at objects of art, science, or history.

THINK AND WRITE

WRITING A REVIEW

Suppose you have just visited Mesa Verde National Park and Jamestown Settlement. Write a paragraph reviewing why such places are important.

WRITING AN ESSAY

Write one paragraph explaining a special event in your community that is important to you. It could be a parade or a holiday celebration.

WRITING A NEWSPAPER ARTICLE

Suppose you went with the Spanish missionaries to Texas. Write an article that reports on the land, the people, and the problems you faced.

BUILDING SKILLS

1. **Making Decisions** What is the first step to take in making a decision?

2. **Making Decisions** Identify a decision you made today and how you made it.

3. **Time Lines** Look at the time line on page 113. Which happened first, the "starving time" or the marriage of Pocahontas?

4. **Bar and Line Graphs** What does the line graph on page 135 show?

5. **Bar and Line Graphs** Suppose you want to show how many students like various kinds of fruit. Would you use a line graph or a bar graph? Why?

YESTERDAY, TODAY &
TOMORROW

At Mesa Verde you can see how the Anasazi lived long ago. At Jamestown Settlement you can see how the colonists and the Powhatan lived. What would you save for people of the future to show how you live today? Why?

READING ON YOUR OWN

Here are some books you might find at the library to help you learn more.

THE MUD FAMILY
by Betsy James
Read of a time when an Anasazi girl made mud dolls that gave rain to her community.

SAN ANTONIO
by Sally Lee
Explore the history, festivals, and neighborhoods of San Antonio.

SARAH MORTON'S DAY: A DAY IN THE LIFE OF A PILGRIM GIRL
by Kate Waters
Join a girl named Sarah as she works and plays in a colonial village in 1627.

UNIT PROJECT

Creating an Infographic

1. Create an Infographic showing how people lived in Jamestown long ago.
2. In a group, discuss facts to include in your Infographic.
3. Decide how you will present these facts. Use the Infographic on pages 84-85 as a guide.
4. Have each group member choose one part of the Infographic to complete.
5. Include colorful drawings to show what life in Jamestown was really like.

Building a Government

WHY DOES IT MATTER?

People in our country work together to make laws that help us live safely and fairly. Some were made a long time ago. Some of the laws were made much more recently. In this unit you will learn about how people and government work to make lives better for people in communities.

As a citizen of the United States of America, you have important rights and responsibilities. By learning about government and citizenship, you will be better able to make a difference to your country and your community.

We the People

WHEN THE WHITE HOUSE IS HOME

The White House belongs to all Americans. But some kids have a special connection to the President's house. It's their home! Young Tad Lincoln liked to read there with his father, Abraham Lincoln. Quentin Roosevelt, Teddy Roosevelt's son, rode his pony in the driveway. "John John" Kennedy enjoyed hiding under the desk of his dad, John Kennedy. And Amy Carter, Jimmy Carter's daughter, played with her nephew in a tree house on the lawn. Kids who live in the White House give up a lot of privacy for the privilege of living there. But White House kids get to make history.

GEO JOURNAL

It's your first night in the White House. Describe your thoughts about being there.

A New Country Is Born

THINKING ABOUT GEOGRAPHY AND HISTORY

As you have read, English colonies grew along the Atlantic coast of North America long ago. Some colonial communities, among them Philadelphia and New York, grew into busy cities.

From the time line and map, you can see that some major events happened in Philadelphia and New York. Match the triangles on the map to the picture that has the same color. In Chapter 6 you will meet some of the people who made Philadelphia and New York important and see how their ideas helped form our country, the United States of America.

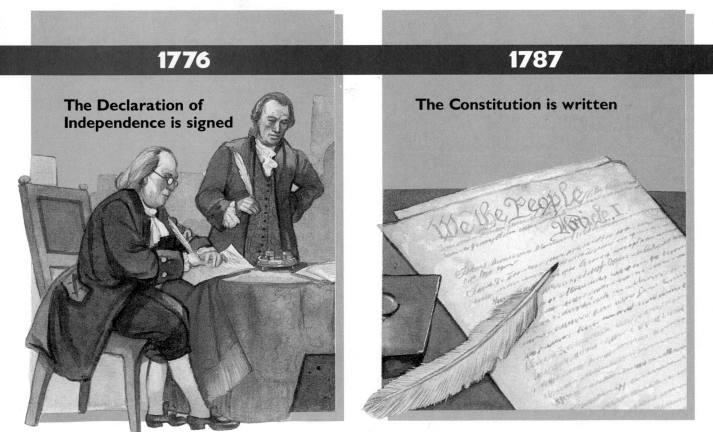

1776

The Declaration of Independence is signed

1787

The Constitution is written

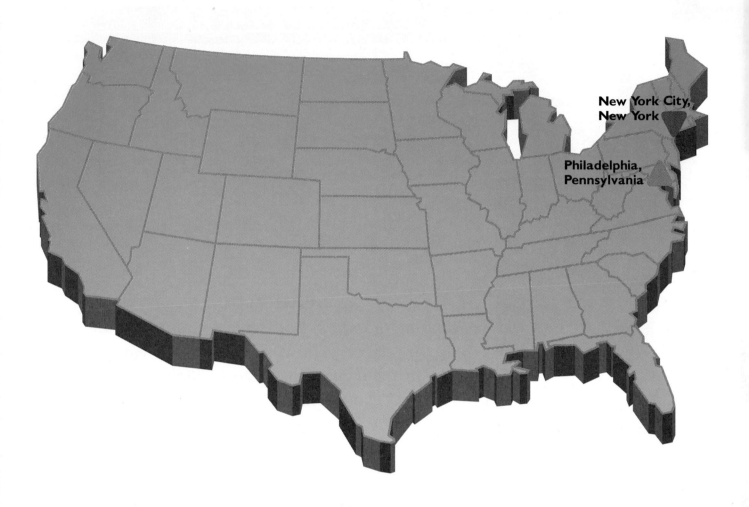

New York City,
New York

Philadelphia,
Pennsylvania

1789

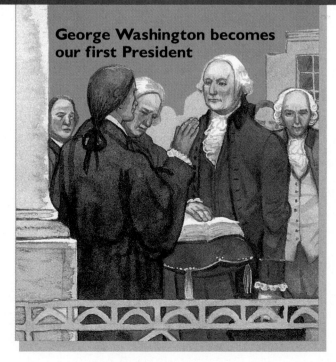

George Washington becomes
our first President

The Bettman Archive

Ben Franklin and Philadelphia

Focus Activity

READ TO LEARN
How did Ben Franklin make a difference in Philadelphia?

VOCABULARY
almanac
tax
American
   Revolution
Declaration of
   Independence

PLACE
Philadelphia,
   Pennsylvania

PEOPLE
Benjamin Franklin
Thomas Jefferson

READ ALOUD

"Most of the shop fronts were painted red, blue, green, or yellow, and the big swinging signs in front of them were brilliant with paint. . . . The people of Philadelphia wore bright colors and had a taste for fine clothes."

Welcome to Philadelphia!

These are the words of a writer named Margaret Cousins. She describes what life was like in the city of Philadelphia, Pennsylvania in the early 1700s. At that time there were 13 English colonies in America. The colonies had many cities. The biggest, busiest city of all was Philadelphia. About 38,000 people lived there, more people than in Boston and New York City put together.

Philadelphia became one of the most important communities in our country's history. Many things happened there that led the colonies to become the United States of America. Let's take a look at what Philadelphia was like back in colonial days.

146

Meet Ben Franklin

Everyone in Philadelphia was talking about one person—Benjamin Franklin. He seemed to be everywhere, doing just about everything.

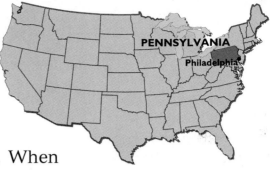

Ben Franklin grew up in Boston, Massachusetts, in a family of 17 children. When he was 12, his father sent him to live and work with his older brother James, a printer. Ben quickly learned a lot about printing. But he did not get along with his brother. When he was 17, he left for Philadelphia.

When he arrived in Philadelphia in 1723, Ben found an exciting city. He talked to everyone and soon made many friends. He loved his new city, and he set out to make it even better.

As a young man, Ben Franklin learned to use the printing press.

Poor Richard's Almanac

Ben quickly found work in Philadelphia as a printer. A few years later, in 1732, he wrote and printed *Poor Richard's Almanac*. An almanac is a book that comes out every year with lots of information in it. His almanac had a calendar, weather predictions, and information about the moon and sun. It was most popular for the helpful advice it gave readers. Read the following sayings from his almanac. Which sayings have you heard of?

From *Poor Richard's Almanac*, written by Benjamin Franklin, 1732-1757.

- Early to bed and early to rise, makes a man healthy, wealthy and wise.

- Lost time is never found again.

- Don't throw stones at your neighbors', if your own windows are glass.

- A penny saved is a penny earned.

- Little strokes fell great oaks.

- Well done is twice done.

- When the well's dry, we know the worth of water.

- The honey is sweet, but the bee has a sting.

Helping His Community

The almanac sold so many copies that soon Ben Franklin was a rich man. He didn't have to work as much as he used to. Franklin decided to spend his time doing things he loved, including helping Philadelphia and the colonies. Look at the chart on this page to learn about some of his many great ideas.

The Inventions of BEN FRANKLIN

Franklin did many experiments with electricity. To save buildings from fires, he invented lightning rods, which conduct lightning straight into the ground.

The first lending library in the colonies was started by Franklin.

The Franklin stove used much less wood and gave off more heat than fireplaces.

Franklin helped organize Philadelphia's first volunteer fire department. Volunteers carried leather pails to help fight fires.

Franklin created bifocal glasses to help people see close-up, for reading, as well as at a distance.

Fighting for Freedom

In Franklin's time the colonies grew and began to have problems with their English rulers. The colonists felt that they should make their own laws. They did not want to pay taxes to the English government. A tax is money that people pay to support the government. By the 1770s many colonists wanted to have their own government.

In 1775 the American Revolution broke out. Fighting began between the colonists and the English. The colonies wanted independence, or to be a free country.

It was the summer of 1776. The leaders of the colonies met in Philadelphia to work together to win the war. Ben Franklin was there. His wise advice and experience were highly valued. Thomas Jefferson from Virginia was also there. Jefferson wrote a statement about why the colonies should be free. It was called the Declaration of Independence. On July 4, 1776, the leaders all agreed to adopt it.

The artist John Trumbull painted *The Declaration of Independence, 4 July 1776* (bottom).

The United States of America

Most Americans were happy about the Declaration of Independence. But the real celebration could not take place yet. Freedom had not yet been won. People from every colony marched off to war against the English. Many battles were fought. Many lives were lost. Finally, in 1781, America won its independence. The 13 colonies were now the states of a new country, the United States of America.

WHY IT MATTERS

Philadelphia was an important city during the American Revolution. Ben Franklin worked to help his city and all the colonies. On July 4, 1776, Ben Franklin was one of 56 leaders to adopt the Declaration of Independence. This date is still important to us today. It is the birthday of our country.

In 1776, the Liberty Bell rang to celebrate the adoption of the Declaration of Independence.

✓ Reviewing Facts and Ideas

SUM IT UP

- Ben Franklin arrived in Philadelphia in 1723. He did many things to help the city.
- Starting in 1775 the American Revolution was fought to free the colonies from England. The colonies wanted to make their own laws and to stop paying taxes to England.
- On July 4, 1776, the Declaration of Independence was adopted.
- In 1781 the American Revolution ended.

THINK ABOUT IT

1. Why did the colonies fight against England?

2. **FOCUS** How did Ben Franklin make a difference in Philadelphia?

3. **THINKING SKILL** _Predict_ what might have happened if the American colonies had lost the American Revolution.

4. **WRITE** Suppose that you are writing your own almanac. Write two sayings that would be helpful to people today.

Our Country's Flag

What is red, white, and blue and has been waving in our country since the American Revolution? It is "Old Glory," our country's flag.

Before 1777 each colony had its own flag. But the colonies came under one flag when they became the United States of America.

The legacy of our "Stars and Stripes" celebrates the land, people, and history of the United States. It is a symbol of the past and future hopes of our country.

As you look at the legacy of our flag, see how it has stayed the same and changed.

In 1969 our "Stars and Stripes" waved far away on the moon.

The rattlesnake was a colonial symbol used in 1775.

Betsy Ross is said to have made our first flag. Today a copy of that flag, with 13 stars and 13 stripes, is flown outside the Betsy Ross House in Philadelphia.

Our First President

READ ALOUD

The American Revolution was over. A new country called the United States was born. But who would lead this country? What kind of government would it have? There was one person many hoped could help the states reach an agreement. That man was George Washington.

Meet George Washington

People had good reason to pin their hopes on George Washington. During the American Revolution, he led the whole army. The army did not have a lot of money or supplies. But Washington's courage and leadership helped win the war. Afterward, he was praised by many people. One army leader described him as ". . . first in war, first in peace, and first in the hearts of his countrymen."

Some people even thought Washington should be crowned the king of the new country. Washington said the new country should not have a king. It should have a leader chosen by the people. Besides, he did not want to be king. He just wanted to go to his home in Virginia when the war ended. "I will rest under my own vine and my own fig tree," he said.

Focus Activity

READ TO LEARN
How did George Washington help our country start a new government?

VOCABULARY
Constitution
elect
compromise
Congress
President
Supreme Court
Bill of Rights

PEOPLE
George Washington
James Madison

A Leader Is Needed

In 1787 the new country was facing new troubles. Many of the problems were about money. All the states were printing money to help pay the costs of the war. Each state had its own kind of money. The states started arguing with each other over these matters. They realized they needed a new government to make laws for printing money.

Leaders from the states decided to hold a meeting in Philadelphia. Their goal was to solve these problems. One of the leaders was George Washington. He was ill, but he knew he was needed once again to help his country.

George Washington and other leaders traveled to Philadelphia in 1787. At their meeting they discussed laws to help the country, including laws for making money.

Leaders came from each state to write the Constitution. James Madison (above) suggested a type of government with three different branches.

Writing the Constitution

The summer of 1787 was the hottest summer anyone in Philadelphia could remember. In spite of the heat, an important meeting was taking place to create a new government.

Imagine what it was like when the leaders met. The men wore wigs, long coats, ruffled shirts, and vests. Their pants came to their knees. Flies buzzed around and could bite right through their knee-high stockings.

Somehow none of that was important. The leaders were forming a new government. Their job was to write a Constitution. The Constitution states the laws and the plan for how the government of our country works.

One of the first things they did was to elect someone to lead the meeting. To elect is to choose by voting. George Washington was elected to be in charge.

A New Plan

Many leaders were at the meeting. Ben Franklin was there. So was James Madison. He spent the whole time taking careful notes. That's how we know what went on at the meeting.

Madison suggested a plan for three branches, or parts, of government. The leaders argued about the plan but worked out some compromises. A compromise is an agreement reached when each side gives up some demands.

When the Constitution was finally signed, Washington called it a miracle. Look at the chart below to see the three branches of our country's government.

Ben Franklin, over 80 years old, was carried to the meeting.

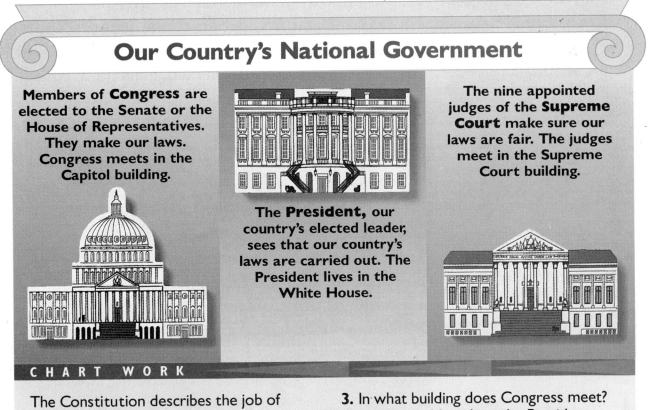

Our Country's National Government

Members of **Congress** are elected to the Senate or the House of Representatives. They make our laws. Congress meets in the Capitol building.

The **President**, our country's elected leader, sees that our country's laws are carried out. The President lives in the White House.

The nine appointed judges of the **Supreme Court** make sure our laws are fair. The judges meet in the Supreme Court building.

CHART WORK

The Constitution describes the job of each branch of government.

1. What are the two parts of Congress?

2. Who is the leader of our country?

3. In what building does Congress meet? In what building does the President work?

4. How do you think the three branches work together?

Our First President

As you can see on the chart on page 157, the Constitution made the President the leader of our country. The President would be different than a king. The President would be elected.

In February 1789, George Washington was elected the first President of the United States. A few months later, he rode to New York City for a special ceremony to become the President. In every town and city he passed through, people surrounded his carriage and cheered. There were parades and celebrations at just about every stop. When he reached New York City, the crowds were so thick that it was hard for carriages to move.

One of Washington's most important jobs was to choose good leaders to help him. Thomas Jefferson was one of the leaders chosen to help run the government. After four years Washington was elected President again.

Wherever George Washington traveled in the colonies, he was often greeted by large crowds of people.

WHY IT MATTERS

George Washington was an important leader in our country's history. He led the American Army during the American Revolution. He also helped write the Constitution. The Constitution is very important to all Americans. It has the most important laws of our country. But people found that it was not enough. It did not protect all people's freedom and rights.

In 1791 the Bill of Rights was added to the Constitution. It lists our most important rights. These include the right to free speech and the right to practice religion freely.

Throughout the history of our country, other changes have been made to the Constitution. But the ideas written in the summer of 1787 still guide us today.

The Constitution and the Bill of Rights still guide our country.

✓ Reviewing Facts and Ideas

SUM IT UP

- George Washington led the American Army in the American Revolution. He became our country's first President in 1789.

- Leaders gathered in 1787 in Philadelphia to write the Constitution. James Madison took notes at the meeting.

- Today, the Constitution is still the plan for how our government works.

- The Bill of Rights was added to the Constitution in 1791.

THINK ABOUT IT

1. What problems did the new country have?

2. **FOCUS** How did George Washington help our country start a new government?

3. **THINKING SKILL** Suppose you had to form a government. How would you _decide_ how to make laws? What would your new government be like?

4. **WRITE** Many people consider George Washington a hero. Write a paragraph about how he might be a hero to you.

THINKINGSKILLS

Comparing and Contrasting

VOCABULARY
compare
contrast

WHY THE SKILL MATTERS

You have just learned about two very important documents in the history of our country, the Declaration of Independence and the Constitution. A document is a written statement that gives information about something. Suppose you wanted to better understand both documents. To do this you might want to compare and contrast them.

To compare things is to see how they are alike. To contrast things is to see how they are different. Comparing and contrasting can help you decide how the Declaration of Independence and the Constitution are important to the history of the United States.

USING THE SKILL

In comparing and contrasting these two documents, your first step might be to think about the Declaration of Independence. You know it was written in 1776. Then think about the Constitution. It was written in 1787, 11 years later. That's one difference. People gathered to write the Declaration of Independence in Philadelphia. They also gathered to write the Constitution in Philadelphia. That's one thing the documents have in common.

The Declaration was written during the American Revolution to simply state the goal of independence. The

The Granger Collection

Constitution was written after the Revolution was over, to set up the laws and plan for the new government. That's another way they are different. Each document was written for a different purpose.

TRYING THE SKILL

When our country was being formed, people did not have cameras. But we can get an idea of the way people looked from paintings and notes. Look at the two paintings

HELPING Yourself

- To **compare** is to see how things are alike. To **contrast** is to see how they are different.

- **Choose one piece of information about the first thing. Then check the second thing for the same information. Is it alike or different?**

of Thomas Jefferson. Use your new skill to compare and contrast the paintings. You can use the Helping Yourself box for some tips as you try this skill.

What should you do first? You could look at the clothes Jefferson is wearing in each painting. How are his clothes alike? How are they different? How else can you compare and contrast the two paintings?

REVIEWING THE SKILL

1. What did you do to compare and contrast the two pictures?

2. What is the difference between comparing and contrasting?

3. Look at the chart of the three branches of government on page 157. How are the President and the Supreme Court alike? How are they different? How do you know?

4. When is it helpful to compare and contrast? Why?

The Granger Collection

161

CHAPTER 6 REVIEW

Major Events

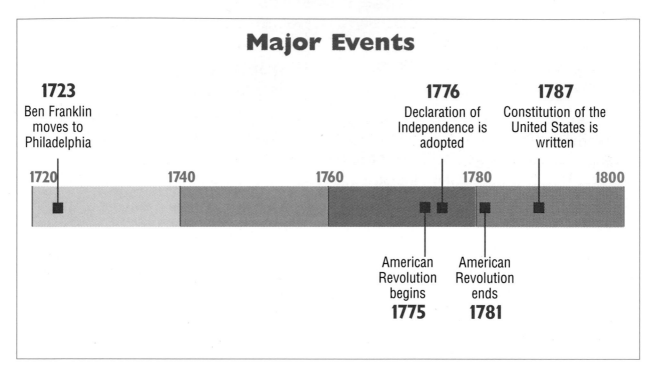

1723
Ben Franklin moves to Philadelphia

1776
Declaration of Independence is adopted

1787
Constitution of the United States is written

1720　　1740　　1760　　1780　　1800

American Revolution begins
1775

American Revolution ends
1781

THINKING ABOUT VOCABULARY

Number a sheet of paper from 1 to 10. For each word listed below, write a sentence using the word correctly. The sentence should show that you know what the word means.

American Revolution
Bill of Rights
compromise
Congress
Constitution
Declaration of Independence
elect
President
Supreme Court
tax

The Granger Collection

THINKING ABOUT FACTS

1. What are some of the things for which Benjamin Franklin is remembered?

2. What is the Declaration of Independence? Who wrote it? When was it adopted?

3. In what year did the American Revolution begin? How long did it last?

4. What important things did George Washington do for our country? Which do you think was his greatest achievement?

5. Into what three different parts does the Constitution divide our government? Name another document important to our freedom. Tell what it does.

THINK AND WRITE

WRITING A NEWSPAPER STORY
Write a newspaper article about the creation of the Constitution. Discuss the meetings, the leaders involved, the disagreements that took place, and how Americans reacted to it.

WRITING AN INTERVIEW
Choose a person from this chapter to interview about the beginning of our country. Write the interview. Include your questions and the answers you think your subject may have given.

WRITING ABOUT A LEGACY
A legacy is something that we value in our lives today that is also a valued part of our past. Our flag is one example of a legacy. Write two paragraphs describing something that you consider to be a legacy.

APPLYING THINKING SKILLS

COMPARING AND CONTRASTING
Answer the following questions to practice the skill of comparing and contrasting.

1. What does it mean to compare and contrast two things?
2. How were Thomas Jefferson and George Washington alike? How were they different?
3. Compare and contrast the pictures of Benjamin Franklin on pages 147 and 157.
4. Compare and contrast the flags on pages 152 and 153. How has our flag changed?
5. What kinds of things might you want to compare and contrast?

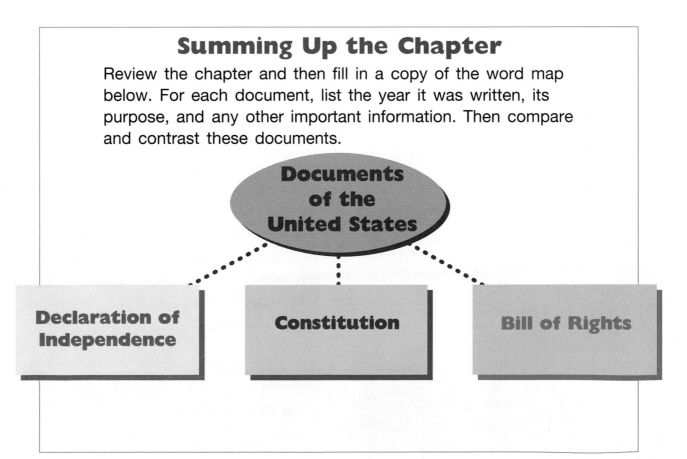

Summing Up the Chapter

Review the chapter and then fill in a copy of the word map below. For each document, list the year it was written, its purpose, and any other important information. Then compare and contrast these documents.

Documents of the United States

Declaration of Independence

Constitution

Bill of Rights

Countries Have Capitals

THINKING ABOUT GEOGRAPHY AND HISTORY

Washington, D.C., is our country's capital. It is the center of our national government. In Chapter 7 you will learn about the beginnings of our capital city. Choosing its location and building it were among the first jobs of the United States government.

Today our capital has memorials and buildings that belong to everybody in the United States. As you will see, these structures honor important people and events in our country's history.

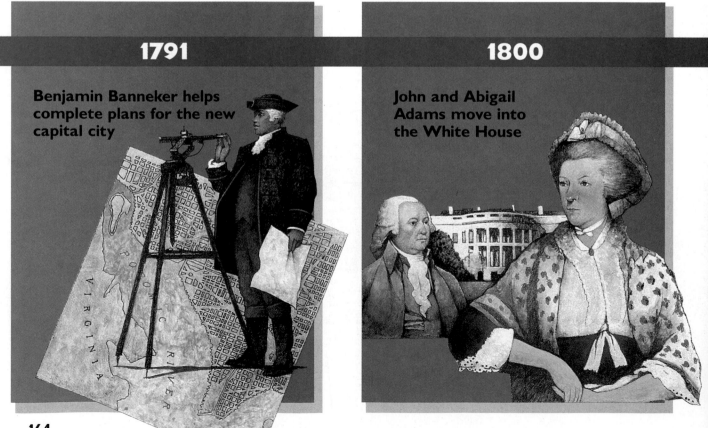

1791

Benjamin Banneker helps complete plans for the new capital city

1800

John and Abigail Adams move into the White House

Washington, D.C.

TODAY

Many people visit the monuments and museums of Washington, D.C.

White House Historical Association

WASHINGTON D.C. 1798

A Capital for the U.S.A.

READ ALOUD

"I pray heaven to bestow [give] the best of blessings on this house and on all that shall hereafter inhabit [live in] it. May none but honest and wise men ever rule under this roof."

Focus Activity

READ TO LEARN
Who helped to build our country's capital?

VOCABULARY
capital

PEOPLE
John Adams
Abigail Adams
Pierre L'Enfant
Benjamin Banneker

PLACES
White House
Washington, D.C.

A Capital Is Needed

The words above were written by President John Adams in 1800. They were written in a letter to his wife, Abigail, the day after he moved into the White House. John Adams was the second President of the United States and the first President to live in the White House.

Just a few years earlier, the leaders of the United States had trouble deciding where to build a capital city for the new country. A capital is the place where the government of a country or state is located.

Thomas Jefferson, who was from the South, thought the capital should be in one of the southern states. Leaders from the North thought Boston or New York would be a good choice. Others thought Philadelphia should be the capital.

Planning a City

In 1790 members of Congress agreed that the capital should not be in any one state. Instead, it should be separate and belong to all the people of the country. Look at this map to see where the new capital was to be. As you can see, its location was a compromise. The new capital was really in the middle of the northern and southern states of our country.

Thirteen Original States

Washington, D.C.

President Washington hired a French builder named Pierre L'Enfant (pee AIR lah FAHN) to draw up plans for the new capital.

L'Enfant came to America in 1777. He was in the army and fought for the colonists during the American Revolution. L'Enfant designed a grand city, with wide streets and magnificent buildings. But he didn't get along with other planners. He left in the middle of the planning. And he took his plans with him!

Here is our capital city long ago. The new streets and buildings were built on land that once was a forest.

167

Life in the New Capital

Luckily, a man named Benjamin Banneker (BAN ih kur) had a good memory. Banneker had been one of L'Enfant's assistants. He had also worked hard on the plans for the new city. He sat down with other planners. Together they redrew L'Enfant's plans.

The new capital was named after George Washington. It was called Washington, D.C. The D.C. stands for District of Columbia.

The first building to be built in the new capital was the White House. In 1800 Abigail Adams was eager to start life in the new house. In her letters to her sister Mary, Abigail described life in the new capital. Read the letter below. What does it tell you about living in Washington, D.C., in 1800?

Benjamin Banneker was honored on a United States stamp.

MANY VOICES PRIMARY SOURCE

Letter written by Abigail Adams in 1800.

My DEAR SISTER:

I expected to find it a new country, with scattered houses over a space of ten miles, and trees and stumps in plenty with a castle of a house. I found the President's House is in a beautiful situation in front of which is the Potomac [River]. . . . The country around is romantic but wild, a wilderness at present.

WHY IT MATTERS

Abigail Adams's letters give us a look into the past. If she could have looked into the future, she might have been very surprised. There have been many changes to the White House since she lived there. Every year has also brought other changes to our country's capital. In the next lesson you will look at Washington, D.C., today.

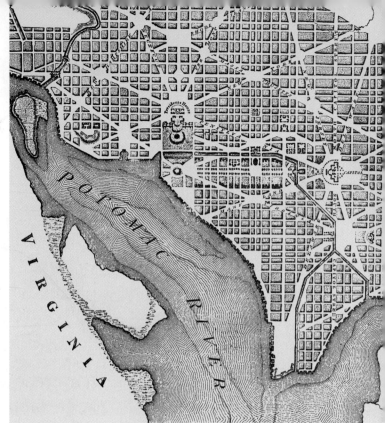

Early plans for Washington, D.C., included wide streets and open areas.

North Wind Picture Archives

✓ Reviewing Facts and Ideas

SUM IT UP

- John Adams was the second President of the United States. In 1800 he and his wife Abigail became the first people to live in the newly built White House.

- The leaders of the country compromised and chose Washington, D.C., as the location for the capital. The new capital city would be in the middle of the country and would not be part of any one state.

- Pierre L'Enfant drew up the first plans for the capital. When he left in the middle of planning, Benjamin Banneker helped to redraw the plans.

THINK ABOUT IT

1. Why did people disagree about where the new capital should be? How did they compromise?

2. **FOCUS** Who helped to build our country's capital?

3. **THINKING SKILL** Suppose you had to choose a location for the United States capital today. Where should it be? How would you *decide*?

4. **GEOGRAPHY** Leaders chose to build the new city along the Potomac River. Most cities at that time were located on or near rivers. Why do you think that was so?

Focus Activity

READ TO LEARN
What interesting things can you see and do in our capital today?

VOCABULARY
memorial

PLACES
Capitol
Washington
  Monument
Jefferson Memorial
Lincoln Memorial
Vietnam Veterans
  Memorial
Lafayette Park

Our Nation's Capital Today

READ ALOUD

"It's great to live in Washington. There are a lot of things to see and do. My favorite place to go to is the National Zoo."

Come See the Capital

Gary Senn is a third grader who lives in Washington, D.C. Not far from his home, the President and other leaders of the United States are busy every day. They are making decisions that are important to the future of our country and the world. Washington, D.C., is home to many people. But it is the capital for all Americans.

Washington, D.C., has changed a lot since it was first built. Many more people live and work here. There are many shops and office buildings where forests once grew. Wide streets have replaced dirt paths and roads. Today cars and buses carry people through the city. There are no more horses and carriages. But you can still see some of the buildings that were built long ago.

Getting Around Town

Look at the map below. Find Anacostia. Here is where Gary Senn and his family live. Gary can walk to his school. To travel to other places in the city, Gary can take the Metro. The Metro is a train system that runs underground. People in Washington are proud of how fast and clean the Metro is.

Not very far from Gary's home is the Capitol. The Capitol is the building where Congress meets. *Capitol,* the word for the building, sounds like *capital,* the word for the city. But, as you can see, these words are spelled differently. Since 1800 Congress has met to make laws inside the Capitol.

Gary Senn is a third grader living in Washington, D.C.

MAP WORK

Washington, D.C., is bordered by the states of Maryland and Virginia.

1. Which different rivers run through Washington, D.C.?

2. In which direction is the National Zoo from Rock Creek Park?

3. Why do you think many people travel by Metro?

A Capital

WASHINGTON D.C.

Washington Monument

Washington, D.C., has many memorials and monuments to help people remember the past. A memorial is something that is a reminder of a person or event. The Infographic on these pages shows some important monuments and memorials in Washington, D.C. Which memorials would you like to visit?

The Washington Monument, the tallest stone structure in the world, is 555 feet high. You can take an elevator to the top for a fantastic view.

The Jefferson Memorial was built in honor of the man who wrote the Declaration of Independence. Thomas Jefferson was also our third President. A large statue of Jefferson is part of this memorial.

to Remember

Lincoln Memorial

The Lincoln Memorial was built in honor of President Abraham Lincoln. He was President during the Civil War. He helped free African Americans from slavery. A large statue of Lincoln looks over the Reflecting Pool.

Vietnam Veterans Memorial

Jefferson Memorial

The names of all American soldiers who died in the Vietnam War are on the walls of the Vietnam Veterans Memorial. People leave flowers and notes to help remember those killed in the war.

173

The Government at Work

Early in the morning Washington, D.C., is already bustling. Thousands of people are going to work. Many of them work for the government.

Right across from the White House lawn is another interesting place in Washington, D.C.—Lafayette Park. This park is public. *Public* means anyone can go there. On many days you can see people holding large signs. They are expressing their opinions. They want the President and other leaders to know how they feel about certain issues. Thanks to our Constitution, people in our country are free to share their opinions.

You might see some people who live in Lafayette Park. They live there because they have no homes. They are a reminder that our country still has problems to solve.

In Lafayette Park people often make signs that express their opinions (left). Many people work for our government in buildings in Washington, D.C. (above).

WHY IT MATTERS

The President of the United States and Gary Senn have at least two things in common. They both live in Washington, D.C. They are both Americans.

Many different people live and work in our country's capital. There are also interesting things to see and do there. Some places will show you how our government works today. There are also memorials and monuments to remind us of important people and events in our country's past.

In different countries around the world, capital cities are important to people. Capitals are not only centers of government. They are also places where people are proud to learn about their country. In the next lesson you will learn about a capital city in Africa.

The President is one of the elected people who work in Washington, D.C.

Reviewing Facts and Ideas

SUM IT UP

- Washington, D.C., is a busy city today. Many people live and work there.

- Memorials and monuments, such as the Washington Monument, remind us of our country's past.

- In Washington, D.C., people work hard trying to make our country a better place for all Americans.

THINK ABOUT IT

1. What is a memorial?

2. **FOCUS** What interesting things can you see and do in our capital today?

3. **THINKING SKILL** *Sort* different places to visit in Washington, D.C., into two groups: memorials and buildings.

4. **GEOGRAPHY** Look at the map of Washington, D.C., on page 171. In what direction would you travel to go from Washington National Airport to the White House?

GEOGRAPHY SKILLS

Reading Grid Maps

VOCABULARY
grid map
index

WHY THE SKILL MATTERS

You have read about some places to visit in Washington, D.C. You have already seen a map of our capital city. But sometimes it is hard to find different places on a map. A **grid map** can help. A grid map has a grid, or a set of crisscrossing lines, to help you locate places on the map.

USING THE SKILL

Look at the grid map below. You can see two sets of lines. One set runs across, the other set runs up and down the map. The two sets crisscross to form boxes, or a grid. This grid map shows you the area in our capital called the National Mall. It is an area where many memorials, monuments, museums, and also government buildings are located.

Suppose you want to find the Library of Congress. It has many books. It is the biggest library in the world. First look at the **index**. An index is a list that tells you where to find information. Indexes are usually in alphabetical order.

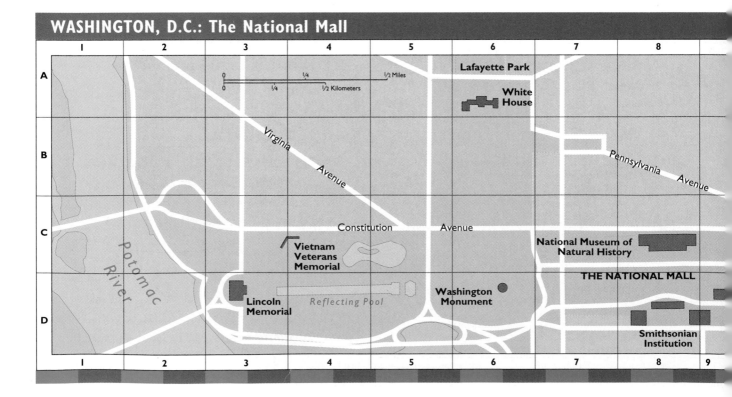

WASHINGTON, D.C.: The National Mall

Look in the index for the Library of Congress. Find D13 next to its name. D13 is the letter and number of a box on the grid. Find the letter D along the side of the map. Then move your finger across until it is over number 13. Your finger is now in box D13. Can you find the library in this grid box?

TRYING THE SKILL

Use the Helping Yourself box as you find more places on the grid

map. To find the Capitol, look in the index. What grid boxes is it in? Find the Capitol on the map. Next look at box D6. What place of interest is located here?

REVIEWING THE SKILL

1. In what box is the Supreme Court located? How did you know?

2. Which buildings can be found in two boxes?

3. Why is it helpful to use a grid map?

INDEX

A Capital in Senegal

READ ALOUD

"Dakar is a great place. Everyone smiles and helps each other."

Focus Activity

READ TO LEARN
What is life like in Dakar, Senegal?

VOCABULARY
mayor

PLACE
Dakar, Senegal

A Capital Connection

These words come from Damian Padilla (puh DEE yuh). He is a 19-year-old ambassador for his school in Washington, D.C. An ambassador is someone who is sent to another country to represent his or her country. Damian went to learn about life in Dakar, Senegal. The country of Senegal is located on the west coast of the continent of Africa along the Atlantic Ocean. Damian also hoped to tell the Senegalese people all about life in Washington, D.C.

Dakar and Washington, D.C., have some things in common. They are both the capitals of their countries. Dakar and Washington, D.C., are also part of a program called Sister Cities. This program links cities in the United States with cities in other countries. People from these cities share ideas. They help each other solve problems.

Governing Senegal

"I had a great time in Senegal," said Damian. "I even met the mayor of Dakar." A mayor is the head of a city government.

Damian learned that the governments of the United States and Senegal have things in common. Senegal's government has a parliament (PAHR luh munt), which is similar to our Congress. It has a supreme court, just as we do. Both countries are also led by a president elected by the people.

Look at the grid map below. In Dakar parliament meets in a building called the Palais (pa LAY) de l'Assemblée (de lah sum BLAY) Nationale (NAH see ah nahl). In which box is it located?

Damian Padilla (left) met the mayor of Dakar (right).

DAKAR, SENEGAL

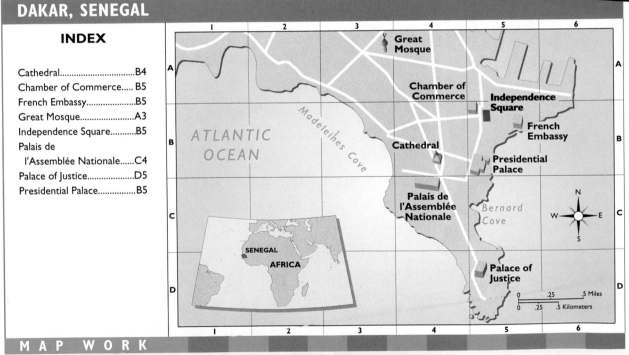

INDEX

ATLANTIC OCEAN

Madeleines Cove

Great Mosque

Chamber of Commerce

Independence Square

French Embassy

Cathedral

Presidential Palace

Palais de l'Assemblée Nationale

Bernard Cove

SENEGAL

AFRICA

Palace of Justice

0 .25 .5 Miles
0 .25 .5 Kilometers

MAP WORK

Dakar is the capital of Senegal, a country in western Africa.

1. In which grid box is the Palace of Justice, or Supreme Court building?

2. How would you find Independence Square on the map?

3. How is Dakar similar to Washington, D.C.?

A Colorful Culture

For Damian one interesting thing about Senegal is its culture. "When I arrived, I first noticed that people wore really colorful clothes. Many children dressed as we do in the United States. Older people wore more traditional clothes. The colors of their clothes were so bright. They seemed to enjoy wearing such amazing colors."

There are many different groups of people in Senegal. The largest group are the Wolof (WUL uf). Their language is the most common one in Senegal. Senegal used to be a French colony, so many people also speak French.

Dakar is located on a peninsula that is nearly surrounded by the Atlantic Ocean. The city is one of Africa's main ports. Goods arrive by ship and are sold in markets. The ocean is also important in another way. People love to go to the beach and swim and play in the warm waters all year round.

A Senegalese woman carries goods from the market (left). People exercise on a beach in Dakar (below).

Living in Two Worlds

You have read about life in Dakar. What do you think someone from Senegal might say about living in the United States? Abdoulaye Diouf (ahb DOO lay DOOF) is a student from Senegal. He lives in Washington, D.C. "I was nervous when I first got here. It was my first time in the United States. But now I'm having fun," he said.

Abdoulaye sees some similarities and differences between the two cities. "In Dakar they are building houses more like American houses," he said. "And in Washington, D.C., the buses are faster."

The Senegalese flag flies over the home of the president of Senegal. It is called the Presidential Palace.

WHY IT MATTERS

Like Washington, D.C., other cities in our country have sister cities around the world. People from these cities learn about and help each other. Both Damian and Abdoulaye learned that, like two sisters, Dakar and Washington, D.C., have a lot in common.

✓✓ Reviewing Facts and Ideas

SUM IT UP

- Dakar is the capital of Senegal.
- The Sister Cities program helps people in different cities around the world meet and work together to solve problems.
- The governments of Senegal and the United States have things in common.
- People speak Wolof and French in Senegal. Wolof is the main language.

THINK ABOUT IT

1. How are the governments of Senegal and the United States similar?

2. **FOCUS** What is life like in Dakar, Senegal?

3. **THINKING SKILL** *Compare* and *contrast* Dakar and Washington, D.C.

4. **GEOGRAPHY** Is Senegal in the Northern or Southern Hemisphere?

CHAPTER 7 REVIEW

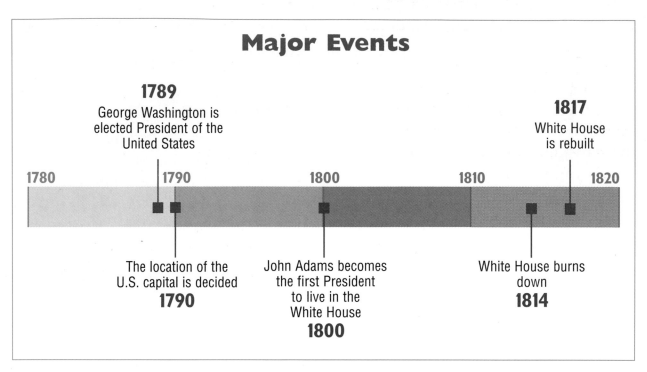

Major Events

1789
George Washington is elected President of the United States

1817
White House is rebuilt

1780   1790   1800   1810   1820

The location of the U.S. capital is decided
1790

John Adams becomes the first President to live in the White House
1800

White House burns down
1814

THINKING ABOUT VOCABULARY

Number a sheet of paper from 1 to 5. Write the word or words that best complete the sentences in the paragraphs below.

capital   index
Capitol   memorials
grid map

     Washington, D.C., is the ___1___ of the United States. There you can visit the ___2___ building where Congress works. You can also see many different ___3___ that honor important people and events.

     When visiting Washington, D.C., it would be helpful to use a ___4___ . It is made up of a set of crisscrossing lines to help you locate different places to visit. To learn where you can find the information on the map, you would look in the ___5___ .

THINKING ABOUT FACTS

1. Why is our capital located where it is?

2. How was Benjamin Banneker important to the building of Washington, D.C.?

3. In what year did President Adams move into the White House?

4. What is the difference between the Capitol and the capital?

5. Why do we build memorials? What are some memorials in Washington, D.C.? What are some memorials in your community?

THINK AND WRITE

WRITING TO PERSUADE

Write a letter about a person from your school or community who you think should be honored. The letter is to persuade local leaders that this person should have a memorial. Include the things this person has done, and the type and location of the memorial you have in mind.

WRITING A JOURNAL ENTRY

Suppose the President has asked you to plan a new capital. Write a journal entry about a day at this new job.

WRITING A TRAVEL BROCHURE

Write a travel brochure about Washington, D.C. List places to visit and describe one.

APPLYING GEOGRAPHY SKILLS

READING GRID MAPS

Answer the following questions using the map on pages 176–177 to practice your skill of reading grid maps.

1. What is a grid map?

2. How is an index helpful in reading a grid map?

3. In which box is the White House located? What building is located in box C8? How did you find the answer to each question?

4. Through which boxes does Virginia Avenue run?

5. When might you use a grid map?

Summing Up the Chapter

Review the chapter before completing a copy of the main idea map below. Fill in at least one fact under every heading. Then write a paragraph explaining the development of Washington, D.C.

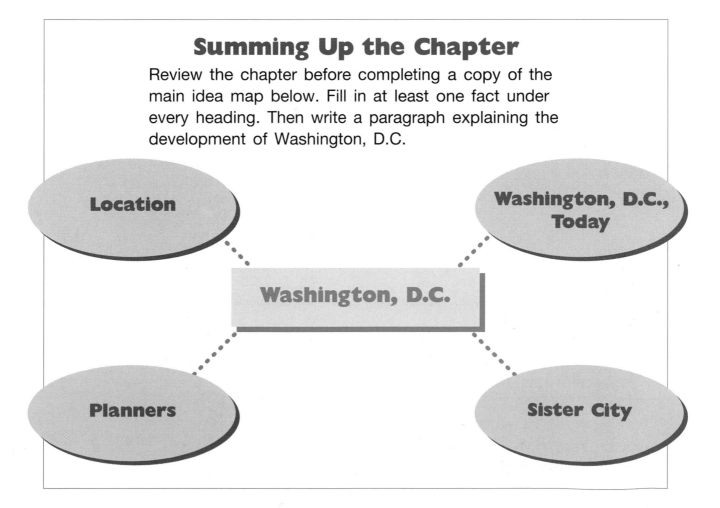

Location

Washington, D.C., Today

Washington, D.C.

Planners

Sister City

CHAPTER
8

Citizens Make Communities Work

THINKING ABOUT GEOGRAPHY AND CITIZENSHIP

Citizens work together to make their communities better places. One way they do this is through government. Large or small, each community and state across our country has a government. In Chapter 8 you will learn what governments do. You will also see other ways people help each other and their communities.

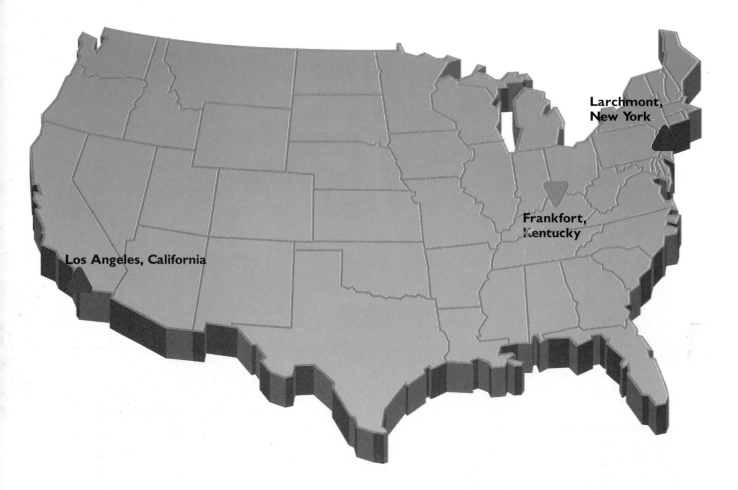

Larchmont, New York

Frankfort, Kentucky

Los Angeles, California

State government in Kentucky meets in the State Capitol.

Local government makes decisions about schools in communities like Larchmont, New York.

Government taxes pay for highways like this one in Los Angeles, California.

VOTE

185

Community Government

READ ALOUD

These are some signs you might see in your community. Have you ever thought about where they come from? Who decides where to put the signs? Who decides on the laws?

State and Local Governments

In the last chapter you read about our country's government. But the country's government does not make all of the laws.

Every state in our country has its own government. At the head of each state's government is the governor. A governor is elected by the people of the state. The governor and other state leaders make laws for the state. The state government is responsible for such things as fixing state highways and cleaning state parks.

A community can make its own laws too. Local government is the government in each city or community. Many local governments are led by a mayor. The mayor chooses people to help run the community. Many cities also have a city council. A city council is a group of elected people who make the laws for the city.

Focus Activity

READ TO LEARN
Why do communities have governments?

VOCABULARY
governor
local government
city council
town meeting

PLACES
Shapleigh, Maine
New England

Welcome to Shapleigh

Potholes, parking, and parks. What do these three things have in common? They are all things a local government takes care of. Does the community want potholes in the local roads to be paved over? If so, how will they be paid for? Are streets too crowded? How can more parking spaces be built? Local governments are responsible for these things. And, as a group of students in Shapleigh (SHAP lee), Maine, found out, local government can also help to build a park.

Look at the map on this page. Shapleigh is a community in the northeast part of our country known as New England. Since colonial times, many communities in this area have held town meetings. Town meetings are a type of local government. They are usually held once a year. People come to a town meeting to decide on the laws and rules that are important to their community. Everyone in the community can come and have a say in what happens. At the end of the town meeting, people vote.

Shapleigh, Maine

NEW ENGLAND

Every year there is a town meeting in Shapleigh, Maine. Community members meet in Town Hall to discuss important issues.

At the Town Meeting

All around New England, early March is an exciting time. The town meetings are about to be held. There will be many discussions and many compromises.

Mr. Jim Brown teaches sixth graders in Shapleigh. A few years ago his students decided that some land in Shapleigh was going to waste. When the yearly town meeting was about to happen, Mr. Brown's students decided to take action. They studied and planned. Then they convinced people at the town meeting that they could build a park on the land. And the result, a beautiful park, has improved their community!

With the help of students and others, a new park was built in Shapleigh.

Students Speak Up

Taking part in the town meeting was important for Mr. Brown's students. "I was surprised," said Adam Pierce. "We made a difference in how people thought about the park in Shapleigh. We changed their opinions."

"It felt good that Shapleigh was getting something out of our hard work," said Wendy Wehmeyer. "I knew it would be nice to have a park for people to enjoy the trees and flowers." A vote by citizens at the town meeting showed that they agreed with Mr. Brown's students.

WHY IT MATTERS

Your community and state have their own governments. They decide on many things that matter to you, like your schools, libraries, parks, streets, and your safety.

You are not old enough to vote yet. Still, you can take part in your government. The next lesson shows you how. You will also see how citizens can improve their communities.

Wendy Wehmeyer and Adam Pierce helped build the new park.

✓ Reviewing Facts and Ideas

SUM IT UP

- The state government makes state laws. A governor is the head of each state government.

- Many local governments have a city council to make laws. Mayors are the heads of many local governments.

- Some communities have town meetings where people vote on important issues.

- Everyone can get involved in community decisions.

THINK ABOUT IT

1. What is a town meeting?

2. **FOCUS** Why do communities have governments?

3. **THINKING SKILL** _Compare_ and _contrast_ local government with state government.

4. **WRITE** Suppose you are going to a town meeting. Write a speech with your classmates about something you would like to tell your community's leaders.

STUDYSKILLS

Using the Library

VOCABULARY

research   nonfiction
reference   fiction
encyclopedia   author
guide word

WHY THE SKILL MATTERS

The students of Shapleigh wanted to learn about gardening before they planted grass and trees in their park. To find the information they wanted, they did **research**. To research is to look for information. The library is often a good place to do research.

USING THE SKILL

At the library there are books of all kinds. Many libraries also have computer and CD-ROM technology. If you need help, a librarian can show you the library's resources.

The Shapleigh students wanted to find information about gardening. If you were going to help them, where would you look?

The first place you might go is the **reference** section. Reference books have many facts in them. You can look things up, but you usually cannot take reference books home.

One useful reference is the **encyclopedia**. Encyclopedias are books or sets of books with facts about people, places, things, and events. If you find encyclopedias on CD-ROM, you can view information on a computer screen.

The topics in an encyclopedia are listed in alphabetical order. If you wanted information on gardening, where would you look? You might use the encyclopedia with the letter G on the cover. Encyclopedias also have **guide words** on the top of each page. Guide words tell the first subject and the last subject that appear on a page.

After reading about gardening in an encyclopedia, you might decide to learn more about planting trees and flowers. Where could you go in the library to do more research?

Next you could go to the **nonfiction** section. Nonfiction books are about real people, places, and events. They are grouped by topics such as environment, history, and science. Suppose the librarian suggests a book called *My Garden Companion* by Jamie Jobb. It is a nonfiction book on growing different kinds of plants. To find it you would look at the environmental books in the nonfiction section of the library.

While you're at the library, you might go to the **fiction** section. Books of fiction are made-up stories of people, places, and events.

Fiction books are grouped on the shelves in alphabetical order by the last name of the author. The author is the person who wrote the book.

TRYING THE SKILL

Suppose you want to research your own community and its government. Where would you begin your research? Use the Helping Yourself box to guide you in using the library.

Which encyclopedia should you use to research your state? Where

would you look in the library for a book about your community?

REVIEWING THE SKILL

1. Where would you go in your community if you needed to do research? Why?

2. What are some of the resources that are in the library? Which ones have you used before?

3. How are guide words helpful in finding information on a page?

4. What is a fiction book? How are fiction books organized on shelves in the library?

Citizens in Action

READ ALOUD

"I pledge allegiance to the flag of the United States of America and to the Republic for which it stands, one Nation under God, indivisible, with liberty and justice for all."

Being a Good Citizen

What do these words mean? You have probably heard and said the Pledge of Allegiance many times. When you "pledge allegiance," you are promising to be loyal. The flag is one of the most important symbols of our country. When you promise to be loyal to the flag, you are really promising to be loyal to your country.

One of the most important things you can do for your country is to be a good citizen. Being a good citizen may mean taking part in your government. What else does being a good citizen mean to you? In this lesson we will see some of the many ways you can be a good citizen in your community and your country.

Focus Activity

READ TO LEARN
What can people do to be good citizens?

VOCABULARY
Pledge of Allegiance

PLACES
Tampa, Florida
Portland, Oregon
Oakland, California

192

Citizens Get Involved

In this book you have read about many communities. All communities have one thing in common. They work best when people work together and help each other.

When you pick up litter, you are helping your community. When you help someone cross the street, you are helping your community. There are many ways to help people.

Alberta Reed lives in Tampa, Florida. She helps people by being a volunteer for a group called Meals on Wheels. Volunteers for Meals on Wheels deliver meals to people who cannot leave their homes.

Once a week Alberta Reed drives to the Meals on Wheels center. She picks up meals and delivers them to people in their homes. "These people cannot go out and shop or cook," she says. "Sometimes the meal I bring them is the only meal they get that day. They really just like seeing someone. I always smile and talk with them."

One way you can help your community is by picking up litter (below). Alberta Reed (top) and other volunteers deliver meals to people in their communities.

Free Bicycles

Good citizens work together to improve their community. In Portland, Oregon, Joe Keating had a great idea on how to be a good citizen and improve community life.

Mr. Keating leads a group called the United Community Action Network. He decided to put free bicycles on the streets of Portland. A person could use a bicycle and then leave it at the end of the trip. Someone else who came along could use it next!

"We wanted to make Portland more livable and to protect the environment," he said. "The bikes worked perfectly for both goals."

Look at the special license plates Mr. Keating and others put on the backs of the bicycles. What do these license plates tell us about being a responsible citizen in the community of Portland?

Free community bicycles are available for use by people on main streets in Portland, Oregon.

FREE COMMUNITY BIKE
Please return to a main street for others to reuse.
USE AT YOUR OWN RISK.
Repair or pickup call:
331-0526
U.C.A.N.

Becoming a Leader

Some good citizens also get involved in government. John Russo lives in Oakland, California. A few years ago he decided he wanted to be elected as a member of the City Council. He worked to tell people his ideas about improving community life in Oakland. He knocked on people's doors. He talked to anyone who would listen to his ideas about making Oakland a better place to live.

Since he was elected, Councilman Russo has been making laws to help find housing for people who don't have homes. He's also trying to get other citizens to do volunteer work.

Students can be active in government too. They can discuss issues with government leaders. "I talk to children all the time," said Councilman Russo. "Even though they can't vote, children are important citizens. They will be the leaders in the future!"

Links to
MATHEMATICS

And the Winner Is . . .

Many people do not vote. They do not think their vote makes a difference. But many elections have been decided by just a few votes.

Suppose you wanted to run for president of your class. One other person is running against you. How many votes would you need to win the election?

Councilman John Russo talks with children in Oakland, California.

America

Good citizens care about their community and their country. When people sing the song "America," they show pride about living in the United States. In what ways do you show pride in our country?

Music by Henry Carey, about 1740
Words by Samuel F. Smith, about 1831

My coun - try, 'tis of thee, Sweet land of lib - er - ty, Of thee I sing. Land where my fa - thers died, Land of the Pil - grim's pride, From ev' - ry ___ moun - tain - side Let ___ free - dom ring.

WHY IT MATTERS

The next time you pledge allegiance or sing a song like "America," think about what it means to be a good citizen. One important thing makes our country and our communities strong: people working together to help each other.

Firefighters and volunteers who visit nursing homes are examples of people who help others.

✓ Reviewing Facts and Ideas

SUM IT UP

- There are many ways to be a good citizen.
- Volunteering to help others is one important part of citizenship.
- Students can be good citizens by talking and writing to their leaders about things that are important to their community.
- Voting is an important part of citizenship.

THINK ABOUT IT

1. Why do communities need good citizens?

2. **FOCUS** What can people do to be good citizens?

3. **THINKING SKILL** Suppose there are two people running for mayor of your town. How would you _decide_ for whom to vote?

4. **WRITE** Think of a project you would like to start in your community. Make a sign asking others to help you with your project.

CITIZENSHIP
VIEWPOINTS

Citizens of the United States vote in booths like this one.

SHOULD VOTING BE REQUIRED?

United States citizens 18 years or older have the right to vote. In most states voters must also register before their first election and any time they move. To register means giving proof of your citizenship and address.

Although United States citizens have the right to vote, many don't use this right. In our country only five out of ten people vote.

Some people suggest that citizens should be made to vote. Suzanne Hee's viewpoint on the next page expresses this idea. Others like Debbie Macon believe that it is best not to vote if you are not informed. Still others, like Joel Rosch, say that voting should be made easier. If Election Day was a national holiday, for example, people would find it easier to vote.

Consider the viewpoints at right, then answer the questions that follow.

Three DIFFERENT Viewpoints

1 SUZANNE HEE
Researcher, Los Angeles, California
Excerpt from Interview, 1994

I think voting should be required. Voting should be what each citizen gives back to society for all that he or she receives from society. I think it is very important for people to know about the issues that affect them and have a say on those issues. I don't think people realize that their votes count.

"... voting should be required."

2 DEBBIE MACON
Community Leader, West Bloomfield, Michigan
Excerpt from Interview, 1994

I believe that every citizen should be encouraged to vote, but not required. In our country freedom of choice is as important as the right to vote. Many times people don't vote because they feel they don't have enough information. If people have enough information, they will vote on their own without forcing them.

"... freedom of choice ..."

3 JOEL ROSCH
Teacher, Raleigh, North Carolina
Excerpt from Interview, 1994

Forcing people to vote is a good idea, but there have to be certain conditions. People should not have to take time off from their jobs. Instead, voting should take place when people have time off. Democracy involves not only rights but responsibilities. If we are going to live in a democracy, going out to vote is a small price to pay.

"... not only rights but responsibilities."

BUILDING CITIZENSHIP

1. What is the viewpoint of each person?
2. How are they alike? In what ways are they different?
3. What other opinions might people have on this issue?

SHARING VIEWPOINTS

Discuss what you agree or disagree with in these and other viewpoints. Be sure to give reasons to support your opinions. Then as a class try to write one statement about which you can all agree.

199

CHAPTER 8 REVIEW

THINKING ABOUT VOCABULARY

On a sheet of paper write the word or term from the list below that matches the statement.

city council Pledge of Allegiance
governor   town meeting
local government

1. We say this when we salute the flag.
2. This type of local government is common in New England.
3. Town meetings are an example of this type of government.
4. This group works with the mayor to make community laws.
5. This person is the elected head of our state government.

THINKING ABOUT FACTS

1. What is the role of the state government?
2. What type of local government does your community have? Who heads your local government?
3. Who are some of the leaders in a local government?
4. Why is the Pledge of Allegiance important?
5. Why do you think people get involved in their local government?

THINK AND WRITE

WRITING A VOLUNTEER LISTING

Think of ways you and your classmates could help others. Write a list on posterboard to display in your classroom. Your list could include ways to help people in class, in school, or in the community. For example, you and your classmates could help improve the school grounds by picking up litter.

WRITING ABOUT A MEETING

When town meetings are held, someone writes a record of what happened. Suppose you are writing a record of a class meeting about classroom rules. Your record must note who was at the meeting, what was discussed, and any decisions that were made.

WRITING A JINGLE

Suppose you work for your state or local government. Your job is to create a jingle, or a saying set to music, that will get people to vote. Write a jingle about the importance of voting, or about voting and citizenship.

USING THE LIBRARY

Answer the following questions to review your skill of using the library.

1. What type of research materials can you find in the library?

2. What is the difference between nonfiction and fiction books? Give an example of each.

3. Where would you look to find out about the history of voting in the United States?

4. How would you go about finding a fiction book by Mark Twain?

5. Why do you think it is important to divide the library into fiction, nonfiction, and reference sections?

Summing Up the Chapter

Review the chapter before completing a copy of the main idea pyramid below. Read the chapter theme at the top and the main ideas in the middle of the pyramid. Fill in the bottom with details that support each main idea. Then answer the following question: Why are good citizens important to a community?

Good citizens take part in their government.

Communities and states have their own government.

Being a good citizen is important to your community and country.

UNIT 3 REVIEW

THINKING ABOUT VOCABULARY

Number a sheet of paper from 1 to 10. Read the definition of each underlined word or words. Write **T** if the definition is true and **F** if it is false. If the definition is false, write a sentence that correctly defines the underlined word or words.

1. Town meetings are a type of local government.

2. A city council is a group of people who are hired to give advice to local governments.

3. The Constitution is a statement about the laws and plans for how our government works.

4. The capital is a building in Washington, D.C.

5. The Declaration of Independence is a statement about why the colonies should be free.

6. A memorial honors an important person or event.

7. To elect is to choose by voting.

8. A tax is money you are paid by the government.

9. A compromise is the constitutional way we run the Supreme Court.

10. The Bill of Rights is a list of our country's most important rights.

THINK AND WRITE ◄▅▅▆▆▶

WRITING ABOUT ART
Describe the memorials and monuments in the Infographic on pages 172–173.

WRITING A PROFILE
Choose one important person from this unit. Write a paragraph describing this person.

WRITING A POEM
Write a short poem or song about our country and the importance of being loyal.

BUILDING SKILLS

1. **Compare and Contrast** What is the first step in comparing and contrasting two things?

2. **Compare and Contrast** Look at the pictures of George Washington on page 155 and Thomas Jefferson on page 160. How are they alike? How are they different?

3. **Grid Map** How does a grid map work?

4. **Grid Map** Look at the grid map on pages 176–177. Where is the Reflecting Pool?

5. **Using the Library** How could you research more information about the memorials in Washington, D.C.?

YESTERDAY, TODAY & *TOMORROW*

George Washington is honored by the Washington Monument and on quarters and dollar bills. In what other ways do we honor him? Do you think we will honor presidents in the future? In what ways might we honor them?

READING ON YOUR OWN

Here are some books you might find at the library to help you learn more.

GEORGE WASHINGTON: A PICTURE BOOK BIOGRAPHY
by James Cross Giblin
An exciting book that tells the story of the father of our country.

DEAR BENJAMIN BANNEKER
by Andrea Davis Pinkney
A biography of the man who helped plan the city of Washington, D.C.

THE STORY OF THE WHITE HOUSE
by Kate Waters
Tour the White House and learn what it was like over two hundred years ago.

UNIT PROJECT

Make a Citizenship Mobile

1. In a group, make a list of what it means to be a good citizen.
2. Have each group member draw and cut out a shape on a piece of colored paper.
3. On each shape, write one thing that a good citizen does.
4. Decorate your shapes with different colors and glitter.
5. Punch a hole in the top of each shape. Attach each shape to a piece of string.
6. Wrap colorful pipe cleaners around a wire hanger. Attach the strings to the hanger.

203

Communities on the Move

WHY DOES IT MATTER?

Our country has a history of movement and change. From colonists long ago to people today, the United States has always been a country on the move. Whether they have come from communities within our country or from far away, people on the move have helped make our country a special place.

Another important part of our country's history is change. As you will see, the changing technology of transportation and communication has helped our country become what it is today: a land of many people and many exciting ideas.

Adventures with

206

ON THE OREGON TRAIL

Your wagon bumps along. So many other wagons have come this way, there are ruts carved into the ground! Sometimes you ride; sometimes you walk. When it gets dark, you help light a fire to cook supper. Is it 1841, or today? It's hard to tell. Modern kids who take part in re-creating the 2,000-mile wagon trip on the Oregon Trail share an experience that thousands of settlers had as they headed west over 100 years ago. They find out what it's like to travel through prairie and desert without a motel in sight.

GEOJOURNAL

Would you like to travel on the Oregon Trail today? Why or why not?

CHAPTER 9

Building New Lives

THINKING ABOUT GEOGRAPHY AND HISTORY

Long ago, people traveled over the oceans to start new communities in the United States. They also moved within our country to start new communities. This is still true today. This time line and map show how our history is filled with people on the move throughout our country.

In Chapter 9 you will learn how our country has grown and changed. You will also meet some of the many people who helped make the United States a special country.

1840s-1850s

OREGON CITY

Many people move west along the Oregon Trail and settle in cities

1880-1920

NEW YORK CITY

People from around the world move to cities in the United States

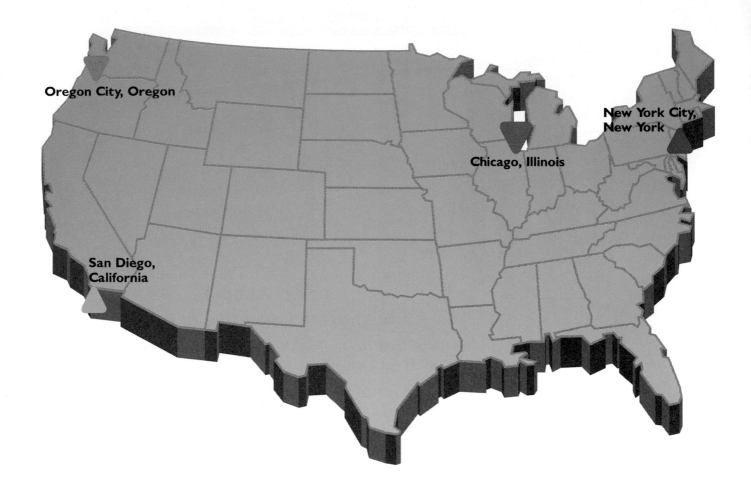

Oregon City, Oregon

New York City, New York

Chicago, Illinois

San Diego, California

1890s–1940s

CHICAGO

African Americans from the South move to Chicago and other cities in the North

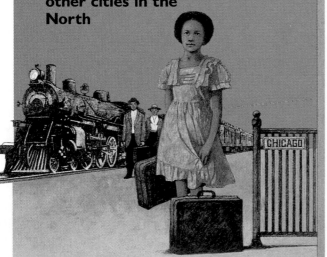

CHICAGO

TODAY

SAN DIEGO

People still move to San Diego and other cities in the United States, looking for a better life

The Oregon Trail

Focus Activity

READ TO LEARN
What was it like to travel west on the Oregon Trail?

VOCABULARY
prairie
pioneer
diary

PLACES
Oregon Trail
Independence, Missouri
Oregon City, Oregon

READ ALOUD

"The prairie, oh, the broad, the beautiful, the bounding [hilly], rolling prairie! Imagine the ocean, when the waves are rolling mountains high, becoming solid and covered with beautiful green grass and you have some faint idea of it."

Leaving Home

These words were written in 1853 by a young woman named Rebecca Ketchum. She was describing the prairie in the middle of the United States. A prairie is flat or rolling land covered with tall grasses. Many Native American groups lived west of the Mississippi River on these prairie lands.

People in the East heard that these areas had rich land for farming. In the 1840s and 1850s, many people left their homes to move west. They became pioneers. Pioneers are people who are among the first to explore and settle an area not known to them. Their adventures are part of our country's history.

Moving West

The map on this page shows some of the routes that thousands of pioneers used to move west. As you can see, the Oregon Trail was one of these routes. Pioneers traveled together in groups of wagons called wagon trains. Why do you think they traveled in groups?

Many wagon trains left from Independence, Missouri. This community had shops that sold supplies and animals for the long journey west.

Many pioneers began their trip west from Independence, Missouri.

TRAILS TO THE WEST, 1840-1860

CANADA

Oregon City

Oregon Trail

CASCADE RANGE

ROCKY MOUNTAINS

Fort Hall

SIERRA NEVADA

California Trail

Sacramento

Old Spanish Trail

Oregon Trail

Santa Fe Trail

Independence

Los Angeles

Santa Fe

PACIFIC OCEAN

APPALACHIAN MOUNTAINS

ATLANTIC OCEAN

Missouri

Mississippi River

River

MEXICO

Gulf of Mexico

0   250   500 Miles
0   250   500 Kilometers

Legend:
— California Trail
— Old Spanish Trail
— Oregon Trail
— Santa Fe Trail
Present-day boundaries are shown.

MAP WORK

Pioneers could take several different trails to travel west.

1. How many trails are shown on this map? Which is the longest trail?

2. At what place do the Santa Fe Trail and Old Spanish Trail meet?

3. Where might a trip on the Oregon Trail be difficult? Why?

A World of Wagons

The wagon trains were a useful way to make the long, difficult journey. The 2,000-mile trip took over five months. The wagons were pulled by oxen, mules, and horses. They crossed rivers and mountains. They ran into snow, rain, and mud. Many pioneers got sick and died along the way.

At night the wagons were set up front-to-end in a big circle. Children would play together in the middle of the circle. People would meet to discuss their problems. Perhaps someone had a broken wagon wheel, another's mule was sick, another was out of flour. Everyone helped each other. Even children had responsibilities. They helped cook and wash dishes. They milked the cows and helped tie up the animals at night. Sometimes children had school lessons from parents or older brothers and sisters.

Settling in for the night often meant a hot meal and rest before the next day's difficult journey.

Corcoran Gallery of Art

Life on the Trail

Life on the trail was oftentimes uncertain. Native Americans lived in many of the areas along the way. In fact, the Oregon Trail was not made by the pioneers. It went along a path that had been used years before by Native Americans. Sometimes Native Americans gave settlers advice about traveling along the trail. But sometimes the two groups fought with each other over the land.

One way we know about the pioneers is from the **diaries** they kept. A diary is a written record of what someone has done or thought each day. Read the following words from a diary written by a 14-year-old girl named Sallie Hester. How was a day on the Oregon Trail different from one of your days?

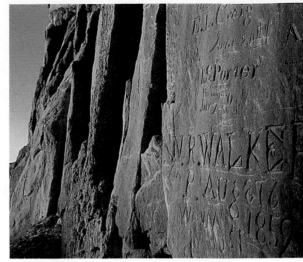

Pioneers carved their names and dates of passage on big rocks to record their journey for others.

Diary written by Sallie Hester, May 21, 1849.

Camped on the beautiful Blue River with plenty of wood and water and good grazing for our cattle. Our family all in good health. We had two deaths in our train within the past week of **cholera** (KAHL ur uh). When we camp at night, we form a **corral** with our wagons. We sleep in our wagons on feather beds. We live on bacon, ham, rice, dried fruits, molasses, packed butter, bread, coffee. Occasionally some of the men kill an antelope and then we have a feast; and sometimes we have fish on Sunday.

cholera: disease of the intestines
corral: fenced-in area for animals

New Communities

After many months and thousands of miles, most of the pioneers reached Oregon. Some of them had lost family and friends along the way. One traveler wrote, "Our journey across the Plains was a long and hard one. We lost everything but our lives."

Most pioneers were planning to settle around Oregon City, Oregon. Many new cities were starting up. Oregon City was the largest. Some people were planning to farm the rich land. Others were planning to open up shops. Some were looking for gold in Oregon and California. Once there, though, life was not easy. Many people arrived with no money and few belongings. They were starting new lives.

Newly arrived pioneers built farms and houses (top). Communities like Oregon City grew quickly (bottom).

Our Country Grows

In 1869 a railroad was built across the country. Soon railroads replaced the Oregon Trail. Today people still move to different parts of the country looking to start new lives. But the ways people travel have certainly changed! How do people travel between communities in our country today?

WHY IT MATTERS

Earlier in this book you read that English settlers came to Jamestown hoping to build new communities in our country. In the same way, the pioneers who traveled west along the Oregon Trail dreamed of building better lives.

The history of our country is filled with stories of people moving to new communities. As you read the next lesson, think about what it would be like to come to a new community, in a new land, to build a better life.

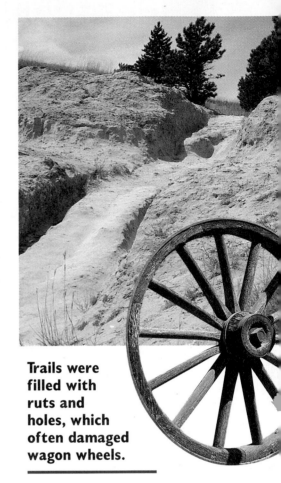

Trails were filled with ruts and holes, which often damaged wagon wheels.

Reviewing Facts and Ideas

SUM IT UP

- In the 1840s and 1850s many pioneers traveled west on the Oregon Trail.

- The route over the prairie and mountains was difficult.

- Stories of people moving to new communities are part of our country's history.

THINK ABOUT IT

1. What was the Oregon Trail?

2. **FOCUS** What was it like to travel west on the Oregon Trail?

3. **THINKING SKILL** Can you _predict_ what responsibilities you might have had on a wagon train? In what ways are they like yours today?

4. **WRITE** Write a diary entry describing a day you spent traveling with your family.

THINKING SKILLS

Classifying

VOCABULARY
classifying

WHY THE SKILL MATTERS

Heading west on the Oregon Trail required careful planning. Travel conditions were very difficult. Pioneers had to plan what to carry with them in their wagons. If a wagon was too heavy to pull, the oxen would get tired and sick. On the other hand, the pioneers were going on a long journey across the country. There were no repair shops or stores with supplies along the way. Pioneers had to bring the things they needed for the trip and for the new homes and farms they were going to build.

One skill that can help in making choices like these is classifying. Classifying is grouping similar things together. Classifying helps to sort many items.

USING THE SKILL

Look at the pictures on the next page. They show some of the different things people wanted to bring with them on the Oregon Trail.

Suppose you were traveling west in the 1840s. Not everything shown in the picture can fit in your wagon. To plan what to take, you could classify the items into things that you will surely need and things that could be given up.

First select an item that you think is necessary. Supplies of food, such as flour and sugar, are necessary. Find other items that are also needed, such as the hammer and nails for repairs. What items are not needed? A favorite old piece of furniture is not absolutely necessary. Could the doll stay behind if there were no room? Continue to sort the items into two groups, those that are needed and those that are not.

TRYING THE SKILL

There is more than one way to classify the items shown in the picture. Suppose your goal is to find items for mending and making clothes. Which items are those? Which items are useful for cooking? Which items would help a child enjoy a long trip?

Use the Helping Yourself box to guide you in classifying.

REVIEWING THE SKILL

1. What is classifying?
2. Which items would you classify as being useful for wagon repairs? Which ones are not useful?
3. Look through the items in your desk or school bag. How could you classify them?
4. Why do you think it is helpful to classify things?

Coming to America

READ ALOUD

"That was the first time I saw the Statue of Liberty, when I was standing on deck. And I had a hat on, and the wind came along and took my hat off. I said to my mother in Italian, 'Mama, there goes my hat!' And I said to her, 'Look at the lady, the lady over there!'"

Journey by Sea

These are the words of Joseph Allatin (a lah TEEN). The "lady" he saw was the Statue of Liberty. Joseph was six years old. His family had left Italy in 1894. The family sailed across the Atlantic Ocean to make new lives in the United States. The Statue of Liberty is in the harbor of New York City. It brought great joy to people like Joseph. It meant that they had arrived in the United States.

The Statue of Liberty is still a symbol that our country welcomes many immigrants. An immigrant is someone who comes to live in a new country. Like the pioneers who moved west in the 1840s and 1850s, immigrants were seeking a new life. During the early 1900s, they came to the United States looking for freedom. They also came because they could not find good jobs in their own country.

Arriving in New York

Once the ships carrying immigrants arrived in New York, they sailed past the Statue of Liberty to Ellis Island. Ellis Island was an immigration center. Officers there decided if people could stay in the United States. Immigrants who were sick might be forced to return to their country.

Many Americans today had a relative who came through Ellis Island. Lauren Buchter (BUHK ter) is 11 years old. Her great-grandfather came from Austria in 1902. He went through Ellis Island and then lived in New York City. Lauren's great-grandmother followed in 1916.

Lauren lives in New York City today. She never knew her great-grandparents. But she likes to learn about her past by talking to her grandfather, Jerry Selinfreund (SE lihn froynd). He was born a few years after his parents came to New York City.

When she asks her grandfather questions, Lauren is listening to oral history. Oral history is telling people what life was like in the past.

Children of all ages arrived with their families at Ellis Island (top). Lauren Buchter learns about the past from her grandfather (below). Here he is as a young boy long ago (left).

The Lower East Side

Like many other immigrants, Lauren's great-grandparents went to live on New York City's Lower East Side. It was very crowded. Most people lived in small, run-down apartment buildings called tenements.

"Even though living conditions were tough, my mother did not mind," said Mr. Selinfreund. "She lived in a tenement. She had to walk up to the fifth floor."

Immigrants came from many countries. They came for different reasons. Lauren's great-grandparents came for religious freedom.

Immigrants on the Lower East Side had different cultures. They also spoke many different languages. Having their children learn English was important. "My mother spoke many languages," Mr. Selinfreund said. "But none of them was English. That was one of the hardest parts. But she was so happy to be in the United States."

The Lower East Side was a community alive with very crowded apartments and busy streets.

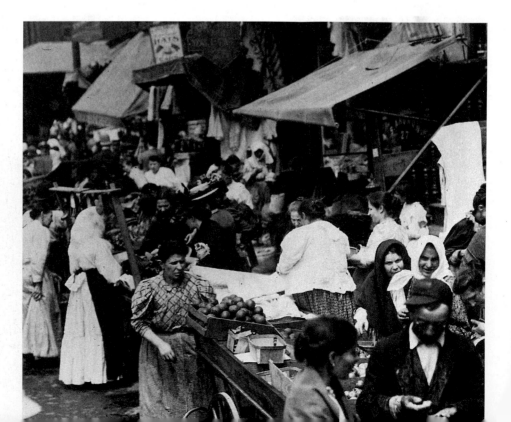

Work and Play

Most immigrants worked very hard. Often they did several jobs to make a living. "My father was a glazier *(window-maker)* and a religious leader," said Mr. Selinfreund. "He also taught dancing. He even drove a taxi and became a button-maker."

Many women and children worked, too. Some worked in factories. Children sold pencils, candy, or newspapers on the streets. But life was not all work for children. The streets were also their playgrounds. They played tag and stickball. Instead of a baseball bat, they used a broomstick. Many neighbors came out to play or watch. But everything stopped when the soda man came by selling cold sodas!

Life was both difficult and fun. Children often worked to earn money to help their families (top). But there was also time to play street games like stickball (bottom).

A Country of Immigrants

Immigrants arrived with suitcases filled with personal items. Their few belongings were all they had to start new lives.

The early 1900s was a time when many immigrants came to our country. They came from many different places around the world. The graph on this page shows you how many people came during this time period. Most came through New York. Others arrived in such cities as Boston and San Francisco.

Immigrants came from many different cultures. The one thing they had in common was hope—hope that life in the United States would be better.

Each group of immigrants has brought many important things to our country. They brought different languages, religions, and other parts of culture. They have made our country rich and strong.

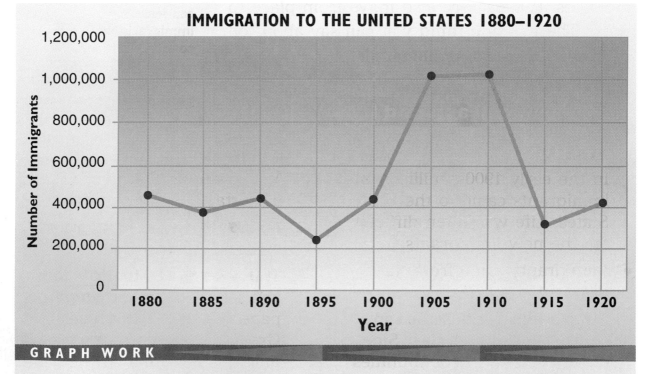

IMMIGRATION TO THE UNITED STATES 1880–1920

GRAPH WORK

The United States grew as more and more immigrants came each year.

1. About how many immigrants came to the United States in 1905? About how many came in 1920?

2. What happened to the number of immigrants who came between 1900 and 1905?

3. What can you say about the pattern of immigration between 1880 to 1920?

Source: U.S. Census Bureau

Oral History

When Lauren is older, she may tell her children about how she lived in New York too. Then she will continue her family's oral history. "It's fun to hear my family stories," said Lauren. "It helps explain who I am today."

Do you have older people in your family or community? Ask them about their lives. Then you, too, will be learning from oral history.

WHY IT MATTERS

In the early 1900s, millions of new people came to the United States. They formed new communities. But immigration was not new for our country. Immigrants have been coming to our country for hundreds of years.

Today people still move here from other countries. People here also move from place to place. There is one thing you can say about our country—it is always changing!

Visitors to Ellis Island can learn about immigration and our country's history.

✓ Reviewing Facts and Ideas

SUM IT UP

- In the early 1900s, millions of immigrants came to the United States. Life was often difficult for the new immigrants.

- Immigrants came from many different countries.

- Many immigrants settled in New York's Lower East Side. Others settled in communities throughout the country.

- One way we learn about the past is through oral history.

THINK ABOUT IT

1. Why was the Statue of Liberty important for immigrants?

2. **FOCUS** Why did immigrants come to America?

3. **THINKING SKILL** *Classify* the years shown on the graph on page 222 into two groups. Group 1 is when over one million people immigrated. Group 2 is when under one million people immigrated. What have you learned?

4. **WRITE** Write a short poem about the Statue of Liberty.

Moving to Northern Cities

READ ALOUD

"The Great Migration is part of my life. I grew up knowing about people on the move. . . . There was always talk in my house of other families arriving from the South."

People on the Move

These are the words of an artist named Jacob Lawrence. He is describing a great journey. It was made by many African Americans in the early 1900s. During this time many African Americans left their homes in the southern part of the United States. They hoped to build new lives in northern cities.

In the last lesson you read about people moving from other countries to the United States. That type of movement, as you know, is called immigration. Another type of movement is called migration. Migration is the movement of people from one part of a country or area to another.

In this lesson you will learn more about Jacob Lawrence. You will also learn about the Great Migration, the movement north of many African Americans.

Focus Activity

READ TO LEARN
What was the Great Migration?

VOCABULARY
migration
Great Migration
Civil War

PLACES
Chicago, Illinois

PEOPLE
Jacob Lawrence
Abraham Lincoln
Martin Luther King, Jr.

The Civil War

Since colonial times most African Americans had been living as slaves. They were forced to work for the people who owned them. They were not allowed to read and write. They were not free people.

Look at the map below. From 1861 to 1865 the Northern and Southern parts of the United States went to war against each other.

This war was called the Civil War. People in the South wanted to be separate from the North. People in the North wanted both sides to stay together as one country. During the war President Abraham Lincoln wanted to end slavery. Finally, in 1865, the war ended. Slavery was over. African Americans were free.

Abraham Lincoln said, "slavery must die that the nation might live."

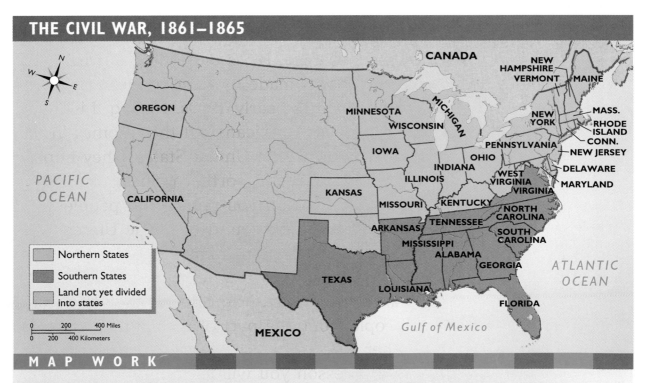

THE CIVIL WAR, 1861–1865

Northern States
Southern States
Land not yet divided into states

0   200   400 Miles
0   200   400 Kilometers

CANADA

NEW HAMPSHIRE
VERMONT
MAINE

OREGON

MINNESOTA
WISCONSIN
MICHIGAN

NEW YORK
MASS.
RHODE ISLAND
CONN.
NEW JERSEY

PACIFIC OCEAN

IOWA
PENNSYLVANIA
OHIO
INDIANA
ILLINOIS
WEST VIRGINIA
VIRGINIA
DELAWARE
MARYLAND

CALIFORNIA
KANSAS
MISSOURI
KENTUCKY
NORTH CAROLINA

ARKANSAS
TENNESSEE
SOUTH CAROLINA

MISSISSIPPI
ALABAMA
GEORGIA
ATLANTIC OCEAN

TEXAS
LOUISIANA
FLORIDA

MEXICO
Gulf of Mexico

M A P   W O R K

During the Civil War the Northern states fought against the Southern states.

1. Locate Texas on the map. Was it part of the Northern or Southern states?

2. Which Northern states shared a border with Southern states?

3. Can you name any states today that did not exist during the Civil War?

Difficult Lives

Although they were free, African Americans living in the South still had a difficult time after the Civil War. There were very few chances for good jobs or education. They still were not treated fairly.

In the early 1900s, African Americans heard there were good jobs and better opportunities in northern cities like Chicago, Detroit, New York, and Philadelphia. Thousands of people moved north hoping for a better life. The Great Migration began.

Many African Americans in the South lived in rural communities where they were not treated fairly.

Starting Over

Starting a new life in the North was exciting for many African Americans. One woman wrote of her life in Chicago, Illinois: "I am well and thankful to be in a city. . . . The people are rushing here by the thousands. The houses are so pretty, we [have] a nice place. Hurry up and come to Chicago. It is wonderful. . . ."

As communities grew in the North, there were more opportunities to find jobs. People worked in iron and steel mills. Some made buildings. Many worked in factories where they made products like bricks and glass. Others worked on railroads. Their lives were improving. As their community grew, some people started their own businesses. Many people were happy with their decision to migrate to the North.

These photos of life in the North were taken in the 1920s by the photographer James Van Der Zee.

Painting the Great Migration

You have read about the artist Jacob Lawrence. About 1917 his parents migrated north to Philadelphia. As a young boy Jacob Lawrence became interested in painting. He knew he wanted to be an artist. Later, in 1941, he made a series of paintings about the Great Migration. Look at the painting on this page. Describe what it tells about the Great Migration.

MANY VOICES PRIMARY SOURCE

Painting by Jacob Lawrence, completed in 1941.

The Phillips Collection

Martin Luther King, Jr.

As African Americans soon found out, life was still difficult in the North. Although they did have a better chance for work and education, they still faced unfair treatment. They often received less pay than a white worker for the same job.

Unfair treatment continued in both the North and South. In the 1950s and 1960s thousands of people joined together to work for change. One African American leader was Martin Luther King, Jr. He spent his life working to make sure all people were treated fairly.

WHY IT MATTERS

You have read about immigration and migration. Our country's history includes many stories of people moving to new communities to build new lives. In the next lesson you will learn how people today still move to the United States with hopes of starting new lives.

Martin Luther King, Jr., wanted to make laws fair for all Americans.

✔️ Reviewing Facts and Ideas

SUM IT UP

- The Civil War was fought between the North and South from 1861 to 1865.
- President Abraham Lincoln helped to end slavery.
- The Great Migration took place during the early 1900s.
- Martin Luther King, Jr., worked to end the unfair treatment of people.

THINK ABOUT IT

1. Why did African Americans migrate to the North?

2. **FOCUS** What was the Great Migration?

3. **THINKING SKILL** How is migration *like* immigration? How is it *different*?

4. **GEOGRAPHY** Look at the map on page 225. In what direction is Maine from Florida?

Legacy

A Family Reunion

During the Great Migration, some members of the Pressley family in South Carolina moved north to Philadelphia.

Today people in this family live in many different communities. Every year they return to South Carolina to have a family reunion. At the reunion they see people they care about. They also learn about their family history. It is a special time.

Today, as in the past, families sometimes move. They may move to new communities in the United States or even to another country.

At the airport Felicia Green welcomes cousins traveling to the reunion from faraway places.

230

Felicia's scrapbook includes a page on fun at the family reunion. Whether it's storytelling (top left), singing or playing baseball, there's lots to do!

It doesn't matter who wins in the tug of war, as long as it's fun for everyone.

231

Immigration Today

READ ALOUD

"I like it in the United States. School is a little bit hard for me now. But it's getting better. I have new friends. But sometimes I miss my old friends."

Moving to a New Country

These are the words of a student named Delores Stivalet (STEE va lay). She and her family moved to San Diego, California, from Veracruz, Mexico, just a few years ago. Delores was 11 years old. It was an exciting time for her and her family.

Maybe you and your family at one time moved to a new community. If so, you know how the move made you feel. Perhaps you were excited, nervous, or a little sad. On the first day of school, you may have been shy.

Perhaps you or someone you know has moved to the United States from another country. Moving to a new country can be very hard. There are many things to learn and many changes to make. In this lesson you will see how immigrants like Delores and her family build new lives in the United States.

Settling in San Diego

For Delores and her family, moving to a new country like the United States was challenging. Her family felt that there were better schools and more jobs for people in the United States. "If you really want to do something in the United States," her father said, "you can do it. That's why we moved here."

Delores's new community in San Diego has a lot in common with Veracruz. They both have busy ports with beautiful beaches. The climate is warm in both cities.

There are also many differences between the two cities. In San Diego, Delores and her family have to learn English. "I am learning to speak English," said Delores. "But we still speak Spanish at home."

Veracruz and San Diego are port cities. In Veracruz a woman sells goods (top). San Diego has many tall office buildings (bottom).

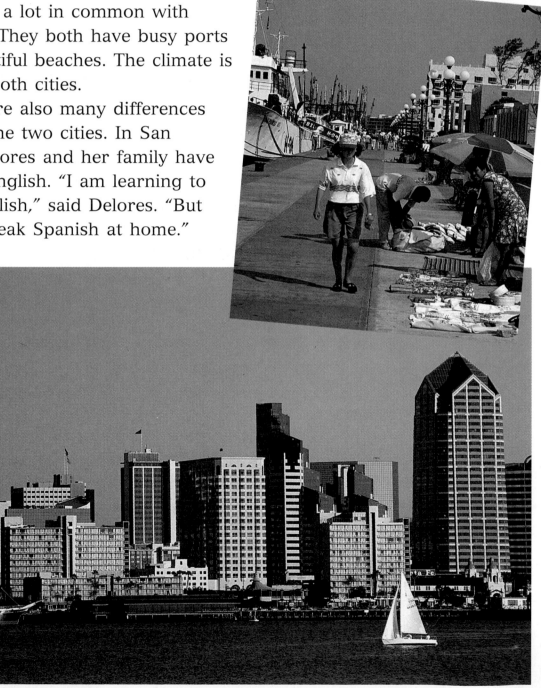

233

Infographic

United States Immigration Today

Immigrants continue to come here from around the world. The United States offers people the chance for a better life. Let's see what some recent immigrants have to say about living in the United States.

> **❝**I never saw snow where I lived in India. It's colder here. I like to go sledding and to make snowmen.**❞**

—Aditya Nochur
(AH deet yah noh CHAWR)

From India
Lives in Cambridge, Massachusetts

> **❝**I missed foods like fried bananas. Someone offered me spaghetti. I said 'No, thank you!' But now I eat it.**❞**

—Oyeyinka Oyelaran
(oh YEAH yin kah oh YEAH la RIN)

From Nigeria
Lives in Winston Salem, North Carolina

> **❝**I was surprised by how big the United States is. It has big airports, big roads and big shopping malls.**❞**

—Joanna Jawdosiuk
(joh AHN uh yahv DOH shook)

From Poland
Lives in Glendale, Wisconsin

Becoming a Citizen

From the Infographic you can see that people immigrate to the United States from different countries around the world. Many of these immigrants, like Delores and her family, hope to become citizens of the United States.

Study the chart below. It shows how some adult immigrants can become citizens of the United States today.

BECOMING A CITIZEN OF THE UNITED STATES OF AMERICA

STEP 5: Receive a certificate of citizenship.

STEP 1: Fill out form about you and your life.

STEP 4: Take an oath of loyalty to the United States. An oath is a statement or promise in which a person swears that what he or she said is true.

STEP 3: Meet with Judge, who can grant citizenship.

STEP 2: Answer questions in English about United States of America history and government.

WHY IT MATTERS

Immigration is even older than our country. From the early English settlers to the Ellis Island immigrants, people kept coming to this land to build new lives. The United States is still growing because of new immigrants and new citizens. The Statue of Liberty stands in New York harbor as a symbol of hope and friendship to all.

Taking the oath is an exciting event for immigrants who hope to build new lives in the United States.

Reviewing Facts and Ideas

SUM IT UP

- Many people immigrate to the United States from different countries around the world.

- Immigrants face a new language and a new way of life in their new country.

- Immigrants continue to help the United States grow.

THINK ABOUT IT

1. Name some countries where immigrants to the United States come from.

2. **FOCUS** What is it like to immigrate to the United States today?

3. **THINKING SKILL** What is the _sequence_ of steps needed to become a citizen?

4. **WRITE** Write a paragraph describing your community to someone who just moved there.

CITIZENSHIP
MAKING A DIFFERENCE

Helping New Immigrants

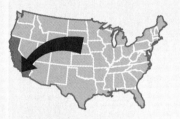

LOS ANGELES, CALIFORNIA—Hee Jin Kang [HEE JIN KAYNG] is 11 years old. She immigrated to the United States from Korea. Hee Jin likes her new home and school. But she misses her family in Korea, especially her grandparents. "My biggest problem," says Hee Jin, "is learning English. It's not easy for me to talk with other students. So it's hard for me to make friends."

Keith Soon Kim is much older than Hee Jin. But he knows how she feels. He, too, was once an immigrant from Korea. He then became a citizen. But he did not forget how hard his early days here had been. He wanted to help new immigrant children. He wanted them to have an easier time learning about the United States.

Mr. Kim decided to work with Korean children in schools in Los Angeles. He started after-school clubs for these students. Club members practice speaking English. They also learn about American culture. Mr. Kim works with the parents of these students, too. Many Korean immigrant parents do not speak English. He helps parents and teachers communicate more easily with each other.

Today Mr. Kim continues to help Korean American immigrants. He started a camp and a leadership program for college students. Mr. Kim works hard to help young people, "because I want them to be good American citizens," he says.

"... I want them to be good American citizens."

Keith Soon Kim

CHAPTER 9 REVIEW

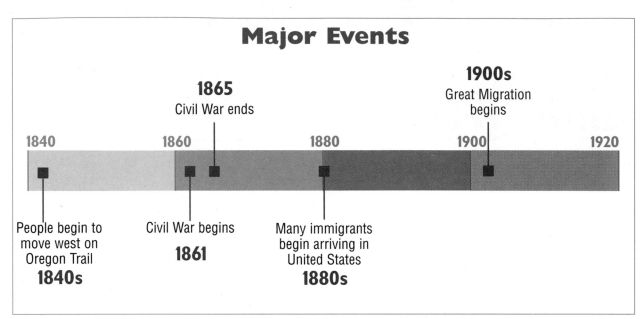

Major Events

1865
Civil War ends

1900s
Great Migration begins

1840   1860   1880   1900   1920

People begin to move west on Oregon Trail
1840s

Civil War begins
1861

Many immigrants begin arriving in United States
1880s

THINKING ABOUT VOCABULARY

Number a sheet of paper from 1 to 10. Beside each number write the word or words from the list that best fit each definition.

Civil War   immigrant   oral history
classify   migration   pioneer
diary   oath   prairie
Great Migration

1. People telling what life was like in the past

2. A statement in which a person swears to tell the truth

3. Flat or rolling land covered with tall grasses

4. To group similar things together

5. The movement of people from one part of a country to another

6. Someone who comes to live in a new country

7. A person who leads the way into a land not known to them

8. The movement north of African Americans in the early 1900s

9. The war between the northern and southern states from 1861–1865

10. A written record of what someone has done or thought each day

THINKING ABOUT FACTS

1. Why did pioneers travel west in groups known as wagon trains?

2. How do diaries help us learn about the past?

3. Why did immigrants come to the United States in the early 1900s?

4. What led to the Great Migration? Did the people who migrated north find what they hoped for?

5. What are some of the steps adult immigrants take to become citizens of the United States?

THINK AND WRITE

WRITING INTERVIEW QUESTIONS
Choose an older person to interview. To prepare, write some questions to ask about the person's childhood.

WRITING A WELCOME GUIDE
Create a guide to your community for new immigrants. Include helpful information such as where to buy groceries, how to get a library card, and how to get emergency help.

WRITING A COMPARISON
Write a paragraph comparing the reasons for two migrations: the move west and the Great Migration.

APPLYING THINKING SKILLS

CLASSIFYING
Review the classifying skill on pages 216–217 before answering the following questions.

1. How do you classify things?
2. How could you classify the things in your school?
3. List items you would take on an overnight camping trip. Classify the items into those needed for survival and those not needed.
4. Look at your list again. How else could you classify the items on it?
5. What are things you classify during a normal day?

Summing Up the Chapter

The movement of people into and within the United States is classified into four groups on the main idea map below. Review the chapter. Then complete a copy of the map by listing several reasons why each group migrated or immigrated. What goal did these groups have in common?

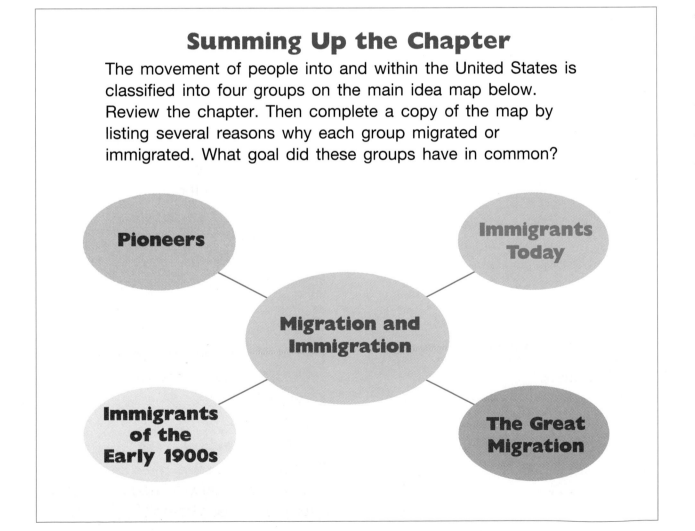

Changing the Way People Live

THINKING ABOUT GEOGRAPHY AND TECHNOLOGY

Two hundred years ago, moving to a new community may have meant a difficult trip and no news from old friends and neighbors. Since then, new methods of transportation and communication have made traveling and staying in touch much easier.

In Chapter 10, you will learn how technology has changed the ways we travel and get news. Technology is not only part of our history, it is part of our lives today and tomorrow.

1807

HUDSON RIVER, NEW YORK

The first steam-powered boat, the *Clermont*, travels upriver from New York City

1839

VANDALIA, ILLINOIS

The National Road, started in the East, reaches Vandalia, Illinois

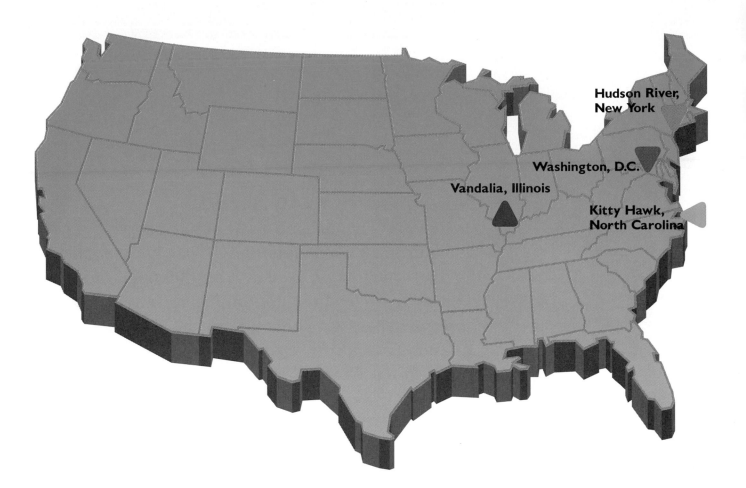

Hudson River, New York

Washington, D.C.

Vandalia, Illinois

Kitty Hawk, North Carolina

1844

WASHINGTON, D.C.
The first telegraph message is sent by Samuel Morse

1903

KITTY HAWK, NORTH CAROLINA
The Wright brothers make the first successful airplane flight

On the Go

READ ALOUD

In the last chapter you read about people moving to new communities. What were some of the ways they traveled? They bumped along in wagons over the Oregon Trail. They sailed long distances on ships across the Atlantic Ocean. They also chugged along in trains to cities in the North.

Transportation Before 1800

You probably travel somewhere almost every day. You may walk, ride a bike, or take a bus to get to school or to visit friends. Maybe you ride in a car or on a train. Can you imagine what your life would be like without these forms of transportation?

Before 1800, people walked to get most places. There were no cars or trains. If people had to go far, they rode on horses or mules, or used wagons pulled by animals. People also used canoes and boats if they had to travel over water.

Often travel over land was difficult because there were few roads in the United States. There were only paths and trails. They were nothing like the wide, smooth roads you often see in our country today.

Focus Activity

READ TO LEARN
In what ways has transportation changed over time?

VOCABULARY
fuel

PEOPLE
Robert Fulton
Peter Cooper
Henry Ford
Wilbur Wright
Orville Wright
Elisha Otis
Amelia Earhart
Eduardo San Juan
Mae Jemison

PLACES
National Road

Steam-Powered Engines

People had always traveled along waterways. But it was hard for boats to travel against the currents of the water. Robert Fulton thought there must be a way that technology could improve travel by water. He worked for years on the idea of using steam engines to power boats. Finally, in 1807, he got to test his idea. People lined the Hudson River in New York to watch Fulton's boat, the *Clermont*. Everyone was excited to see the boat move up the river.

The National Road

In the early 1800s people began to build new roads. Some of these new roads were covered with stone. Other roads were made from logs and planks of wood. Each new road made it easier to travel between places. One road became the busiest of all. It was called the National Road. It was built over many years, by many people. From the map below you can see that it helped people to move west.

This drawing shows Robert Fulton's steamboat, the *Clermont*, chugging up the Hudson River.

THE NATIONAL ROAD, 1839

Legend
— National Road
— Other Road
⊛ National Capital
★ State Capitals
• Other Cities

MAP WORK

The National Road made it easier for people to travel between places in the United States.

1. About how long is the National Road?

2. In what direction does it run?

3. How do you think the National Road was important in the growth of the West?

243

Railroads from Coast to Coast

It was not long before steam engines were also used in other forms of transportation. Around 1825 steam engines in the United States were used for the first time to power railroad trains. Before then trains were pulled by horses.

One of the first railroad engines was called the *Tom Thumb*. Peter Cooper built the engine so it would be able to travel over hills and around curves. Cooper was proud of the *Tom Thumb*. He wanted people to know how fast his engine was. He set up a race. His engine would race against a "gallant gray" horse pulling a train car. When the day came for the big event, Cooper was disappointed! The mighty *Tom Thumb* broke down. The horse went on to cross the finish line.

But the age of the railroad was coming. Soon steam-powered railroads ran between most big cities. They made it easier for people to travel. Railroads also made it easier to move goods across the country.

The year is 1885. These construction workers are in front of railroad tracks built along the Cascade Mountains.

The Auto and the Airplane

With roads and steamboats and railroads, traveling long distances kept getting easier. Soon another invention changed the way people traveled between communities.

In 1908 a man named Henry Ford made a car he called the Model T. For the next several years Ford worked on making cars cheap enough so that many people could afford to buy them. People could now travel on their own to different places in less time than ever before. How do you think automobiles changed the way people live in your community?

Another invention that changed the way we live was the airplane. Wilbur and Orville Wright were brothers who owned a bicycle shop. Together they completed the world's first airplane flight in Kitty Hawk, North Carolina. Airplanes made people think that anything was possible.

Henry Ford's Model T (top) and the Wright Brothers airplane (bottom) changed forever the way people travel.

245

Faster and Further

Transportation and technology are always changing. Today people travel in space. There are even machines that have landed on the moon and the planet Mars. Look at the chart below. It shows that the history of transportation has many exciting people and events. What did Eduardo San Juan (ed WAHR doh san WAHN) do?

PEOPLE IN TRANSPORTATION

Elisha Otis **invented an elevator with a safety clamp in 1852. This led to the first passenger elevator and encouraged the building of skyscrapers.**

In 1932 Amelia Earhart **was the first woman to make a cross-Atlantic flight alone. In 1937, she disappeared on a flight around the world.**

Eduardo San Juan, **a scientist and engineer, designed the lunar rover vehicle. Called the "moon buggy," it carried astronauts across the moon's surface in 1971 and 1972.**

Mae Jemison **became an astronaut in 1988. She was the first African American woman to prepare, launch, and travel in space shuttles.**

CHART WORK

Many people have helped to shape the way we travel today.

1. Who was the first woman to fly alone in a plane across the Atlantic Ocean?

2. How do you think elevators changed the way people live in communities?

3. In what ways is the work of Eduardo San Juan and Mae Jemison similar?

Public Transportation

Sometimes new types of transportation bring new problems. Most forms of transportation today use fuel. Fuel is something that is burned to provide power. Gas and oil are examples of fuel. But burning fuel can cause pollution and use up our natural resources.

Today people are working to solve these problems. Public transportation is one solution that saves fuel. When people ride buses and trains instead of taking their own cars, there are fewer vehicles on roads. How do you think public transportation helps the environment?

WHY IT MATTERS

The United States has always been a country of people on the move. Today people move faster and further than ever before. Transportation is one way to bring people closer together. In the next lesson you will see other ways that bring people in communities closer together.

Public transportation is helpful in fighting pollution by saving fuel.

✓ Reviewing Facts and Ideas

SUM IT UP

- In the 1800s Americans began to build many roads.

- Robert Fulton developed steam engines to power boats.

- Steam engines were also used for railroad trains.

- Henry Ford made cars that many people could afford.

- The Wright Brothers made the first successful airplane flight.

- New types of transportation change the way people live.

THINK ABOUT IT

1. How did the steam engine change transportation?

2. **FOCUS** In what ways has transportation changed over time?

3. **THINKING SKILL** *Classify* into groups different ways people travel. Make a chart. What headings could you use?

4. **GEOGRAPHY** Look at the map on page 243. What direction is Vandalia from Cumberland?

247

GEOGRAPHY SKILLS

Reading Transportation Maps

VOCABULARY
transportation map

WHY THE SKILL MATTERS

By the middle of the 1800s there were several different ways for people to travel. You can see these different ways by reading a transportation map. A transportation map shows the routes people can use to travel from place to place. Transportation maps often show roads, railroads, and other kinds of transportation all on the same map.

Use the Helping Yourself box on the following page to guide you in reading transportation maps.

USING THE SKILL

Look at the map on the next page. It shows some other ways people traveled in the United States in 1860. Look at the map key. Find the symbols for roads, railroads, and canals. Canals are waterways dug across the land and used for boat travel.

Look at the painting of the Erie Canal below. Canals helped people move goods between bodies of water. A trip that had taken up to six weeks on rough trails and rivers took about a week on the Erie Canal. Find the Erie Canal on the map on the next page. It connects the Hudson River and Lake Erie.

Suppose that you wanted to travel from Cumberland, Maryland, to Vandalia, Illinois. The red line shows you that the National Road connected these two cities. With your finger follow the route from Cumberland to Vandalia on the map. You will pass through Maryland, Virginia, Pennsylvania, Ohio, Indiana, and Illinois. The brown line shows you that a railroad connected Cumberland and Vandalia.

The Granger Collection

TRYING THE SKILL

The map shows more than one way to get from one place to another. Suppose you wanted to travel north from Augusta, Georgia, to Boston, Massachusetts. What were two ways you could get there? If you wanted to take a train trip from the city of Philadelphia, where were two places you could go?

REVIEWING THE SKILL

1. What types of transportation are shown on the map below?

2. In what ways can people travel now that were not possible in 1860?

3. What kinds of transportation could people use to travel from Augusta to Montgomery in 1860? How do you know?

4. Look at the cities on the map. In 1860 most cities were near railroads or along the water. Why do you think that was so?

5. When is it helpful to use a transportation map?

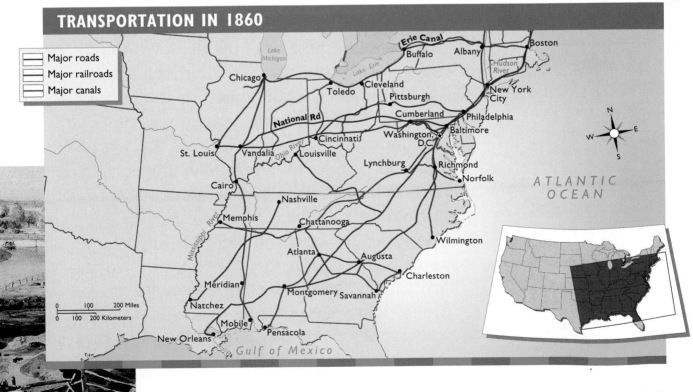

TRANSPORTATION IN 1860

Major roads
Major railroads
Major canals

Lake Michigan, Chicago, Toledo, Cleveland, Pittsburgh, Cumberland, Lake Erie, Erie Canal, Buffalo, Albany, Hudson River, Boston, New York City, Philadelphia, Baltimore, Washington, D.C., National Rd, Cincinnati, St. Louis, Vandalia, Ohio River, Louisville, Lynchburg, Richmond, Norfolk, Cairo, Nashville, Memphis, Chattanooga, Mississippi River, Atlanta, Augusta, Meridian, Montgomery, Savannah, Natchez, Mobile, Pensacola, New Orleans, Charleston, Wilmington, ATLANTIC OCEAN, Gulf of Mexico

0   100   200 Miles
0   100   200 Kilometers

Keeping in Touch

READ ALOUD

The whole family gathered in the living room. Everyone was so excited as the switch was turned on. Slowly, like a miracle, a picture appeared on the screen and voices came out of the box.

Your grandparents probably remember a scene like this from the first time they watched television. In this lesson you will read about how television and other inventions have changed our lives.

Focus Activity

READ TO LEARN
In what ways has communication changed over time?

VOCABULARY
communicate
pony express
telegraph
satellite

PEOPLE
Samuel Morse
Alexander Graham Bell
Guglielmo Marconi

Communicating Long Ago

From the earliest days people have found ways to communicate. To communicate is to pass along feelings, thoughts, or information to someone. Today there are many ways to communicate with people around the world. What did people do before telephones, radios, and televisions? People used other ways to get information and share ideas.

Newspapers long ago were an important source of news. But they were expensive and hard to get. Town criers stood on street corners and yelled out the main news stories. News stories were also posted in public places where people could read them.

Riding the Pony Express

Pioneers often left friends and family behind as they moved to new communities and built new lives. These people wanted news from their families and old communities.

In the 1800s mail service was not reliable. But in 1860 a group of men developed a mail service called the pony express. The pony express was a team of daring horseback riders. They rode across the western United States to deliver mail from one place to another. They would hand off the mail to another rider, who would continue the route. Look at the map below. Find the route of the pony express. People in Sacramento, California, could get mail from people in St. Joseph, Missouri, in just 10 days.

Pony express **riders traveled by horse both day and night, no matter what the weather.**

Buffalo Bill Historical Center

THE PONY EXPRESS, 1860–1861

CANADA

VERMONT MAINE

NEW HAMPSHIRE
MASSACHUSETTS

OREGON

Missouri River

MINNESOTA

WISCONSIN

MICHIGAN

NEW YORK

RHODE ISLAND
CONNECTICUT

Snake River

IOWA

PENNSYLVANIA

NEW JERSEY

Sacramento   Carson City   Salt Lake City

Platte River

INDIANA
ILLINOIS

OHIO

DELAWARE
MARYLAND

St. Joseph

Ohio River

VIRGINIA

CALIFORNIA

Colorado River

MISSOURI   KENTUCKY

ATLANTIC
OCEAN

ARKANSAS   TENNESSEE

NORTH
CAROLINA

Rio Grande

PACIFIC
OCEAN

MISSISSIPPI

ALABAMA

SOUTH
CAROLINA

GEORGIA

TEXAS

LOUISIANA

FLORIDA

—— Pony Express Route

★ State Capital

• Other City

☐ Land not yet divided into states

0   250   500 Miles
0   250   500 Kilometers

MEXICO

Gulf of Mexico

MAP WORK

At each city riders used fresh horses to carry the mail to the next city.

1. About how many miles is the trip from St. Joseph to Carson City?

2. Along what river does the pony express route travel?

3. Where might the trip be most difficult for riders?

Communication by Wire

Links to
LANGUAGE ARTS

What's in a Word?

The word telegraph has two parts. Both come from the ancient Greek language. *Tele* means "far off" and *graph* means "to write." When put together they form the word *telegraph*—"far off writing."

List as many words as you can that contain *tele* or *graph*.

The pony express was a new step for communication. But soon an invention was to change everything. Samuel Morse was one of the early inventors of the machine called the telegraph. The telegraph used special codes to send words long distances over wires. In 1844 Morse had workers run a wire from Washington, D.C., to Baltimore, Maryland. He then sat in the Capitol building and tapped out the first telegraph message: *"What hath* [has] *God wrought* [made]*!"* The telegraph worked! By 1861 telegraph wires ran across the country. People could now get news from far away places in minutes. The pony express was no longer needed.

It was not too much longer before another invention changed how people communicated. In 1876 Alexander Graham Bell built a working telephone. People could now speak to each other directly from far away places.

This telegraph register (left) was used by Samuel Morse (right) in 1844. It received and printed codes sent by wire.

252

On the Air

The telegraph and the telephone were exciting inventions. Messages could travel in seconds! But there was one problem. The messages had to run through wires. It was impossible to connect all places around the world with wires.

Guglielmo Marconi (goo LYEHL moh mahr KOH nee) was an Italian inventor. He wanted to find a way to send signals without using wires. He studied the ideas and inventions of other people who had been working on the same idea. Finally, in 1895 Marconi invented the wireless telegraph. Now, even ships at sea could send signals back and forth to each other. The wireless telegraph then led to the invention of the radio.

Later, scientists invented a way to send pictures through space. That led to the invention of the television. Today, televisions and radios are in many homes. We can instantly see clear pictures and hear voices from all over the world.

The radio (above) was a popular form of communication before television. Alexander Graham Bell (bottom) built this telephone in 1875.

Latest Connections

Look at the time line. You can see that people have continued to look for new ways to improve communication. In the 1960s the first communications satellites were used. A satellite is a spacecraft that is used to connect radio, telephone, and television communications. Satellites make it possible for people to communicate in seconds across oceans to other countries.

Can you think of other machines that people use to communicate with each other? Computers and faxes are used every day to send and receive information.

Satellites are used by scientists to help them learn about faraway places like the sun, Venus, and Mars.

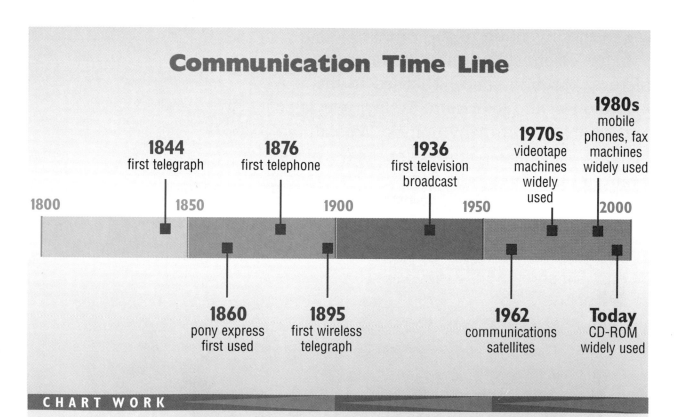

Communication Time Line

1844 first telegraph	**1876** first telephone	**1936** first television broadcast	**1970s** videotape machines widely used	**1980s** mobile phones, fax machines widely used	

1800 — 1850 — 1900 — 1950 — 2000

1860 pony express first used

1895 first wireless telegraph

1962 communications satellites

Today CD-ROM widely used

CHART WORK

Every year people are finding newer and faster ways to communicate with each other around the world.

1. What happened in 1860?

2. How many years after the invention of the telephone was the mobile phone being used by people?

3. Can you think of an invention in communication that might be in people's homes in the future?

WHY IT MATTERS

It has always been important for people to communicate. It used to take days to get a message across the country by pony express. Now it can happen in less than a second.

Over the years people have found new and better ways to share ideas and information. As people communicate more quickly with each other, they learn more about communities and the world around them. By communicating more easily around the world every day, people learn about many cultures and new ideas. By working together to understand each other and to use new ways of communication, people can solve many problems in our world today.

Just fifteen years ago, few people used personal computers. Today they are used by many people at work and home.

✓/ Reviewing Facts and Ideas

SUM IT UP

- People have always found ways to communicate.

- The pony express used horses and daring riders to speed mail across the western part of the country.

- Samuel Morse invented a way to send messages across wires.

- Guglielmo Marconi invented a way to send messages without wires.

- Radios and televisions soon followed. Communication continues to improve today with satellites and computers.

THINK ABOUT IT

1. How did people receive news long ago?

2. **FOCUS** In what ways has communication changed over time?

3. **THINKING SKILL** Make your own time line about some of the changes in communication. Put the events in the correct *sequence*.

4. **WRITE** Write a newspaper headline about the invention of the personal computer.

255

Focus Activity

READ TO LEARN
What is the English Channel Tunnel?

VOCABULARY
channel

PLACES
France
England
English Channel

A Tunnel in Europe

READ ALOUD

"Fog in Channel. Continent Cut Off."

These words appeared in a newspaper headline in England long ago. It describes what happened when fog prevented ships from sailing across the English Channel.

But thanks to technology, things have changed. Today people do not have to rely on ships and planes to cross the English Channel.

Two Countries and a Channel

In 1994 the first passengers boarded the *Eurostar* train. They were about to take a special trip. It was the first time France and England were connected by railroad. Look at the map on the next page. England is an island off the continent of Europe. It is separated from the rest of Europe by the English Channel. A channel is a narrow waterway between two larger bodies of water. The English Channel connects the Atlantic Ocean and the North Sea.

England and France are only about 21 miles apart at their closest points. But to travel between these two countries, people had to take a ship or fly. Now the English Channel Tunnel has connected them in a new way.

256

A Dream of Many Years

For over 200 years people have dreamed of linking England with France. In 1802 a French scientist came up with a plan for two long tunnels with a little island in between. The horse-drawn carriages could stop at the island to get fresh horses! The plan never came to life. Over the years many other plans were made. However, some people in England were afraid to connect their country with the rest of Europe. They thought they were safer as an island. But in 1986 the decision was made to build the tunnel. It took eight years to complete.

A ferry trip across the English Channel includes a view of these chalk cliffs at Dover, England.

THE ENGLISH CHANNEL TUNNEL

Map Legend:
- English Channel Tunnel
- Railroad
- Ferry Route
- Highway
- ✈ Airport
- ⊛ National Capital
- ○ Other City

MAP WORK

Before the English Channel Tunnel was built, people traveled between England and France by ferry or plane.

1. About how far is it from Folkestone to Calais?

2. What are two ways to get from Calais to Paris?

3. What might be some differences in traveling by ferry instead of by tunnel?

Special machines dug a tunnel below the channel (left). When the digging was done, English and French workers had a big party (right).

Building the Tunnel

Finally we reach the breakthrough site. The two machines that dug this tunnel started from opposite sides of the Channel and worked toward the middle. [The] cutter-head—a huge wheel with . . . teeth—chews into the last trace of rock separating England from France.

These are the words of a writer named Cathy Newman. She was describing the moment when workers broke through the rock that separated the two halves of the tunnel. It was an important moment. The digging of the tunnel was completed. French and English workers hugged each other.

A special machine called the "tunnel-boring machine" was used to dig the tunnel. Many pounds of earth were dug up from the bottom of the English Channel to make the tunnel. That earth was then piled along the English and French coasts. These areas will be used to build parks.

All Aboard!

The English Channel Tunnel is more than one tunnel. It is really three tunnels. Trains from England to France run through one tunnel. Trains from France to England run through the second tunnel. The third tunnel is just for workers and service crews. The service crews help keep the tunnel safe.

Two different trains run through the tunnel. *Eurostar* is the train for passengers without cars. The other train is called *Le Shuttle* (le shuh TELL). It carries people with their cars. It also carries trucks filled with goods that will be sold in other countries.

The tunnels are actually dug in the ground below the bottom of the English Channel (right). Trains (below) travel through the tunnel faster than cars on the highway.

A Big Change

Because of the tunnel, people in England and France can do business with each other more easily. Goods can be trucked from one country to the other without having to be loaded and unloaded onto a boat or plane.

The French and English have different cultures, different histories, and different languages. But now they can visit each other more easily. The poem below was written by a ten-year-old English boy named Adam Westgarth. In what ways do you think he is excited about the tunnel?

MANY VOICES LITERATURE

The Channel Tunnel
Poem written by Adam Westgarth in 1994.

At last, the Channel Tunnel has arrived
We have been waiting,
Anxiously, curiously for a long while.
Deep, deep down we will **burrow**
Into the sea,
Like a mole underground.
From London to Paris we can travel
With no delay;
Just straight down the tracks,
Going at tremendous speed
As quick as a flash,
We will be there.

—————————————

burrow: dig

WHY IT MATTERS

In this chapter you have read about changes in transportation and communication. Each of these changes has brought people closer together in different ways.

Trains, planes and automobiles have allowed people to travel between places faster than ever. The telegraph allowed people to send messages quickly to each other over wires. Today the computer lets people around the world communicate quickly without wires. And in Europe the English Channel Tunnel makes it easier for people in England and France to share ideas and lives every day.

THE WORLD'S LONGEST RAIL TUNNELS

MILES

Seikan (Japan) · Channel Tunnel (England-France) · Oshimizu (Japan)

GRAPH WORK

Japan has two of the three longest tunnels in the world.

1. About how long is the Seikan Tunnel?
2. Can you think of one way a tunnel might be better for travel than a bridge?

Reviewing Facts and Ideas

SUM IT UP

- England is separated from the rest of Europe by the English Channel.
- For hundreds of years people dreamed of ways to connect England and France.
- The English Channel Tunnel has made it easier to travel between England and France.

THINK ABOUT IT

1. What are two ways to cross the English Channel today?
2. **FOCUS** What is the English Channel Tunnel?
3. **THINKING SKILL** List in _sequence_ some of the new kinds of transportation that have been invented since 1800.
4. **GEOGRAPHY** Look at the world map in the Atlas on pages R10 and R11. What are some other places a tunnel might be built?

HERE WE GO

Modern ways of transportation help people travel between communities quickly. But for many people transportation is more than just traveling from one place to another. Transportation is also a legacy of fun and excitement. Look at the pictures here. See why being on the move has been fun for people of all ages, yesterday and today.

Look out pony express! In some communities today, people still use horses as a main form of transportation. Others ride horses just for fun.

Moving on! In the 1920s children rode carts they made from wooden boxes and baby carriage wheels (left). Today children keep rolling with in-line skates.

Whether paddling a canoe on a warm river or ice skating on a frozen lake, people enjoy having fun on the go in all kinds of weather.

CHAPTER 10 REVIEW

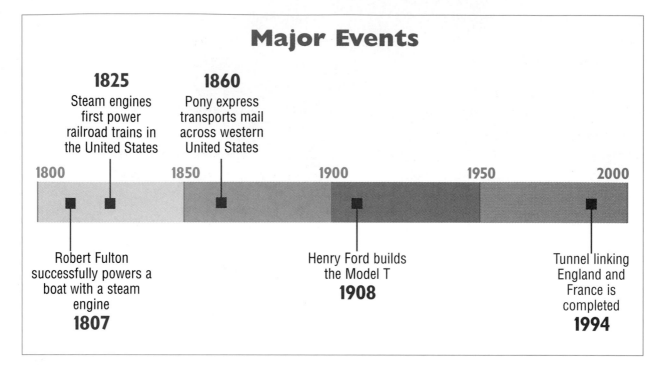

Major Events

1825
Steam engines first power railroad trains in the United States

1860
Pony express transports mail across western United States

1800   1850   1900   1950   2000

Robert Fulton successfully powers a boat with a steam engine
1807

Henry Ford builds the Model T
1908

Tunnel linking England and France is completed
1994

THINKING ABOUT VOCABULARY

Number a sheet of paper from 1 to 5. Write the word or words that best complete each sentence in the paragraph below.

Channel
communication
pony express

satellites
telegraph

Various means of transportation and __1__ have developed over time. In 1844, the __2__ first sent messages over wires. Later, in 1860 the __3__ delivered mail across the western U.S. In the 1960s __4__ enabled people to communicate around the world in seconds. And in the 1990s some high-speed trains travel below the English __5__.

THINKING ABOUT FACTS

1. What types of transportation were available before 1800? Name several types of transportation developed since then. Which do you think influenced people's lives the most? Why?

2. What environmental problem is partly caused by modern transportation? What is one way to help prevent this problem?

3. What was the pony express? What invention replaced it?

4. What are four ways people communicate today? Which of these ways were not available to people before 1800?

5. How has the English Channel Tunnel changed the lives of people in England and France?

THINK AND WRITE

WRITING A JOURNAL ENTRY
Suppose you are Robert Fulton or one of the Wright brothers. Write a journal entry about the first time your invention worked.

WRITING TO CONVINCE
Write a letter to convince people that they need the wireless telegraph. Explain why this invention is needed when people can already send messages over telegraph wires.

WRITING A RADIO REPORT
Write a radio report about the English Channel Tunnel. Explain what it is, why it is important, and why people like or dislike it.

APPLYING GEOGRAPHY SKILLS

READING TRANSPORTATION MAPS
Answer the following questions about the map on page 249 to practice your skill of reading transportation maps.

1. What do transportation maps show?

2. What types of transportation are shown on the map key?

3. What kind of transportation can you use to get from Chicago to St. Louis?

4. Which cities are not on a railroad line? How could you travel there?

5. How are transportation maps different from grid maps? How are they alike?

Summing Up the Chapter

The chart below shows major changes in transportation and communication since 1800. Complete a copy of the chart by listing the missing development or person most responsible for it. How have we benefited by these changes in transportation and communication?

Person	Development
Robert Fulton	
	telegraph
Alexander Graham Bell	
	wireless telegraph
	Model T automobile
Wright Brothers	
Eduardo San Juan	"moon buggy"
French and English (1994)	

UNIT 4 REVIEW

THINKING ABOUT VOCABULARY

Number a sheet of paper from 1 to 10. Beside each number write the word or words from the list below that best completes each sentence.

channel
diary
fuel
immigrants
migration

oath
oral history
pioneers
pony express
prairie

1. Much of our pollution is caused by burning _____ .

2. Many _____ traveled west in wagon trains on the Oregon Trail.

3. By reading a _____, we can learn about someone's personal life.

4. When people become citizens of the United States they must take an _____ of allegiance.

5. Many _____ came to the United States hoping to begin new lives.

6. The _____ north of African Americans began around 1900.

7. Some bodies of water are connected by a _____ .

8. By listening to _____, we can learn what life was like in the past.

9. It was difficult for the _____ riders to cross the western United States to deliver mail.

10. Flat or rolling land covered with tall grasses is known as _____ .

THINK AND WRITE ◄▬▬▬▬▬D

WRITING A JOURNAL ENTRY

Suppose that you are crossing the United States by wagon train with your family in the 1850s. Write a journal entry describing what life is like during your trip West.

WRITING AN ADVERTISEMENT

Choose one of the developments in communication or transportation discussed in Chapter 10. Then create an advertisement to convince people that this development will make their lives better.

WRITING ABOUT PERSPECTIVE

Write a paragraph about how your life might be different today if there were no buses, cars, airplanes, computers, or even telephones.

BUILDING SKILLS

1. **Classifying** What is the first step to take when classifying items?

2. **Classifying** Classify items in your classroom into three groups.

3. **Transportation Maps** Look at the map on page 257. What are two ways to get from London to Dover?

4. **Transportation Maps** Look at the map again. How can you travel from Calais to Lille?

5. **Transportation Maps** When might you or your family need to use a transportation map?

YESTERDAY, TODAY &
TOMORROW

In this unit, you have read about changes in where and how people lived in the past. Why do people move to new places today? What further changes in communication and transportation could we make in the future?

READING ON YOUR OWN

Here are some books you might find at the library to help you learn more.

THE FIRST RIDE: BLAZING THE TRAIL FOR THE PONY EXPRESS
by Jacqueline Geis
The story of the Pony Express and how it blazed a trail through dangerous territory.

THE GLORIOUS FLIGHT
by Alice and Martin Provensen
Louis Bleriot has a wish: He wants to fly. Read how he makes his dream come true.

GRANDFATHER'S JOURNEY
by Allen Say
A Japanese immigrant struggles with his love for both the United States and Japan.

UNIT PROJECT

Make Travel Stamps

1. Think of three ways people traveled long ago.
2. Design one stamp for each kind of travel. Use different colored construction paper for each stamp.
3. Decorate your stamps to make them more exciting.
4. Glue each stamp onto a piece of cardboard.
5. Write a description of each stamp on the cardboard. Tell why this form of transportation was important long ago.
6. Share your stamps and descriptions with a partner.

People walked.

People rode horses or mules.

Working Together

WHY DOES IT MATTER?

As you know, people are an important resource in our country. The work that people do contributes to our country's growth. In this unit you will learn about the different types of jobs people have to make a living. You will also learn how people use money.

Some people help other people for a living. Still others turn natural resources into products that people can use. As you will see, most jobs require people to work together.

Kidz Biz

Being young didn't stand in Chris Webb's way when he created "Imagination Industries." This teenager from Vermont makes teddy bears that move—and he sells them. Other "businesskids" have also come up with great ideas. Casey Golden, of Colorado, makes biodegradable golf tees from grass seeds, apple sauce, and other materials. Brandi Champion, of Maryland, creates dolls out of mops. Celesly Shabi, of Arizona, weaves traditional Navajo rugs, a skill she learned from her mom. What business would you like to go into?

GEO JOURNAL

Write and draw an advertisement to sell a product you invent yourself.

271

CHAPTER
11

Work and Money

THINKING ABOUT GEOGRAPHY AND ECONOMICS

Long ago people made or grew most things they needed. Today things have changed. Most people work at jobs to make money to buy things they need and want. In Chapter 11 you will see the many different jobs people have in communities around our country and in other countries too.

Spokane, Washington

Dallas, Texas

Tokyo, Japan

In Spokane, Washington, work around the house may include raking leaves.

Basketball players in Dallas, Texas, have a difficult job, but one that is fun and exciting.

Around the world there are many kinds of jobs, such as selling newspapers in Japan.

273

Jobs and Money

READ ALOUD

Mr. Skip Flythe (Flīth) works in a bicycle shop. He has sold hundreds and hundreds of bicycles to children. "I'll tell you something," he says. "There's nothing more exciting than selling a bike to a child."

Making a Living

Mr. Flythe has worked at the Flythe Cyclery shop in Raleigh (RAW lee), North Carolina for many years. His grandfather first opened the store back in the 1920s. What if his grandfather walked into the store today? He might be surprised at how it has changed. The style of bicycles has changed. And so have the prices. Bicycles are much more expensive today. But some things have remained the same. The sign on the front hasn't changed. There are still plenty of bicycles in the store. And, like his grandfather, Mr. Flythe provides goods for the people of Raleigh to buy. Goods are things that people make or grow. Mr. Flythe also offers a service by selling and repairing goods such as bicycles. A service is a job that helps others by providing something they need or want.

Focus Activity

READ TO LEARN
Why do people earn, save, and spend money?

VOCABULARY
goods
services
employer
interest
consumer
economy

PLACE
Raleigh, North Carolina

Why People Work

"I've been in this business ever since I was a little boy," says Mr. Flythe. "Whenever I was free, I was in the store with my grandfather. Then the business was my father's. Now it's mine. And one of my sons seems interested in joining the business. I've been warning him—it's a lot of hard work. But he still seems interested!"

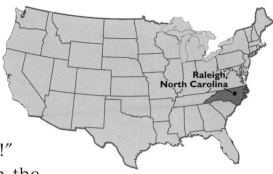

Maybe Mr. Flythe's children will work in the bicycle shop. Or maybe they'll do some other work to earn money. Most people work to earn money. Then they use that money to pay for a place to live. They also use it to buy food, pay for visits to the doctor, and buy clothes and books. What are other reasons people need money?

Like his grandfather long ago, Mr. Flythe provides a service by selling bicycles to people in Raleigh.

Mr. Flythe does not work all by himself. He needs other people to help him sell and repair bicycles. So he hires other people to work for him. This means he is an employer. An employer is someone who hires and pays other people to work. There are six other people who work at Flythe Cyclery.

Saving Money

Elissa Zellinger is a 14-year-old girl who lives in Raleigh. She has visited Flythe Cyclery many times to look at the bicycles. "Looking at those bikes kept me going," says Elissa. Slowly, she has saved her allowance and money from jobs outside her home.

Elissa was saving her money in a piggy bank. Her parents had a better idea. They took her to a bank and helped her open an account. If you save money in a bank, the bank gives you extra money called interest. The interest is payment for lending money to the bank. "I need every extra penny of interest," says Elissa.

Mr. Flythe has used banks for his business too. He keeps the money the store earns in the bank. He has also borrowed money from the bank to help the business grow. He pays interest to the bank for his loan.

How did the piggy bank get its name?

The answer has nothing to do with pigs! The name comes from *pygg*, (pronounced like the word *pig*), an old Scottish word for a kind of clay used to make jars. People stored money at home in these jars. The jars made from this clay became known as pyggy banks. Later the name changed to piggy banks and the jars were even shaped like pigs.

Elissa Zellinger worked at different jobs to earn money to buy a bicycle.

Being a Consumer

Finally Elissa saved enough money. She did some research to find out which bikes were the best buys. Elissa wanted to be a smart consumer. Consumers are people who buy goods and services. "I've worked hard to save money," says Elissa. "I want to make sure I don't throw it away!"

Mr. Flythe knows what Elissa means. "Children who have earned and saved their own money are my best consumers. I give a free workshop for children on bicycle safety and repair. Children who have saved their money are always the ones who take my class!"

Elissa loves her new bike. She even knows how to fix a tire or a slipped chain. She also knows she has to wear her helmet and be alert when she rides her bicycle. And she has also learned a lot about how our economy works. Economy is the making and consuming of goods and services.

Elissa is a smart consumer. She asked many questions before deciding which bicycle to buy.

277

WHY IT MATTERS

Flythe Cyclery is part of Raleigh's economy. Mr. Flythe and his employees provide a service and sell goods. They also earn money. They spend that money in their community. That money helps other businesses grow.

Some people do jobs that don't earn money. For example, some people work in their homes raising their families. That's an important job too. Everyone who works contributes something to a community and to its economy.

Elissa plays a role in her community's economy by earning money and buying goods.

✔ Reviewing Facts and Ideas

SUM IT UP

- Goods are things people make or grow.
- A service is a job that helps other people by providing something they need or want.
- People who buy goods are called consumers.
- Interest is money paid for a loan.
- Economy is the making and consuming of goods and services.

THINK ABOUT IT

1. What is the difference between an employer and a consumer?

2. **FOCUS** Why do people earn, save, and spend money?

3. **THINKING SKILL** _Compare_ and _contrast_ Mr. Flythe's job with the job of a teacher or principal.

4. **WRITE** Suppose you want to earn money over the summer. Write a brochure advertising what services you can offer your neighbors. Make sure your brochure tells why people should hire you and what you will charge.

The Pencilmania Business

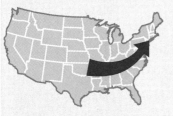

NEW YORK CITY, NEW YORK— Would you like a monster pencil holder, an eraser shaped like a clown, or a holiday bunch of lollipops and pencils? Jason Walder and José Rodriguez can help you. They are 12-year-old students at Public School 169 in New York City. They're in classes for students who have special learning needs. And they are "super salesmen" of a program called Pencilmania.

Pencilmania is a made-up word that means "crazy about pencils." Students in Pencilmania need not be crazy about pencils, but they are serious about learning to run a business. Every day at lunch, they sell pencils and gift items.

The students give some of the money they earn to the Make a Wish Foundation to help children who are very sick. The money also pays for class trips to museums and concerts.

"Selling the pencils is just one part of the business," Jason learned.

The students use catalogs and decide what and how many of each kind of pencil to order. When the pencils arrive, they make sure they have received everything they ordered. They advertise their goods with posters, fliers, and announcements over the school loudspeaker.

José enters the daily earnings on a computer. "I also help decide how much each item should sell for so we can make money. But what I like most is helping the customers decide what they want. And I like to count money. It helps me in math."

The hard work is rewarding. Jason explained, "I am proud I learned how to make good decisions." And José added, "We learned how to work together to get our job done."

Pencilmania

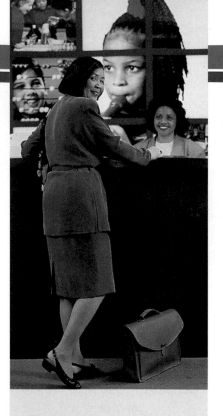

People at Work

Focus Activity

READ TO LEARN
What are some different ways a person can make a living?

VOCABULARY
publishing
editor
designer
producer

READ ALOUD

"When I was a child, I didn't think much about where textbooks came from. I didn't think about who wrote them or how they were printed. Now I think about textbooks a lot! Working on textbooks is how I make my living."

Where Did This Book Come From?

These are the words of Iris Kim. She works at the publishing company in New York City that made this book. Publishing companies make books, magazines, CD-ROMs, and other things people can read. Ms. Kim is an editor. An editor helps with all the steps involved in making a book.

Like Ms. Kim at your age, you may not have given thought to your textbooks. But many people work hard to make the books that appear on your desk at the start of each school year. For Ms. Kim and the people she works with, making textbooks is more than just a way to make a living. They hope that readers, like you, will learn from the books. In this lesson you will learn some of the steps involved in making a book like this one.

Planning a Book

One of the first steps in making a textbook is to decide what the book should be about. The authors and editors make this decision together. Ms. Kim does research to find interesting and important topics for the textbooks she helps plan. Textbook authors and editors also pay attention to what teachers want their students to learn. The authors and editors learn what people have liked about their books in the past. It is also important to find out what changes to the book people would like to see in the future.

As an editor Iris Kim must research information. She also discusses writing ideas with writers and other editors.

How Does It Read?

After the first version of the book is written, many changes are made. The editor reads each lesson and makes suggestions about how to improve them. "Then I try to make all the changes work," says Ms. Kim. "I used to do my work on a typewriter. Now I use computers and other new technologies. I can make many more changes in much less time. I try to make each lesson interesting for students to read!"

Sometimes more information is needed, so Ms. Kim does more research. Sometimes all the information will not fit in the lesson. Then Ms. Kim must decide what information to leave out. There are also pictures and maps. Deciding what is most important is the editor's job. Computers help editors keep track of what is on each page.

After Ms. Kim receives a page from a writer, she makes many corrections and changes.

Planning a Book
One of the first steps in making a textbook is to decide what the book should be about. The

LESSON 2

People at Work

READ ALOUD
"When I was a child, I didn't think much about where textbooks came from. I didn't think about who wrote them or how they were printed. Now I think about te Working on textbooks is hov living."

MASTER

Focus Activity

READ TO LEARN
What are som different ways person can ma living?

VOCABULARY
publishi-

How

After the first v
many changes a
lesson and mak
improve them
changes wor
work on a
and other
more cha
it even

Som
Ms. Ki
infor
Kim
Th
w

LESSON 2

Work
People
At work

READ ALOUD
"When I was a kid, I didn't think much about where text books came from. I didn't think about who wrote them or how they were printed. Now, I think about text books a lot! Working on text books is how I make my living."
For Iris Kim, working on text books is more than just a way to make a living. She hopes that readers, like you, will learn from them!

At a Publishing Company

280

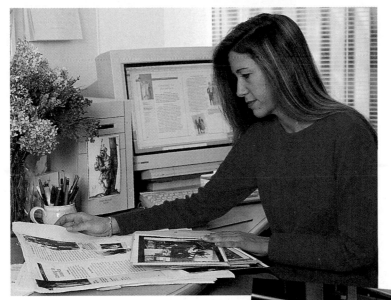

The **designer** decides where the photos and drawings will go on each page (top). The pages are then sent to the printer and made into a book (bottom).

How Does It Look?

Next, designers look at the pages. Designers make sure that each page looks right. They use a computer to help them decide where pictures will fit. "I try to make these pages exciting to look at," says a designer of this book. "Learning should be fun, so I choose pictures and designs that I think children will enjoy and learn from."

Then there are people who make sure the book will be printed correctly. All in all, about 75 people have worked on the book you are holding in your hands right now! By making a textbook that will be used by consumers, Ms. Kim and others are producers. A producer is a maker of goods or services.

Infographic

At the Workplace

Look around you. Almost everything you see is the result of someone's job. People built your school building. People made your desk and your pencils. Read this Infographic. What are the different jobs in your community?

Dena Abergel

Ballet Dancer
New York City, New York

Dancing is what makes me most happy in the world. Not everybody gets to do what they love. I began to study dancing intensely at age 10. The most rewarding part is performing.

Denice Burnham

Veterinarian
Orofino, Idaho

I take care of dogs, cats, and other pets. I like working with children to teach them how to care for their pets because children are usually the ones who know their pets best.

Alfredo Estrada

*Third-Grade Teacher
El Paso, Texas*

There's a lot of work involved in teaching. I like the challenge of trying to make learning exciting. I use computer games to teach writing, spelling, and math. I also use laser discs to teach science.

Leon Harris

*Television Anchorperson
Stone Mountain, Georgia*

I make news stories understandable. A story can happen and within minutes I'm talking about it. When I get nervous I just imagine I'm talking to my son.

Kim Guyette

*Furniture Maker and
Woodworker
Waterbury Center, Vermont*

I build tables from start to finish. Working with wood is challenging because you don't know exactly how each piece will come out.

I Like My Job!

For people to do a good job, it's important that they enjoy their work. Read the story below about a man who loves his job.

UNCLE JED'S BARBERSHOP

Story by Margaree King Mitchell, 1993.

Jedediah Johnson was my granddaddy's brother. Everybody has their favorite relative. Well, Uncle Jedediah was mine.

He used to come by our house every Wednesday night with his clippers. He was the only black barber in the county. Daddy said that before Uncle Jed started cutting hair, he and Granddaddy used to have to go thirty miles to get a haircut.

After Uncle Jed cut my daddy's hair, he **lathered** a short brush with soap and spread it over my daddy's face and shaved him. Then he started over on my granddaddy.

I always asked Uncle Jed to cut my hair, but Mama wouldn't let him. So he would run the clippers on the back of my neck and just pretend to cut my hair. He even spread lotion on my neck. I would smell wonderful all day.

---

lathered: filled with soap

286

WHY IT MATTERS

In this lesson you have met people doing different things to earn a living. All of these people depend on other people to do their jobs. "I wouldn't be able to do my job by myself," says Ms. Kim. "Authors, designers, artists, and other editors all work on books with me. And the most important people of all are the students who read them. Without them, I wouldn't be able to work on books like this one at all!"

Ms. Kim and many other people have worked together to make this textbook.

✓ Reviewing Facts and Ideas

SUM IT UP

- Publishing companies make books. Authors, editors, and designers are some of the people who work on books.

- Technology has changed the way editors and designers do their jobs.

- A producer is a maker of goods and services.

- There are many different ways to make a living. People need to work together to do their jobs.

THINK ABOUT IT

1. What is a producer?

2. **FOCUS** What are some different ways a person can make a living?

3. **THINKING SKILL** Look around your classroom. List some jobs needed to produce the things you observe. _Classify_ the jobs into at least three groups. What do these groups tell you about making a living?

4. **WRITE** Write a letter to the editor of this book telling what you like and don't like about the book.

Working AT Home

Museum of the City of New York

Working at home is a legacy that goes back long ago. People often lived above their shop or business or had a workshop in their backyard.

Today many people still work at home. As in the past some people work at home to care for their family and home. Still others work at home using computers and other high-tech machines to help run a business.

Cooking, cleaning and managing expenses are some of the many tasks homemakers do.

A pioneer family in the 1800s worked together for food and shelter.

Modern technology like telephones, computers, and faxes enable people to keep in touch with businesses from home.

Craftmakers often work at home. Dressed as a colonist, a woman shows how candles were made (left). Today, an Arapaho woman sews quilts (below).

THINKINGSKILLS

Identifying Cause and Effect

VOCABULARY

cause   effect

WHY THE SKILL MATTERS

In the last lesson you read about how technology has changed publishing. It is now easier for authors, editors, and designers to do their jobs. People can work all over the country, using fax machines and computers to send their work in.

New technology is one **cause** of these changes. A cause is something that makes something else happen. Some of the changes are **effects** of the new technology. An effect is what happens as a result of something else.

Understanding cause and effect connections helps you to make good decisions. For example, you know that opening your window on a cold day will cause cold air to come into the room. That will have the effect of making the room colder. You can then decide if you want to open the window or not. Look at the Helping Yourself box for some tips on how to find causes and effects as you read.

USING THE SKILL

One way to understand the connection between events is to look for clues as you read. Some words and phrases that may show you a cause are *because of*, *as a result of*, and *since*. Some that indicate effects are *as a result*, *so*, and *therefore*. As you read the story that follows, look for words to help you identify causes and effects.

> *Lisa Groome just took a new job. Since she is still learning how to do her new job, Lisa has to work late.*
>
> *Lisa is more excited about her work than she was at her old job. It is more rewarding. As a result, Lisa is happier.*

In the first paragraph, the word *since* connects two ideas. One idea is that Lisa is learning her new job. The other idea is that she is working late. *Since* shows you that Lisa's learning the job is the cause of her working late. Working late is an effect of learning the job.

Read the second paragraph again. Notice the phrase *as a result*, which indicates an effect. *As a result* shows that Lisa's happiness is an effect of her new job being more rewarding. The rewarding job is the cause of her happiness.

TRYING THE SKILL

Suppose that your mother or father is going to take a new job. Since the new job pays more money, your family will be able to save money for an exciting vacation. But the new job is located in another town, so you and your family will have to move.

What is the cause of your family being able to take a vacation? What is the effect of the job being in another town? How can you tell?

REVIEWING THE SKILL

1. What is a cause? What is an effect?

2. Suppose your community builds a new library. What might be some effects of the library on your community?

3. As a result of technology, editors can change what is written more easily. Is the technology a cause or an effect? How do you know?

4. Why is it helpful to think about cause and effect when making a decision or solving a problem?

Life in Japan

Focus Activity

READ TO LEARN
How do people live and work in Japan?

VOCABULARY
journalist
high-tech

PLACE
Tokyo
Japan

READ ALOUD

It is early Monday morning in Tokyo, Japan. Tokyo is one of the largest cities in the world. The subway platform is crowded. A train pulls into the station, silent and fast. The doors open and people start moving into the cars. Then the "pusher" comes along. He gently pushes people into the train to pack it more tightly. In Tokyo, the work day has begun.

A Growing Country

Tokyo (TOH kee yoh) is the capital of Japan. Japan is a small country in terms of land. Japan is a large country in terms of population. About 125 million people live in Japan. That number is about half the number of people living in the United States of America. To understand how crowded Japan is, picture half the people in our country moving to Montana!

Japan has been called "the land of the rising sun" because it is in the most eastern part of the continent of Asia. People there are among the first in the world to see the sun rise each day. Today "the land of the rising sun" has another meaning. The Japanese have worked hard to build up their country. So, they might see their country as a rising sun growing every day.

On the Job in Japan

Tsutomu Yamaguchi (tsew TOH mew yah mah GEW chee) is a journalist. A journalist writes for a newspaper, a magazine, or for a television news program. Mr. Yamaguchi lives in Japan and writes for a newspaper called the *Yomiuri Shimbun* (yoh mee ur ree SHIM bewn). "Working as a journalist is very challenging and exciting," says Mr. Yamaguchi. "I like finding stories and responding quickly to the news."

Mr. Yamaguchi also finds his job to be very hard at times. "The news is endless," he says. "And it is difficult to work on sad stories."

Just as Ms. Kim's job as an editor in the United States has changed because of technology, so has Mr. Yamaguchi's job. "We are very proud of our technology. We can get news stories and information faster than ever before. There is more information to understand," says Mr. Yamaguchi. "But it is still people who write the stories and make the decisions."

Mr. Yamaguchi is a journalist who has worked in Japan and around the world.

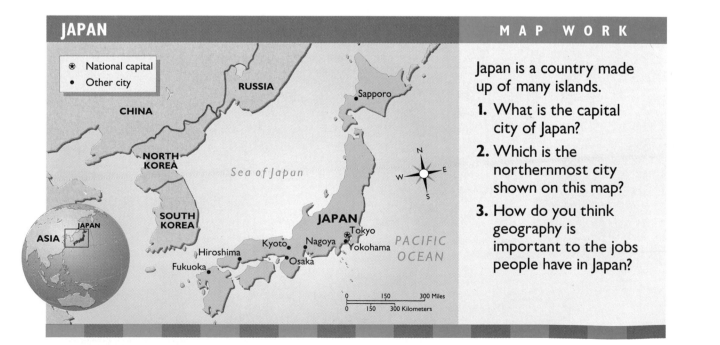

JAPAN

- ✹ National capital
- • Other city

RUSSIA · CHINA · NORTH KOREA · Sea of Japan · SOUTH KOREA · JAPAN · Sapporo · Tokyo · Kyoto · Nagoya · Yokohama · Hiroshima · Osaka · Fukuoka · PACIFIC OCEAN · ASIA · JAPAN

0   150   300 Miles
0   150   300 Kilometers

MAP WORK

Japan is a country made up of many islands.

1. What is the capital city of Japan?

2. Which is the northernmost city shown on this map?

3. How do you think geography is important to the jobs people have in Japan?

Kabuki theater, like Noh theater, is a very old tradition that is still popular in Japan.

Old and New

If you look around your home, the chances are you'll find something made in Japan. Like American companies, Japanese companies are also known for making high-tech products. High-tech is the use of the latest technology to make electronic and other goods. Japan makes cars, televisions, computers, video and recording machines, and other high-tech goods.

Japan has changed as quickly as technology has changed. It has kept much of its old culture as well. Look at the pictures on this page. They show some parts of Japanese culture. In his free time Mr. Yamaguchi likes to take part in a kind of theater called *Noh*. Actors in Noh theater wear masks that have been part of Japanese culture for hundreds of years. Mr. Yamaguchi also likes to make pottery. "In recent years, though, I haven't had time. I work long hours," says Mr. Yamaguchi. "When I have free time, I like to spend it with my family."

Many people read the *Yomiuri Shimbun* (left). Baseball is popular in Japan.

A Changing Country

"In some ways, Japan is becoming more and more like other countries," says Mr. Yamaguchi. "My son is fifteen years old and his favorite music is American. But in other ways, Japan will always be different. For one thing, no other country speaks Japanese. It is a difficult language."

WHY IT MATTERS

You have read about some people who work for an American publishing company. You have also read about someone working for a Japanese newspaper company. What are some of the differences? Some things are very similar. Both work places have been changed by technology. And in both countries, as everywhere, people are the most important resource.

Japanese traditions like this style of house remain strong today, but Japan is changing as contact with other countries continues.

✓/ Reviewing Facts and Ideas

SUM IT UP

- Japan is a small country with a large population.
- Journalists write for newspapers, magazines, or television news programs.
- Japan is known for making high-tech products.
- Japan has kept much of its traditional culture.

THINK ABOUT IT

1. What does a journalist do for a living?
2. **FOCUS** How do people live and work in Japan?
3. **THINKING SKILL** What is the *cause* of Mr. Yamaguchi's being able to receive information more quickly? What are the *effects* of technology on his job?
4. **WRITE** Write a two-paragraph newspaper article about something that happened at your school this week.

CHAPTER 11 REVIEW

THINKING ABOUT VOCABULARY

Number a sheet of paper from 1 to 10. Beside each number write the word or term from the list below that best completes each sentence.

consumer	high-tech
designer	interest
economy	journalist
employer	producers
goods	service

1. A good _____ makes sure that all the information in a news story is correct.

2. Some _____ products include fax machines and CD-ROMs.

3. People who produce and consume goods and services help our _____ to grow.

4. An _____ is someone who hires and pays other people to work.

5. A savings account in a bank earns extra money called _____.

6. When you buy something you are acting as a _____.

7. A _____ makes sure pages in a book look good.

8. _____ make things that consumers buy.

9. Books, cars, and sneakers are all examples of _____ people buy.

10. A doctor provides a _____ by helping people stay healthy.

THINKING ABOUT FACTS

1. Why do most people work?

2. What is the difference between goods and services?

3. What does it mean to be a smart consumer?

4. Why are people the most important resource in any economy?

5. Describe two ways in which Japan has kept its traditional culture.

THINK AND WRITE

WRITING A HOW-TO PARAGRAPH
Write a paragraph describing the steps involved in making a textbook such as this one.

WRITING A RESUME
A resume is a list of the jobs people had, with a description of each job. Write a short resume about yourself. Describe the different jobs or responsibilities you have.

WRITING ABOUT HOME
Look at the Legacy lesson on pages 288-289. Write a paragraph describing how working at home is different today than long ago.

APPLYING THINKING SKILLS

IDENTIFYING CAUSE AND EFFECT
Read the paragraph below and answer the questions that follow.

Twinkles Sports Shop was losing business because a huge new discount store was selling products at a lower price. It seemed that everyone was buying balls, bats, and skateboards there. Fortunately, the owner of Twinkles had an idea. She invited Muscles Malone, a famous football hero, to sign autographs and give tips on kicking and catching. As a result, Twinkles is full of customers now and sales are better than ever.

1. Define cause and effect.
2. What caused Twinkles Sports Shop to lose business?
3. What was the effect of Muscles Malone coming to Twinkles?
4. What do you think might be the effect of two stores selling the same products?
5. Why is it important to be able to tell the difference between causes and effects?

Summing Up the Chapter

Read the headings on the diagram below. Then review the chapter to find at least two pieces of information to include under each heading. When you have filled in a copy of the diagram, use it to write a sentence or two about how our economy works.

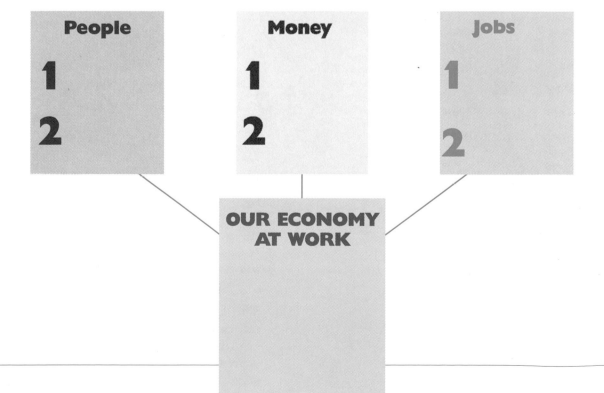

CHAPTER 12

Producing Goods

THINKING ABOUT GEOGRAPHY AND ECONOMICS

Many things that people need are made from natural resources. The availability of these resources influences what can be produced. So, caring for our resources is important not only to people who work with them but to all of us. In Chapter 12 you will see how people work to turn resources into many different products.

Amsterdam, Netherlands

Port Arthur, Texas

Saõ Paulo, Brazil

The United States exports computers to countries around the world.

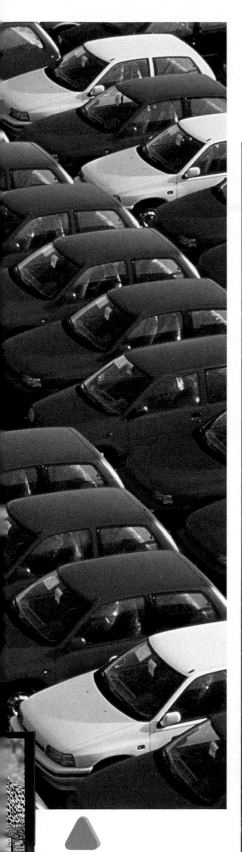

Automobiles are imported to the Netherlands.

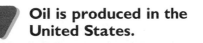
Oil is produced in the United States.

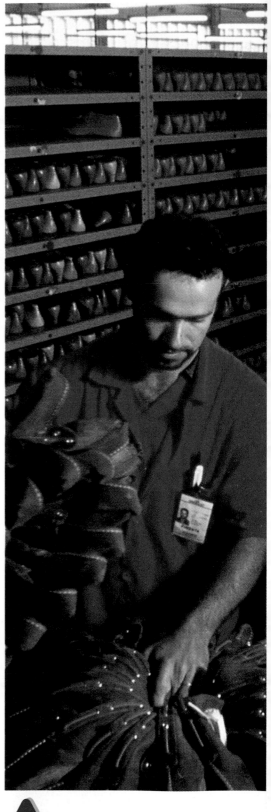

Shoes made in Brazil are traded throughout the world.

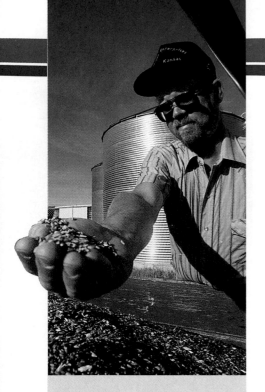

On the Farm

Focus Activity

READ TO LEARN
How is wheat produced on farms?

VOCABULARY
agriculture
harvest
fertilizer
product map
process

PLACE
Norton, Kansas

READ ALOUD

"Sometimes my job is hard on my children. I come home tired and dirty. But the children bring me lunch and help in the fields. They see me working with the land, growing things. They learn a lot about nature, the economy, and hard work. I think they're proud of me."

Jon Lofgreen is a farmer. Across our country, there are many different kinds of farming. In this lesson you will see what life on one farm in Kansas is like.

A Farm in Kansas

Sometimes Jon Lofgreen just likes to stand in the middle of his wheat farm near Norton, Kansas. Kansas has good soil and a good climate for growing crops. Mr. Lofgreen looks around and sees his land surrounding him in all directions. Crops such as wheat and alfalfa grow on that land. Four hundred cows also graze on that land. This land has supported the Lofgreen family for over 100 years. But sometimes when Mr. Lofgreen stands and looks across his farm, he's not thinking about that. He's just looking at the beauty of the wheat blowing in the wind, covering the rolling hills.

Busy All Year

Of course, agriculture doesn't leave much time for gazing or standing around. Agriculture is the business of growing crops and raising animals. "We do several different kinds of farming here," says Mr. Lofgreen. "But most of the land is used for growing wheat. The harvest is gathered in about ten days at the end of June. But the rest of the year is spent getting ready for those ten days!"

The harvest is the ripe crops that are gathered. It takes planning, hard work, and help from nature to produce a good harvest. "Toward the end of September, we plant the crop in the brown soil. We use machines to plant the wheat and spread fertilizer," says Mr. Lofgreen. Fertilizers are chemicals that are used to help plants grow.

In the winter the wheat freezes. The fields turn brown again, but the plants are still working. They are producing seeds. In the spring the plants begin to turn dark green.

There are many jobs to do on a farm. Seth Lofgreen feeds a calf (below). Mr. Lofgreen loads wheat stored in a silo (bottom).

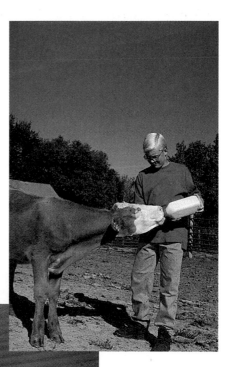

301

Farm Products

By mid–June, the wheat has turned from dark green to light green, and then to a golden color. The wheat is ready to be gathered. Farmers use a machine called a combine to cut the wheat, clean it, and put it in a holding tank. From there, trucks haul the wheat to storage tanks. Finally it is sold to companies that grind the wheat into flour. The flour is then made into bread, cakes, pasta, and other foods. These foods are then sold all over the world.

Wheat is just one of many crops grown in our country. Look at the product map below. A product map shows the places where goods are made or grown. This map shows crops that are grown in the United States.

Wheat is used to make many products you might eat, such as breads and cereals.

UNITED STATES FARM PRODUCTS

Legend:
- Corn
- Cotton
- Fruits and Vegetables
- Dairy
- Wheat

MAP WORK

Farmers throughout the United States supply many different types of products.

1. What are some of the different crops grown in the United States?

2. What products are grown in Florida?

3. In what ways do you think states in our country rely on each other for food products?

From milking cows to growing cranberries, farmers rely on technology to help make their work easier and faster.

New Ways of Farming

Sometimes Mr. Lofgreen is out in the fields, riding the combine or giving directions to workers. Other times he sits at a computer to do his farming. Here's what he says about how farmers today depend on technology to make a living. "I look at my computer and I can know in a second that wheat is selling for $3.69 a bushel. My computer helps me make decisions about when and where to sell my crop. I can see what's happening with other crops, in other parts of the world."

Look at the pictures on this page. Some farmers raise cattle. Others grow cranberries. Many farmers are now using new technology like computers and high-tech combines to help raise their crops and animals.

Links to **HEALTH**

Why Eat Wheat?

Many breakfast cereals contain grains such as wheat. Grains are the seeds of cereal plants. Wheat and other grains give you important vitamins and minerals. They help your muscles, blood, nerves, bones, and teeth stay healthy.

Look at the nutrition labels on the containers and packaging of foods you eat. Which foods list wheat as one of the first three ingredients?

303

Throughout the history of our country, the harvest has been important to people. Some people celebrate the harvest with dancing and singing. Read the following song. Have you ever planted any of these crops?

Harvest

Georgia Folk Song

1. Time to gath - er har-vest. ___ Oh, Em-ma, oh! ____
2. Dig-ging sweet _ po - ta - toes. ___ Oh, Em-ma, oh! ____
3. Dig-ging ru - ta - ba - gas. ___ Oh, Em-ma, oh! ____
4. Dig-ging big _ fat par-snips. ___ Oh, Em-ma, oh! ____

You turn a - round, dig a hole in the ground, ___

Oh, Em - ma, oh!

To Your Table

Farmers rely on each other. "The alfalfa I grow helps feed cattle on someone else's farm," points out Mr. Lofgreen. "The food on my table comes from another farm."

Many people other than farmers help make the food you see at your table. Some people **process** the food. To process is to change something into a different form. People process wheat to make bread and oranges to make orange juice. People at factories put the food into packages. Truckers drive the packages to stores. Stores sell the products to consumers.

WHY IT MATTERS

Native Americans farmed corn and other crops hundreds of years ago. Today Mr. Lofgreen makes a living from farming, as his great-great grandparents did. Farming is one of the important ways people make a living in our country.

Milk from cows is **processed** to make cheese and other dairy products.

Reviewing Facts and Ideas

SUM IT UP

- Agriculture is the business of growing and raising crops. One example of agriculture is wheat farming.

- There are many different kinds of farming in our country.

- There are many different jobs involved in getting food from the farm to your table.

THINK ABOUT IT

1. What are two ways people earn their living in agriculture?

2. **FOCUS** How is wheat produced on farms?

3. **THINKING SKILL** What do you think might *cause* a bad harvest? What *effect* would this have on farming?

4. **GEOGRAPHY** Look at the product map on page 302. What kinds of farming are done in California?

STUDY SKILLS

Reading Flow Charts

VOCABULARY
flow chart

WHY THE SKILL MATTERS

For ten busy days in June, wheat is harvested on Jon Lofgreen's farm. But he and the other workers are busy the rest of the year too. As you have read, more than one step is involved in growing wheat. The order in which these steps are taken is important. A **flow chart** can be used to show the sequence of steps that are followed to produce a final product. Flow charts show the steps of an activity in order. Look at the Helping Yourself box for some tips on how to read flow charts.

USING THE SKILL

Suppose you want to see the sequence of steps in growing wheat. Look at how the flow chart below shows these steps and their order.

To read the flow chart, first look at its title. What is this flow chart about? Next notice that each step has a picture and a label. How many steps are shown in this flow chart?

The steps of an activity are shown in order in a flow chart. As you can see here, the first step in growing wheat is plowing the field. An arrow leads you to the next step—which is planting the wheat. The steps that follow are harvesting the wheat and finally selling it.

It is very important to follow the steps in order. If you plow the field after planting the wheat, you will not end up with much wheat to harvest!

GROWING WHEAT

1 Plow field.   **2** Plant wheat.   **3** Harvest wheat.   **4** Sell wheat.

TRYING THE SKILL

You have learned about some of the steps followed by wheat farmers. Farmers grow wheat in order to sell it. One wheat product is pasta. The flow chart on this page shows some of the steps in making pasta.

What is the first step in making pasta? What happens after flour is emptied into a bin? What happens after dough is formed into big sheets?

- **A flow chart shows all of the steps of an activity in order.**
- **Study the title, pictures, and labels.**
- **Follow the arrows to read flow charts in order.**

REVIEWING THE SKILL

1. What is a flow chart?

2. Look at the flow chart for making pasta. What is the last step shown?

3. Suppose you are making a flow chart of the steps you follow in making a sandwich. What would you show as the first step?

4. When is it helpful to read a flow chart?

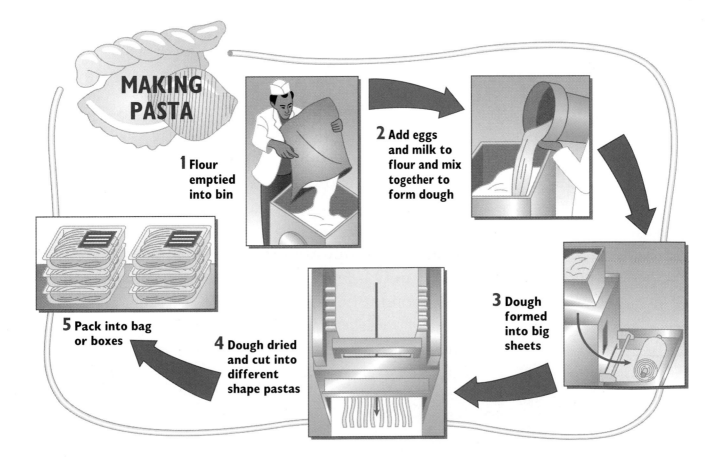

MAKING PASTA

1 Flour emptied into bin

2 Add eggs and milk to flour and mix together to form dough

3 Dough formed into big sheets

4 Dough dried and cut into different shape pastas

5 Pack into bag or boxes

Mining the Land

READ ALOUD

Every state has certain symbols. For example, you may know the name of your state bird or state tree. Did you know that some states also have a state mineral? In this lesson you will read about why minerals are so important to people in our country.

Focus Activity

READ TO LEARN
What are some ways we get and use mineral resources?

VOCABULARY
renewable resource
nonrenewable resource
public property
private property

An Important Resource

Look at the pictures at the bottom of page 309. They show some everyday objects. Can you guess what these objects have in common? They all are made from the same mineral, copper.

Like farmers, miners also make their living from the land. They remove minerals from the land. There is one important difference, though. Many of the resources that farmers use are renewable resources. A renewable resource is one that can be replaced by nature, if used carefully. The soil and water used to grow wheat are renewable resources. Minerals are nonrenewable resources. That means they cannot be replaced. Once nonrenewable resources are used up they are gone forever.

Working in a Mine

Andy Romero knows a lot about the importance of natural resources. He is a copper miner in a community in Arizona. From the picture here you can see that Mr. Romero drives a truck in an open-pit mine. Copper that lies close to Earth's surface is removed by open-pit mining. "Natural resources like copper help keep our company in business and are important in making products people need," Mr. Romero says.

There are also other ways to mine copper. Some companies send miners deep down below the surface to dig for copper. Look at the chart on the next page to see what happens after copper is mined.

Andy Romero (top) drives a big truck at a mine. He is one of the many people who make copper available for all types of products (bottom). Copper is one of several minerals used to make a penny.

309

World of Resources

Copper is just one resource that people remove from Earth. Iron, gold, silver, limestone, coal, and oil are also mined. Our country is very rich in natural resources.

Some resources are on public property. Public property is land that has been set aside for all people to use. National parks and forests are public property.

Other resources are on private property. Private property is land that is owned by people or companies. Some people own land to build homes on it. Mining companies have bought a lot of land in order to mine it.

Minerals include (clockwise from top) gold, iron pyrite, and forms of copper.

FROM COPPER TO WIRE

1 Mine rocks that contain copper.

2 Separate copper from rock.

3 Melt copper and make it pure.

4 Cast copper into bars.

5 Roll bars into rods.

6 Stretch rods into wire.

7 Coil wire onto spool.

CHART WORK

There are several steps involved before copper is made into wire.

1. What is the first step in the process of making copper wire?

2. What happens after the copper is made pure?

3. What are two questions you could ask to learn more about making copper products?

Boom Town to Ghost Town

Earth's resources provide jobs for many people. Sometimes "boom towns" grow when a resource is discovered. Many people move quickly to these towns to try to make money mining gold, oil, or other resources. Once the resource runs out, the jobs disappear.

People cannot make natural resources. But some companies make products that are like those found in nature. For example, plastic is sometimes used instead of metal.

WHY IT MATTERS

There are many mining jobs. People have to find where the minerals are. Some people are in charge of safety in the mines. Other people change minerals into forms people can use.

We use natural resources in many different ways. But we must use them carefully to be sure they will be here for a long, long time.

This ghost town in California was once a busy community. People hoped to get rich by finding valuable minerals.

✓ Reviewing Facts and Ideas

SUM IT UP

- Mining is the removing of minerals from the earth.

- Renewable resources can be replaced by nature. Once nonrenewable resources are used, they are gone forever.

- Public property is land that has been set aside for all people to use. Private property is land that is owned by people or companies.

THINK ABOUT IT

1. Give an example of public property in your community. Give an example of private property.

2. **FOCUS** What are some ways we get and use mineral resources?

3. **THINKING SKILL** Suppose oil was discovered near your town. What might be some of the *effects* of this discovery?

4. **WRITE** Write a paragraph describing the process of making wire.

On the Assembly Line

Focus Activity

READ TO LEARN
How do factories work?

VOCABULARY
manufacturing
factory
assembly line
robot
mill

PLACE
Detroit, Michigan

READ ALOUD

Suppose your class is making teddy bears to sell at a fair. Instead of each person making a complete bear, everyone has a special job. For example, one person will cut the fabric. Another will sew on the faces. Your class has just discovered a smart way to make a product. In this lesson you will read more about smart ways companies make things.

A Factory in Detroit

Whether you're making teddy bears or cars, you are manufacturing. Manufacturing is the business of making things. Manufacturing used to be done mostly by hand in factories. A factory is a place where things are manufactured. Today manufacturing is often done by people as well as by high-tech machines in factories.

Marge Gendron works in manufacturing at an automobile company in Detroit, Michigan. Most cars are built on assembly lines in factories like hers. An assembly line is a line of workers and machines all working together to make a final product. Different tasks are done at each stop along the way.

312

Assembly Lines Long Ago

The cars that roll off the assembly line today look very different from the first cars in our country. The assembly line is not a new idea for the automobile industry. In fact, assembly lines got their start in the early 1900s as a way to make cars.

At first only a few people could afford to buy cars. Cars took so much time to build that they were very expensive. But Henry Ford knew that many people would want to buy cars if they were less expensive. He started one of the first assembly lines. Soon it took less time to make cars. Then the price of cars went down and people rushed to buy them. In 1924 a Model T cost $290.

From filling bottles (top) to making automobiles (bottom), people had different jobs on assembly lines long ago.

Henry Ford Museum

Making a Car Today

The assembly line Marge Gendron works on today is different from the one Henry Ford first used. Today's assembly lines use robots. Robots are machines made to do tasks. Marge feels lucky that her job is still done by people. "Otherwise," she says, "I'd be out of work!"

From the chart below you can see that a car has many parts. Ms. Gendron works at the "bumper station." There she checks that the bumpers are safely made. She also makes sure the bumpers have no scratches or paint marks. If she finds a problem, it is also her job to fix the bumper. One hour after she checks the bumper, it is attached to a finished car.

Marge Gendron works in a factory where she checks automobile bumpers.

PARTS OF A CAR

Window

Windshield Wiper

Steering Wheel

Gas Tank

Engine

Door Handle

Tire

Hubcap

Headlight

Seat

Door

Battery

Bumper

Proud of a Product

Marge Gendron has been working at the same company for almost 30 years. "Sometimes it's been rough to do the same job day after day," she says. "Each bumper weighs about 30 pounds. That's a lot of bending and lifting. I feel proud when I see people driving our cars. I like to think that we do a good job. My best friend works next to me. I also like to hear people say we make beautiful cars."

Look at the pictures on this page. What do they tell you about how manufacturing is changing the jobs people like Marge Gendron do?

Robots do many jobs on assembly lines, including welding (top) and safety testing (bottom).

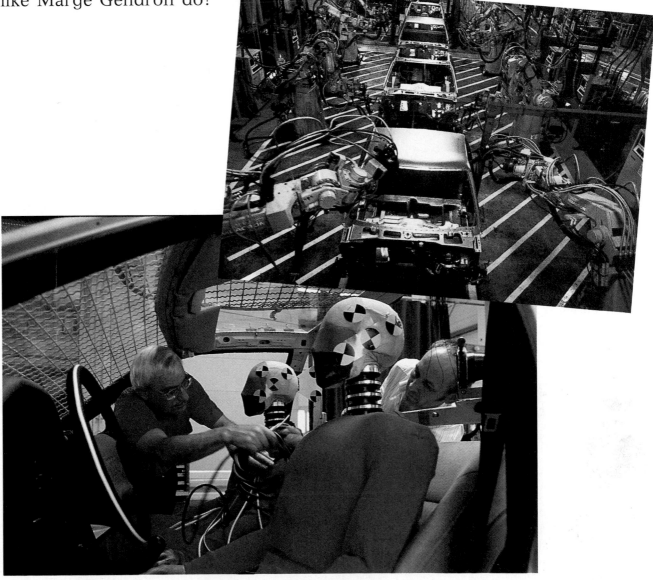

Manufacturing Today

Cars are just one of the many products manufactured in our country. Many companies are in the manufacturing business. Manufacturing is one of the biggest kinds of business in our country. Millions of people work in manufacturing. They make thousands of different products. Some of the most important products are transportation equipment, such as trains, cars, and buses. Chemicals, machines, medicines, food, toys, computers, and books are some other examples.

Not all things are manufactured on assembly lines. Can you think of something in your school that was not manufactured on an assembly line? How about your school building? It was most likely built by workers using tools, not on an assembly line. Or perhaps the blanket in your bedroom was made by hand by someone in your family.

Not all products are made in a factory. The house you live in and baked goods you eat were most likely made by hand.

A Manufacturing Town

The jobs people have are not only important to them, but they are also important to their family and community. The story below is about a steel **mill** in West Virginia. A mill is a place where people use machines to make natural resources into finished products. How do you think the jobs that people do at this steel mill influence the community?

No Star Nights

**Excerpt from the story
by Anna Egan Smucker, 1989.**

We went to school across from the mill. The smokestacks towered above us and the smoke billowed out in great puffy clouds of red, orange, and yellow, but mostly the color of rust. Everything—houses, hedges, old cars—was a rusty red color. Everything but the little bits of **graphite**, and they glinted like silver in the dust. At recess when the wind whirled these sharp, shiny metal pieces around, we girls would crouch so that our skirts touched the ground and kept our bare legs from being stung.

We would squint our eyes when the wind blew to keep the graphite out. Once a piece got caught in my eye, and no matter how much I blinked or how much my eye watered it wouldn't come out. When the eye doctor finally took it out and showed it to me, I was amazed that a speck that small could feel so big.

---

graphite: soft, black mineral

Using Resources

In manufacturing products, people need to use natural resources. Trees are used to make paper. Sand is used to make glass. Iron is used to make steel. Coal and oil are used to make the energy that runs the factories. So in manufacturing, people must also be sure to use resources carefully.

WHY IT MATTERS

A factory hires people like Marge Gendron to make products. It also creates jobs for even more people outside of the company. Suppose a company makes computers. Other people are hired to ship the computers. Still other people are needed to sell the computers. And someone else may design programs to be used on the computer. As you can see, most of the jobs in your community and around our country are connected to each other in many ways.

Nuts and bolts are manufactured from natural resources like iron.

Reviewing Facts and Ideas

SUM IT UP

- Manufacturing is the business of making things.

- Many factories use assembly lines to make things faster and less expensively. On an assembly line different steps are done in order to make a finished product.

- Manufacturing is one of the most important types of businesses in our country today.

THINK ABOUT IT

1. List ten different things manufactured in our country today.

2. **FOCUS** How do factories work?

3. **THINKING SKILL** *Classify* these items—books, water, coal, cars, trees, computers, copper. Are they manufactured, or are they natural resources?

4. **GEOGRAPHY** Many types of manufacturing companies are located near big cities. Why do you think this is so?

CITIZENSHIP
MAKING A DIFFERENCE

Inventor and Friend

HOUSTON, TEXAS—One day Josh Parsons, age 10, made a close friend. It started with baseball. Josh's father coached Josh's Little League team, the Mustangs.

One day just before the season started, Mr. Parsons told Josh about a boy named David Potter. David wanted to try out for the Mustangs. He was a very good hitter and catcher. "This was unusual," Josh says, "because he has arms only to the elbows." When David was 4 years old, he lost his hands and lower arms in an accident.

Like Josh, David loved baseball. On his own he learned to swing a bat. He also taught himself to catch a ball. He used a glove attached to his elbow. But David could not find a way to throw a ball.

"I had an idea," says Josh. "I thought of making something to help him throw. It could be shaped like a scoop. I told my idea to my Dad. We made a model of it."

Josh and his father went to David's house. They wanted to show him the invention. "I didn't know him. He didn't know me. At first he was shocked. Then he tried the throwing arm on. It fit perfectly over his elbow. We went into his yard and my dad threw the ball to him. He threw it back. The arm worked!"

With his new throwing arm, David tried out for and won a place on the Mustang team. Today both boys are still playing baseball. And Josh is still inventing. He made another throwing arm for a boy in Montana. "This one," says Josh "is good for throwing snowballs in the winter and baseballs in the summer."

Josh Parsons

"I thought of making something to help him . . ."

Partners in Trade

Focus Activity

READ TO LEARN
Why is trade important?

VOCABULARY
trade
domestic trade
export
import
international trade

PLACE
Canada

READ ALOUD

"There's so much that we share that it's time we're aware, It's a small world after all."

You've read a lot in this book about how important our natural resources are. People in communities work together to share them and to make the most of them. People are also working to protect natural resources. In this lesson you will see how the words to the above song are true.

Not Only Baseball Cards

What do you think of when you hear the word trade? Perhaps you think about swapping sandwiches with a friend. Or you may think about trading baseball cards. For businesses and governments, *trade* means something a little different. Trade is the buying and selling of goods and services. In some ways, though, trade is not that different from trade in the lunchroom or in the schoolyard. People and countries trade for the same reasons. They trade because each side has something the other wants.

320

Trade Across Borders

Earlier in this chapter you read that Kansas has good soil and a good climate for agriculture. But it does not have many big cities with manufacturing. Detroit, Michigan has a lot of automobile factories. But it does not grow much wheat. So people in Kansas buy cars made in Detroit. People in Detroit eat bread made from wheat grown in Kansas. This exchange is called domestic trade, or trade within one country.

Most countries can't produce everything they need. Instead they import goods that are made or grown in another country. To import is to buy goods from another country. Then often they export what they've made or grown to other countries. To export is to sell and ship goods to another country.

One of our country's biggest trading partners is Canada, our neighbor to the north. We import fish, wood, and other products from Canada. We export computers, fruits, and other products to Canada.

The United States imports products like fish and wood from Canada and exports products including computers and automobiles.

Infographic

U.S. Trade Around the World

International trade is the importing and exporting of goods between countries. Look at this Infographic to see some of the products the United States trades with other countries of the world.

Computers

Wood

Airplanes

Computers

Gold

Clothing

CANADA

RUSSIA

UNITED STATES

ITALY

JAPAN

Computers

Corn

NIGERIA

ARGENTINA

AUSTRALIA

Oil

Medicines

Wool Products

Leather Products

Cellular Phones

Airplanes

KEY

Exports   Imports

322

The World at Home

Look at the picture on this page. If you visited a port, you might see many different products being imported and exported from around the world. Sugar might come from sugarcane grown in the Philippines or India. Coffee probably comes from beans grown in Colombia in South America. The wheat being loaded might be headed for Japan or Russia.

WHY IT MATTERS

People in communities in the United States and around the world depend on each other in many ways. One of these ways is trade. By working with each other in the years ahead, people in all communities can continue to make our planet a better place to live and work.

The port of Los Angeles handles trade between the United States and other countries.

✔ Reviewing Facts and Ideas

SUM IT UP

- Trade is the business of buying and selling goods and services.
- To export is to sell goods to another country. To import is to buy goods from another country.
- The United States trades with Canada and other countries all over the world.
- Domestic trade is trade within one country.
- International trade is importing and exporting of goods between countries.

THINK ABOUT IT

1. What is the difference between imports and exports?
2. **FOCUS** Why is trade important?
3. **THINKING SKILL** Suppose the United States could not trade with other countries. What are some _effects_ this might have on life in our country?
4. **GEOGRAPHY** Look at the map on page R10. What ocean would a ship carrying coffee have to cross to get from Colombia to the western United States?

CHAPTER 12 REVIEW

THINKING ABOUT VOCABULARY

Number a sheet of paper from 1 to 10. Beside each number write the word or term from the list below that matches the statement.

agriculture   import

assembly line   manufacturing

factory   process

fertilizer   robot

harvest   trade

1. The buying and selling of goods and services
2. A place where things are manufactured
3. The business of making things
4. The ripe crops that are gathered
5. The business of growing crops and raising animals
6. Chemicals used to help plants grow
7. To change into a different form
8. Machine made to do tasks instead of people
9. To buy goods from another country
10. A line of workers and machines all working together to make a final product

THINKING ABOUT FACTS

Number a sheet of paper from 1 to 5. Write **T** if a statement is true. If it is false, rewrite it to make it true.

1. In Kansas the wheat harvest is usually ready during the summer.
2. Today many farmers in the United States make use of computers and high-tech combines to help grow their crops.
3. Minerals like copper are examples of renewable resources.
4. The use of assembly lines lowers the cost of making products such as cars and trucks.
5. Domestic trade is trade between countries.

THINK AND WRITE

WRITING ABOUT A FARM

Write a story in which you describe what it might be like to live and work on a Kansas wheat farm.

WRITING ABOUT BUSINESS

Write a paragraph explaining why the assembly line helped reduce the cost of making automobiles.

WRITING A SHORT STORY

Write a story about a young boy or girl who lives near a copper mine. Describe how the mine and the people who work there are important to their community. You can refer to "Many Voices" on page 317 for help.

APPLYING STUDY SKILLS

READING FLOW CHARTS

Answer the following questions about the chart on page 310 to practice your skill of reading flow charts.

1. Explain how to read a flow chart.

2. What is the first step shown on the flow chart? What is the last step?

3. What happens right after the copper is separated from rock?

4. What happens just before the melted copper is rolled into rods?

5. Why is a flow chart a good way to explain how wire is made?

Summing Up the Chapter

Review the chapter to find information about each type of work shown in the theme diagram below. Next fill in a copy of the diagram with a main idea about each type of work. Then write a short paragraph describing one way in which goods are produced from natural resources.

Farming

Mining

Theme

Goods are produced in many ways. In the U.S. and other countries, they come from different natural resources

Manufacturing

Trade

UNIT 5 REVIEW

THINKING ABOUT VOCABULARY

consumers	imports
designer	product map
employer	public property
export	robots
fertilizer	services

Number a sheet of paper from 1 to 10. Beside each number write **C** if the underlined word is used correctly. If it is not, choose the word or term from the list above that correctly completes the sentence.

1. During a sale, Andy's Bike Shop is always filled with <u>employers</u>.

2. The more money you save in a bank, the more <u>interest</u> you earn.

3. We enjoy camping on <u>private property</u> such as national parks.

4. Today <u>consumers</u> are used in factories to make cars and trucks.

5. One of the first <u>assembly lines</u> made automobiles.

6. The United States <u>imports</u> computers and cars from Japan.

7. A <u>journalist</u> makes sure that every page in a book looks good.

8. A <u>flow chart</u> shows the places where goods are made or grown.

9. The <u>economy</u> is the making and consuming of goods and services.

10. The farmer brings his <u>harvest</u> to be sold at the market.

THINK AND WRITE

WRITING ABOUT JOBS
In this unit you read about a variety of jobs. Write a paragraph explaining why you might choose to have any one of these jobs.

WRITING A PARAGRAPH
Suppose that you lived long ago, before the use of money. Write a paragraph describing how farmers might have obtained goods and services.

WRITING ABOUT WORKING TOGETHER
You have seen how people work together in many ways. Write a paragraph describing how the United States trades with other countries.

BUILDING SKILLS

1. **Cause and Effect** List three words that show causes. List three words that show effects.

2. **Cause and Effect** What is one effect of saving your money in a bank?

3. **Cause and Effect** What is one effect of using an assembly line?

4. **Flow Charts** Why is a flow chart a good way to learn about how things are made?

5. **Flow Charts** Look at the flow chart on page 307. What happens after the dough is dried and cut?

YESTERDAY, TODAY &
TOMORROW

Assembly lines, computers, robots, and high-tech machines have changed farming and manufacturing. Name two ways a farmer might use a robot in the future. How might a farmer use computers?

READING ON YOUR OWN

Here are some books you might find at the library to help you learn more.

COWS IN THE PARLOR
by Cynthia McFarland
Where does milk come from? Visit Clear Creek Farm and learn about dairy farming.

AUNT LILLY'S LAUNDROMAT
by Melanie Hope Greenberg
Step into Aunt Lilly's laundromat and learn about working hard and keeping dreams alive.

IF YOU MADE A MILLION
by David Schwartz
Here's your chance to learn about making and spending a lot of money.

UNIT PROJECT

Have a Career Fair

1. Have each group member choose one career they would like to research.
2. Write several facts and draw pictures for each career on a piece of cardboard.
3. Make a display showing the different careers in your group.
4. Share displays in a Class Career Fair. Have group members describe why they chose each career.

SPECIAL SECTION
EXPLORING YOUR COMMUNITY

Welcome to Toms River, New Jersey! It's the end of the school year for Mrs. Green's third-grade class at Walnut Street Elementary School. In social studies, the students have studied communities. Now the class wants to do something very special.

More and more people move to Toms River every year. So Mrs. Green's class decided to make a Community Welcome Center. It will be on display at their school. Making the Welcome Center will be a great way for Mrs. Green's class to learn about their community. It will also help people who are new to the community to learn about Toms River.

You can learn how to make your own Community Welcome Center. Read this section to learn how to do it.

Toms River

NEW JERSEY

Making a Map

Main Street. Walnut Street. Water Street. Getting around from place to place in a community can be tricky. Two students, Rashad and Jaime, wanted to make a big, colorful community map of Toms River for the Welcome Center. With the help of their school librarian, they found a map of Toms River.

Rashad and Jaime then used this map to help make the community map you see here. Their map includes their school and a few parks. What places would you include in a map of your community?

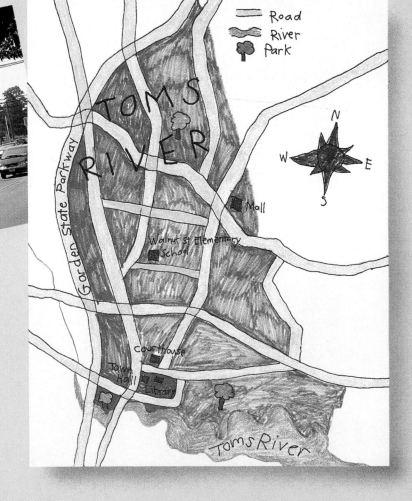

Main Street

Helping Our Environment

Joseph, Cyndi, and Jaclyn wanted the Welcome Center to include a poster about protecting their environment. So first they researched information about the environment. They spoke with people in the state government who could tell them about environmental problems. They learned about water pollution problems in Toms River. They also learned how they could help fight water pollution. Look at their poster below. What does it say about fighting pollution in Toms River? What would you want to say in a pollution poster for your community?

KEEP TOMS RIVER CLEAN

The History of Toms River

Why is Toms River called Toms River? Ryan was curious. So he did some research at the local historical museum to answer this question. He found out that no one knows for sure. Some people think Toms River was named by an English settler called Captain William Toms in the 1660s. Others think that Toms River is named for a man named Tom Luker. This man married the daughter of a local Native American chief. Still others think it is named for a Native American known as "Old Indian Tom." He lived in the area in the late 1700s.

One thing was certain, though. Ryan was excited about all the information he gathered at the museum. What questions about your community would you like to research?

From the Collection of Richard Steele/Ocean County Library

Ocean County Cultural & Heritage Commission

Photos Taken Around 1900

Toms River Time Line

Ryan did research on a computer to find history books and old newspaper articles about Toms River. He also looked at the library's old pictures of life in Toms River long ago. He even interviewed a town historian who told him about a group of Native Americans, the Lenni Lenape (LEN ee len ah PAY).

With the help of his classmates, Ryan sequenced all this information to make a history time line. What would a time line of your community look like?

A Video Look at Work

Sarah knew that many people move to communities like Toms River to find jobs and make a living. She decided that she would make a video of the different people and their jobs in Toms River.

With the help of people at the Chamber of Commerce, Sarah contacted different workers. She then interviewed them on videotape to learn about their jobs. By including her video in the Welcome Center, Sarah wants to help people learn about the different jobs in Toms River. What would you include in a video about jobs in your community?

Dr. Zimmerman
Astronomer

Robert J. Novins Planetarium/Ocean County College

Dr. J.M. Rush
Principal

South Toms River Elementary School

Ms. Wauters
Environmental Lawyer

Fun All Year!

Winter, spring, summer, or fall—there are many ways people have fun in Toms River. Nathan decided to make a calendar of these events. He read local newspapers and magazines. He spoke with his schoolmates. Soon he had plenty of information to include in his calendar.

Look at Nathan's Community Calendar of Events. How are these events like those in your community? How are they different?

Wooden Boat Festival

Community Calendar of Events

SEASON	EVENT
Spring	Masterpiece Theater Founders' Day
Summer	Ice Cream Festival Wooden Boat Festival Crab Races
Fall	First Day of School Halloween Parade
Winter	Holiday Performances First Night Celebration Musical Theater Shows

Being a Good Citizen

Mrs. Green's class learned about government and citizenship this year. So Yifan (ee FAHN) and Anna volunteered to do projects about local government leaders and people who are making a difference in Toms River.

Yifan read the community newspaper to learn about local government leaders. He then visited Town Hall and spoke with community leaders. Yifan decided to make a chart of how the government in Toms River works. What project would you choose to learn about your community government?

Anna decided to interview a person who is making a difference in Toms River. She spoke with community leaders. They told her about a special teacher in Toms River. With the help of Mrs. Green, Anna interviewed this teacher. Whom would you like to interview in your community?

CITIZENSHIP
MAKING A DIFFERENCE

Computers for All

In this interview Anna spoke with a teacher named Mrs. Clare Devine. Anna met with Mrs. Devine at the computer lab at North Dover Elementary School in Toms River. The lab is a big room with many computers. Mrs. Devine teaches students how to use the computers. She and her students started a program to teach older Americans how to use computers.

Q: Why did you start this program?

Mrs. Devine: I know that many people, especially older people, are nervous or afraid of working with computers. They did not grow up using them in school, as children do today. My students know a lot about computers. I thought they would enjoy teaching others.

Q: What do older Americans learn in the classes?

Mrs. Devine: Each class shows the older people a different way to use the computer. Also, the students show them their favorite computer games. We also taught them how to "talk" to someone on the Internet.

Q: Do older Americans like the classes?

Mrs. Devine: Yes, I think so. This year at the last class, they bought ice cream for everyone.

Q: What do you like best about this project?

Mrs. Devine: Everyone wins. Older people see that working with computers is not as hard as they thought. Many children don't spend much time with older people. Working together, students and older people get to know each other.

North Dover Elementary School

337

Hello Around the World

The Welcome Center helps newcomers to the community learn about Toms River. It also helps people who have lived there for a long time. Both Danny and Marisa had another idea for the Welcome Center. They have pen pals in other countries. They wanted to tell their pen pals about Toms River. So they decided to send letters and pictures about the Welcome Center. They also thought it would be great to include a Welcome Kit like the one in the picture on page 339. The kit contains things such as a small community map, a calendar of events, and a listing of important phone numbers. What would you want someone in another country to know about your community?

Communities Are Special

This year in social studies, Mrs. Green's class learned a lot about communities in the United States and around the world. They read about the geography of different places. They learned about the history of different communities. They also learned about people who make a difference to their community.

By making the Welcome Center below, Mrs. Green's class learned that their community is a special place. When you explore your own community, you will see that it, too, is special.

REFERENCE SECTION

The Reference Section has many parts, each with a different type of information. Use this section to look up people, places, and events as you study.

R4 Atlas

An atlas is a collection of maps. An atlas can be a book or a separate section within a book. This Atlas is a separate section with maps to help you study the geography in this book.

NORTH AMERICA: Political

ASIA

EUROPE

ARCTIC OCEAN

Chukchi Sea

Bering Sea

Bering Strait

Ellesmere Island

ICELAND

Queen Elizabeth Islands

GREENLAND (DEN.)

ALASKA (U.S.)

Beaufort Sea

Banks Island

Parry Islands

Baffin Bay

Yukon River

• Fairbanks

Great Bear Lake

Victoria Island

Baffin Island

• Anchorage

Davis Strait

Mackenzie River

• Nuuk

Gulf of Alaska

• Iqaluit

• Juneau

• Yellowknife

Great Slave Lake

Labrador Sea

Hudson Bay

Lake Athabasca

Vancouver Island

• Edmonton

Saskatchewan River

CANADA

Newfoundland

PACIFIC OCEAN

• Vancouver

Columbia R.

Lake Winnipeg

Gulf of St. Lawrence

• Seattle

Lake Manitoba

• Winnipeg

• Quebec

• Portland

Snake R.

Lake Superior

• Montreal

Ottawa ⊛

Missouri River

• Minneapolis

Lake Michigan

Toronto •

St. Lawrence River

• Boston

ATLANTIC OCEAN

Great Salt Lake

• Salt Lake City

UNITED STATES

• Chicago

Detroit •

Lake Huron

Lake Ontario

Lake Erie

• New York

• San Francisco

Platte River

• Denver

Colorado River

Arkansas River

St. Louis •

Ohio River

• Philadelphia

⊛ Washington, D.C.

• Los Angeles

• Phoenix

• Atlanta

BERMUDA (U.K.)

• Dallas

Mississippi River

• Ciudad Juárez

Rio Grande

Houston •

• New Orleans

Miami •

THE BAHAMAS

ANTIGUA AND BARBUDA

Nassau ⊛

St. John's

ST. KITTS AND NEVIS

Gulf of Mexico

• Monterrey

Havana ⊛

CUBA

PUERTO RICO (U.S.)

San Juan

DOMINICAN REPUBLIC

MEXICO

HAITI

Roseau

DOMINICA

• Guadalajara

Port-au-Prince

Santo Domingo

ST. LUCIA

JAMAICA

Mexico City ⊛

Kingston

ST. VINCENT AND THE GRENADINES

GRENADA

BELIZE

⊛ Belmopan

Caribbean Sea

TRINIDAD AND TOBAGO

GUATEMALA

HONDURAS

Guatemala City ⊛

Tegucigalpa •

San Salvador ⊛

NICARAGUA

EL SALVADOR

⊛ Managua

Panama City

COSTA RICA

San José •

PANAMA

SOUTH AMERICA

⊛ National capital   • Other city

0   500   1,000 Miles

0   500   1,000 Kilometers

N W E S

R4

Caribbean Sea

CENTRAL AMERICA

Gulf of Panama

Barranquilla

Maracaibo

Valencia

Caracas

⊛ Georgetown
Paramaribo

Lake Maracaibo

VENEZUELA

GUYANA

Cayenne

Medellín

Orinoco River

SURINAME

FRENCH GUIANA (FR.)

Bogotá

COLOMBIA

Cali

Negro River

⊛ Quito

ECUADOR

Manaus

Amazon River

Belém

Guayaquil

Iquitos

Madeira River

Tocantins River

Tapajós River

PERU

Xingu River

Recife

Trujillo

BRAZIL

Callao Lima

Salvador (Bahía)

Cuzco

Lake Titicaca

São Francisco River

Arequipa

BOLIVIA

La Paz

Brasília

Sucre

Belo Horizonte

PACIFIC OCEAN

Paraguay River

Rio de Janeiro

Antofagasta

PARAGUAY

São Paulo

Tucumán

Paraná River

Asunción

CHILE

Paraná River

ATLANTIC OCEAN

Córdoba

Pôrto Alegre

Valparaíso

Rosario

Uruguay River

URUGUAY

Santiago

Buenos Aires

Montevideo

ARGENTINA

Rio de la Plata

Concepción

Colorado River

N
W ⊛ E
S

| ⊛ National capital | • Other city |

0   250   500 Miles

0   250   500 Kilometers

FALKLAND ISLANDS (U.K.)

Strait of Magellan

Punta Arenas

SOUTH GEORGIA (U.K.)

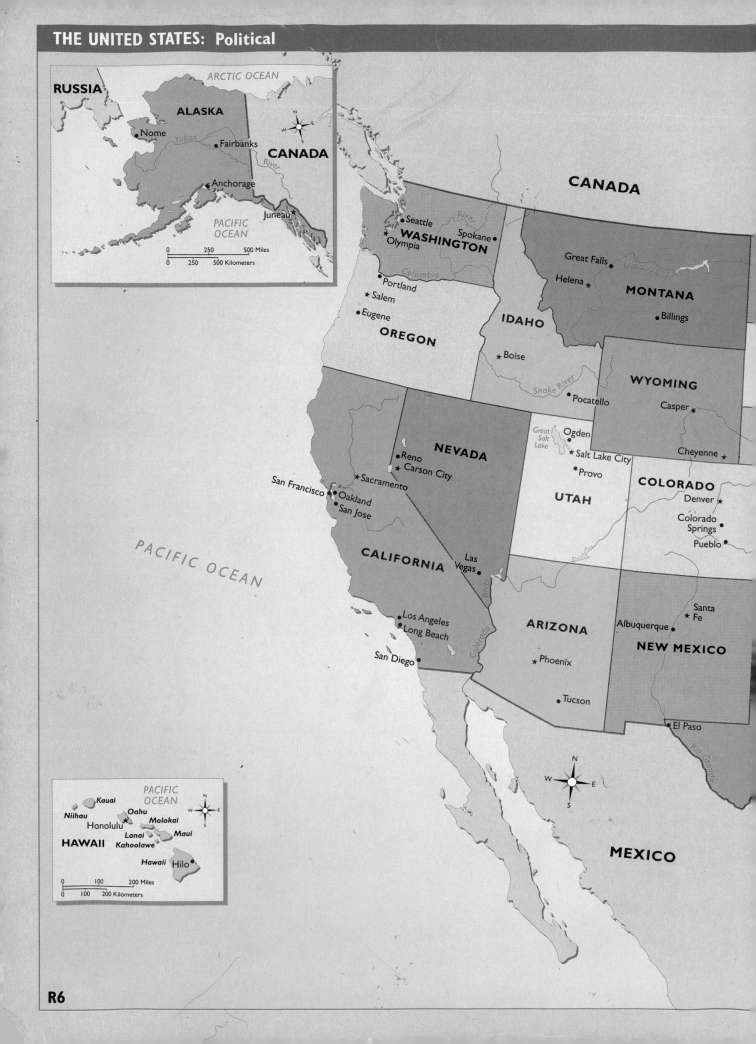

RUSSIA

ARCTIC OCEAN

ALASKA

Nome

Fairbanks

Yukon

CANADA

Anchorage

Juneau ★

PACIFIC
OCEAN

| 0 | 250 | 500 Miles |
| 0 | 250 | 500 Kilometers |

CANADA

Seattle

Spokane

★ **WASHINGTON**

Olympia

Columbia

Great Falls

Missouri River

Helena ★

MONTANA

Billings

Portland

★ Salem

Eugene

OREGON

IDAHO

★ Boise

Snake River

Pocatello

WYOMING

Casper

Great
Salt
Lake

Ogden

Salt Lake City ★

Cheyenne ★

Reno

NEVADA

★ Carson City

Provo

COLORADO

San Francisco

★ Sacramento

Oakland

San Jose

UTAH

Denver ★

Colorado
Springs

Pueblo

PACIFIC OCEAN

CALIFORNIA

Las
Vegas

Colorado River

Los Angeles

Long Beach

San Diego

ARIZONA

Phoenix ★

Santa
★ Fe

Albuquerque

NEW MEXICO

Tucson

El Paso

Rio Grande

PACIFIC
OCEAN

Kauai

Niihau

Oahu

Honolulu ★

Molokai

Lanai Maui

Kahoolawe

HAWAII

Hawaii

Hilo

| 0 | 100 | 200 Miles |
| 0 | 100 | 200 Kilometers |

MEXICO

RUSSIA

ARCTIC OCEAN

BROOKS RANGE

ALASKA

ALASKA RANGE

CANADA

Bering Strait

Yukon River

▲ Mt. McKinley
20,320 ft.
(6,194 m)

Bering
Sea

250   500 Miles

250   500 Kilometers

CANADA

Puget
Sound

▲ Mt. Rainier
14,410 ft.
(4,391 m)

Mt. St. Helens
8,366 ft.
(2,550 m)

COAST RANGES

CASCADE RANGE

Columbia River

▲ Mt. Hood
11,235 ft.
(3,424 m)

COLUMBIA PLATEAU

Snake River

Missouri   River

Yellowstone River

ROCKY

Granite Peak
12,799 ft.
(3,900 m)

BLACK
HILLS

Cape Mendocino

▲ Mt. Shasta
14,162 ft.
(4,316 m)

Sacramento River

COAST

SIERRA NEVADA

CENTRAL VALLEY

Lake
Tahoe

San Joaquin River

GREAT

BASIN

Great Salt
Lake

GREAT
SALT LAKE
DESERT

WASATCH   RANGE

TETON RANGE

MOUNTAINS

Kings Peak
13,528 ft.
(4,123 m)

GREAT

PLAINS

San Francisco Bay

PACIFIC OCEAN

RANGES

▲ Mt. Whitney
14,491 ft.
(4,418 m)

DEATH
VALLEY

MOJAVE
DESERT

Lake
Mead

Colorado   River

COLORADO
PLATEAU

Humphreys Peak
12,633 ft.
(3,850 m)

Mt. Elbert
14,433 ft.
(4,398 m)

Pikes Peak
14,107 ft.
(4,301 m)

Wheeler Peak
13,065 ft.
(3,982 m)

Salton
Sea

SONORA
DESERT

Gila   River

Pecos   River

Guadalupe Peak
8,751 ft.
(2,667 m)

Gulf of California

Rio Grande

MEXICO

PACIFIC
OCEAN

Kauai

Oahu

Maui

HAWAII

Hawaii

▲ Mauna Kea
13,796 ft.
(4,205 m)

100   200 Miles

100   200 Kilometers

CANADA

Lake of the Woods

MESABI RANGE

Lake Superior

GREAT

LAKES

St. Lawrence River

WHITE MTS.

Mt. Washington
6,288 ft.
(1,917 m)

GREEN MTS.

Cape Cod

Lake Huron

Lake Michigan

Lake Ontario

ADIRONDACK
MTS.

Hudson River

Long Island

Mississippi

CENTRAL PLAINS

Lake Erie

ALLEGHENY
PLATEAU

APPALACHIAN MOUNTAINS

Susquehanna River

Delaware Bay

River

Platte River

River

Wabash River

Ohio River

Potomac River

Chesapeake Bay

ATLANTIC COASTAL PLAIN

Missouri

Cape Hatteras

Arkansas

INTERIOR PLAINS

River

OZARK
PLATEAU

ALLEGHENY MOUNTAINS

Mt. Mitchell
6,684 ft.
(2,037 m)

PIEDMONT

River

River

OUACHITA
MOUNTAINS

Mississippi

Tennessee

River

River

Savannah River

ATLANTIC OCEAN

Red

River

Brazos

River

Alabama

Chattahoochee

GULF COASTAL PLAIN

Colorado River

Mobile Bay

Mississippi Delta

Galveston Bay

Gulf of Mexico

Lake
Okeechobee

Bahama Islands

N
W   E
S

0   150   300 Miles
0   150   300 Kilometers

Florida Keys

Straits of Florida

CUBA

R9

ARCTIC OCEAN

GREENLAND)
(DENMARK)

ALASKA (U.S.)

CANADA

**NORTH
AMERICA**

UNITED STATES

BERMUDA
(U.K.)

ATLANTIC
OCEAN

MEXICO

See inset below

Caribbean Sea

MIDWAY ISLANDS
(U.S.)

HAWAII (U.S.)

PACIFIC OCEAN

VENEZUELA

GUYANA
SURINAME

FRENCH GUIANA
(FRANCE)

COLOMBIA

0°   Equator

GALÁPAGOS ISLANDS
(ECUADOR)

ECUADOR

**SOUTH
AMERICA**

WESTERN
SAMOA

AMERICAN SAMOA
(U.S.)

FRENCH POLYNESIA
(FRANCE)

PERU

BRAZIL

TONGA

BOLIVIA

PARAGUAY

URUGUAY

CHILE **ARGENTINA**

FALKLAND ISLANDS
(U.K.)

ANTARCTICA

Central America and West Indies

Gulf of Mexico

FLORIDA
(U.S.)

THE
BAHAMAS

TURKS AND
CAICOS IS. (U.K.)

ATLANTIC OCEAN

CUBA

VIRGIN ISLANDS
(U.K.)

ST. KITTS
AND NEVIS

CAYMAN ISLANDS
(U.K.)

JAMAICA

HAITI

DOMINICAN
REPUBLIC

ANTIGUA AND
BARBUDA

PUERTO RICO
(U.S.)

GUADELOUPE
(FRANCE)

MEXICO

VIRGIN ISLANDS
(U.S.)

DOMINICA

BELIZE

MARTINIQUE
(FRANCE)

ST. LUCIA

GUATEMALA

Caribbean Sea

ST. VINCENT AND
THE GRENADINES

HONDURAS

BARBADOS

EL SALVADOR

ARUBA
(NETHERLANDS)

NETHERLANDS
ANTILLES
(NETHERLANDS)

GRENADA

NICARAGUA

TRINIDAD AND
TOBAGO

PACIFIC
OCEAN

N
W   E
S

COSTA
RICA

PANAMA

VENEZUELA

0   250   500 Miles
0   250   500 Kilometers

COLOMBIA

GUYANA

ARCTIC OCEAN

SPITSBERGEN
(NORWAY)
SVALBARD IS.
(NORWAY)

ICELAND

RUSSIA

ASIA

See inset below

North
Sea

EUROPE

AZORES IS.
(PORTUGAL)

GEORGIA
ARMENIA
TURKEY

KAZAKHSTAN

MONGOLIA

UZBEKISTAN
KYRGYZSTAN
TURKMENISTAN
TAJIKISTAN

NORTH
KOREA
SOUTH
KOREA

JAPAN

MOROCCO

TUNISIA

LEBANON
ISRAEL

SYRIA
JORDAN

AZERBAIJAN
IRAQ
IRAN

AFGHANISTAN

CHINA

PACIFIC OCEAN

CANARY IS.
(SPAIN)

ALGERIA

LIBYA

EGYPT

KUWAIT
QATAR
SAUDI
ARABIA

BAHRAIN

PAKISTAN

NEPAL BHUTAN

HONG KONG

TAIWAN

WESTERN SAHARA
(MOROCCO)

UNITED
ARAB
EMIRATES

INDIA

WAKE ISLAND
(U.S.)

MAURITANIA

MALI

NIGER

CHAD

SUDAN

OMAN

YEMEN

MYANMAR
(BURMA)

MACAU (PORT.)

NORTHERN
MARIANA IS. (U.S.)

MARSHALL ISLANDS

CAPE VERDE
SENEGAL
GAMBIA
GUINEA-
BISSAU
SIERRA LEONE

BURKINA
FASO

NIGERIA
BENIN

AFRICA

ERITREA

DJIBOUTI

BANGLADESH

LAOS
THAILAND

VIETNAM

PHILIPPINES

GUAM (U.S.)

FEDERATED STATES
OF MICRONESIA

PALAU

LIBERIA
GHANA
TOGO
CÔTE D'IVOIRE
SÃO TOMÉ AND PRÍNCIPE
EQUATORIAL GUINEA

CENTRAL
AFRICAN REP.

CAMEROON

ETHIOPIA

SOMALIA

SRI
LANKA

CAMBODIA
BRUNEI
MALAYSIA

KIRIBATI

GABON

UGANDA
KENYA

MALDIVES

SINGAPORE

Equator

NAURU

0°

CONGO

RWANDA
ZAIRE
BURUNDI

INDONESIA

PAPUA
NEW
GUINEA

SOLOMON
ISLANDS

ATLANTIC
OCEAN

ANGOLA
MALAWI
ZAMBIA
MOZAMBIQUE

TANZANIA

SEYCHELLES

COMOROS

INDIAN
OCEAN

TUVALU

VANUATU

FIJI

NAMIBIA
ZIMBABWE
BOTSWANA

MADAGASCAR

MAURITIUS

AUSTRALIA

NEW
CALEDONIA
(FRANCE)

N
W   E
S

SOUTH
AFRICA

SWAZILAND
LESOTHO

NEW
ZEALAND

0   1,000   2,000 Miles
0   1,000   2,000 Kilometers
Scale accurate at Equator

ANTARCTICA

FINLAND

NORWAY

SWEDEN

ESTONIA

North
Sea

Baltic
Sea

LATVIA

IRELAND

UNITED

KINGDOM

DENMARK

LITHUANIA
RUSSIA

RUSSIA

NETHERLANDS

BELARUS

ATLANTIC
OCEAN

BELGIUM

GERMANY

POLAND

LUXEMBOURG

CZECH
REPUBLIC

UKRAINE

FRANCE

LIECHTENSTEIN

SLOVAKIA

SWITZERLAND

AUSTRIA

HUNGARY

MOLDOVA

N
W   E
S

SLOVENIA

PORTUGAL

ANDORRA

MONACO

SAN
MARINO

CROATIA
BOSNIA AND
HERZEGOVINA

ROMANIA

GEORGIA

SPAIN

CORSICA
(FR.)

ITALY

YUGOSLAVIA

BULGARIA

Black Sea

BALEARIC IS.
(SP.)

ALBANIA

MACEDONIA

GIBRALTAR (U.K.)

Mediterranean
Sea

SARDINIA
(IT.)

GREECE

TURKEY

ASIA

SICILY
(IT.)

SYRIA

0   250   500 Miles
0   250   500 Kilometers

MALTA

CRETE (GR.)

CYPRUS

LEBANON

R11

Dictionary of GEOGRAPHIC TERMS

HILL (hil) Rounded, raised landform; not as high as a mountain.

GULF (gulf) Body of water partly surrounded by land; larger than a bay.

PENINSULA (pə nin′sə lə) Land that has water on all sides but one.

MESA (mā′sə) Landform that looks like a high, flat table.

LAKE (lāk) Body of water completely surrounded by land.

PLAIN (plān) Large area of flat land.

PORT (pôrt) Place where ships load and unload goods.

CANAL (kə nal′) Waterway dug across the land to connect two bodies of water.

BAY (bā) Body of water partly surrounded by land.

HARBOR (här′bər) Protected place by an ocean or river where ships can safely stay.

BEACH (bēch) Land covered with sand or pebbles next to an ocean or lake.

ISLAND (i′lənd) Land that is surrounded on all sides by water.

MOUNTAIN (moun´tən) High landform with steep sides; higher than a hill.

CANYON (kan´yən) Deep river valley with steep sides.

VALLEY (val´ē) Area of low land between hills or mountains.

RIVER (ri´vər) Long stream of water that empties into another body of water.

PLATEAU (pla tō´) High flat area that rises steeply above the surrounding land.

COAST (kōst) Land next to an ocean.

CLIFF (klif) High steep face of rock.

OCEAN (ō´shən) A large body of salt water.

Gazetteer

This Gazetteer is a geographical dictionary that will help you to pronounce and locate the places discussed in this book. The page numbers tell you where each place appears on a map or in the text.

A

Africa (af′ri kə) A continent located in the Eastern and Southern hemispheres. (m. G5, t. 59)

Antarctica (ant ärk′ti kə) A continent in the Southern Hemisphere. (m. G5)

Arctic Ocean (ärk′tik ō′shən) A large body of water located in the Northern Hemisphere. (m. G5)

Argentina (är jən tē′nə) A country in southern South America. (m. 322, t. 322)

Asia (ā′zhə) A continent in the Eastern and Northern hemispheres. (m. G5, t. 292)

Atlantic Ocean (at lan′tik ō′shən) A large body of water located to the east of North and South America. (m. G5, t. 37)

Australia (ôs trāl′yə) An island continent in the Southern Hemisphere between the Pacific and Indian oceans. (m. G5, t. 322)

B

Baltimore (bôl′tə môr) Port city on the Chesapeake Bay in the state of Maryland. (m. 243, t. 252)

Belgium (bel′jəm) A country in Western Europe on the North Sea. (m. 257)

Bothell (bäth′əl) A suburban community near Seattle, Washington. (t. 18)

Brazil (brə zil′) The largest country in South America. (m. R5, t. 299)

C

Calais (ka lā) City that is connecting point for English Channel Tunnel in France. (m. 257)

Canada (kan′ə də) A very large country located in the northern part of North America, bordering the United States. (m. 211, t. 321)

Capitol (kap′i təl) The building in Washington, D.C., where Congress meets. (m. 171, t. 171)

Chesapeake Bay (ches′ə pēk bā) A bay, partly enclosed by Maryland and Virginia. (m. 99, t. 99)

Chicago (shi kä′gō) A port city in northeastern Illinois. It is the largest city in the state. (m. 23, t. 227)

Colombia (kə ləm′bē ə) A country in the northwestern part of South America. (m. R5, t. 323)

Cuajimalpa (kwä hē mäl′pə) A suburban community near Mexico City, Mexico. (t. 25)

Cumberland (kəm′bər lənd) The most eastern city on the National Road. It is located in Maryland. (m. 243, t. 248)

pronunciation key

a	at	ī	ice	u	up	th	thin	
ā	ape	îr	pierce	ū	use	th	this	
ä	far	o	hot	ü	rule	zh	measure	
âr	care	ō	old	ù	pull	ə	about, taken,
e	end	ô	fork	ûr	turn		pencil, lemon,
ē	me	oi	oil	hw	white		circus
i	it	ou	out	ng	song		

D

Dakar (dä kär′) The capital and largest city in the country of Senegal. (m. 179, t. 178)

Detroit (di troit′) The largest city in Michigan. It is an important automobile manufacturing center. (m. 23, t. 312)

E

Eastern Hemisphere (ēs′tərn hem′is fîr) The half of Earth east of the Atlantic Ocean that includes Europe, Africa, Asia and Australia. (m. 58, t. 58)

Ellis Island (el′is ī′lənd) A small island located near New York City. It was the first stop for millions of immigrants who came to the United States from 1892 to 1954. (t. 219)

England (ing′glənd) Part of the United Kingdom, an island country off the continent of Europe. (m. 257, t. 256)

English Channel (ing′glish chan′əl) A narrow waterway between England and France. It connects the Atlantic Ocean and the North Sea. (m. 257, t. 256)

Equator (i kwā′tər) An imaginary line around the middle of Earth between the Northern Hemisphere and the Southern Hemisphere. (m. G4, t. G4)

Erie Canal (îr′ē kə nal′) A narrow waterway located in New York State connecting the Hudson River with Lake Erie. (m. 249, t. 248)

Europe (yùr əp) The smallest of Earth's seven continents. (m. G5, t. 256)

F

Folkestone (fōk′stən) City that is the connecting point for the English Channel Tunnel in England. (m. 257)

Four Corners (fôr kôr′nərz) The only place in the United States where four states meet. The states are Arizona, New Mexico, Utah, and Colorado. (m. 79, t. 78)

France (frans) A country in western Europe on the Atlantic Ocean and the Mediterranean Sea. (m. 257, t. 256)

G

Galveston (gal′və stən) A port city located on the Gulf of Mexico in the southeast part of Texas. (m. 10, t. 9)

H

Hudson River (hud′sən riv′ər) A river that flows in the eastern part of New York State. (m. 249, t. 243)

I

Independence (in di pen′dəns) A community in Missouri that marked the beginning of the Oregon Trail in the 1840s. (m. 211, t. 211)

India (in′dē ə) A country located in South Asia. (R11, t. 234)

Indian Ocean (in′dē ən ō′shən) A large body of water located east of Africa. (m. G5)

Italy (it′ə lē) A country in southern Europe. (m. 322, t. 322)

J

Jamestown (jāmz′toun) A community in southeastern Virginia along the James River. Settled in 1607, it was the first permanent English colony established in North America. (m. 99, t. 98)

Jamestown Settlement (jāmz′toun set′əl mənt) A living history museum showing how the English colonists and the Powhatan lived in the 1600s. (t. 108)

Japan (jə pan') A country of islands in the Pacific Ocean off the eastern coast of Asia. (m. 293, t. 292)

Jefferson Memorial (jef'ər sən mə môr'ē əl) A building in Washington, D.C. dedicated to the memory of President Thomas Jefferson. It was completed in 1943. (t. 172)

L

Lafayette Park (läf ē et' pärk) A public park located near the White House in Washington, D.C. (m. 176, t. 174)

Lake Erie (lāk îr'ē) The most southern of the five Great Lakes. It is located on the border between Canada and the United States. (m. 41, t. 248)

Lake Huron (lāk hyür'ən) The second largest of the five Great Lakes. It is located on the border between Canada and the United States. (m. 41)

Lake Michigan (lāk mish'ə gən) The third largest of the five Great Lakes. It is located between the states of Michigan and Wisconsin. (m. 41)

Lake Ontario (lāk on târ'ē ō) The smallest of the five Great Lakes. It is located on the border between Canada and the United States. (m. 41)

Lake Superior (lāk sə pîr'ē ər) The largest of the five Great Lakes. It is located on the border between Canada and the United States. (m. 41)

Lincoln Memorial (ling'kən mə môr'ē əl) A building in Washington, D.C., that honors President Abraham Lincoln. (m. 176, t. 173)

M

Mesa Verde (mā'sə vûr'dē) The ruins of an Anasazi community built into the side of a cliff and located in the southwestern part of the state of Colorado (m. 79, t. 80)

Mesa Verde National Park (mā'sə vûr'dē nash'ə nəl pärk) A national park in the state of Colorado that was an Anasazi community long ago. (m. 89, t. 88)

Mexico (mek'si kō) A country in North America that borders the southern United States. (m. 25, t. 24)

Mexico City (mek'si kō sit'ē) The capital of Mexico. (m. 25, t. 25)

Mississippi River (mis ə sip'ē riv'ər) One of the longest rivers in North America. It flows south from northern Minnesota into the Gulf of Mexico. (m. 40-41, t. 37)

N

National Mall (nash'ə nəl môl) An area in Washington, D.C. where many monuments, memorial, museums, and government buildings are located. (m. 176-177, t. 176)

National Road (nash'ə nəl rōd) A highway built in the 1800s that ran from Cumberland, Maryland to Vandalia, Illinois. It opened the way for people to move west. (m. 243, t. 243)

New England (nü ing'glənd) The northeastern part of the United States. It includes Maine, Vermont, New Hampshire, Massachusetts, Connecticut, and Rhode Island. (m. 187, t. 187)

New Orleans (nü ôr'lē ənz) The largest city in the state of Louisiana. It is an important Mississippi River port. (m. R7, t. 17)

New York City (nü yōrk sit'ē) The largest city in the United States, located in southeastern New York. (m. 249, t. 218)

Nigeria (nī jîr' ē ə) A country in West Africa. (m. 322, t. 234)

North America (nôrth ə mer'i kə) A continent in the Northern and Western hemispheres. (m. G5, t. 59)

Northern Hemisphere (nôr′thərn hem′i sfîr) The half of Earth north of the equator. (m. 59, t. 58)

North Pole (nôrth pōl) The place farthest north on Earth. (m. G5)

Norton (nôr′tən) A farming community in northern Kansas. (m. 302, t. 300)

O

Oakland (ōk′lənd) A port city in western California. It is on San Francisco Bay directly opposite the city of San Francisco. (m. R6, t. 195)

Oregon City (ôr′i gən sit′ē) A city located in the northwestern part of Oregon. In the 1840s it marked the end of the Oregon Trail. (m. 211, t. 214)

Oregon Trail (ôr′i gən trāl) A route that pioneers used in their move west in the 1840s. It ran from Independence, Missouri to Oregon City, Oregon. (m. 211, t. 211)

P

Pacific Ocean (pə sif′ik ō′shən) A large body of salt water bordering the west side of the United States. (m. G5, t. 37)

Paracas (pə räk′əs) A fishing community located in the country of Peru in South America. (m. 53, t. 52)

Peru (pə rü′) A country on the western coast of South America. (m. 53, t. 52)

Philadelphia (fil ə del′fē ə) A port city in southeastern Pennsylvania. It is the largest city in the state. (m. 147, t. 146)

Phillipines (fil′ə pēnz) An island country located in Southeast Asia, separated from the mainland by the South China Sea. (m. R11, t. 323)

Poland (pō′lənd) A country in Eastern Europe on the Baltic Sea. (m. R11, t. 234)

Portland (pôrt′lənd) A port city in northwestern Oregon on the Columbia River. (m. R6, t. 194)

R

Raleigh (rô′lē) The capital city of the state of North Carolina. (m. 275, t. 274)

River Walk (riv′ər wôk) A riverside park along the San Antonio River in Texas. It has sidewalks, trees, restaurants, and shops. (m. 120, t. 118)

Rochester (räch′ə stər) A rural farming community located in northern Indiana. (m. 23, t. 19)

Rocky Mountains (rok′ē moun′tənz) The longest mountain range in North America. It stretches from Alaska into Mexico. (m. 40, t. 38)

Russia (rush′ə) A country in Eastern Europe and Northern Asia. (m. 322, t. 322)

S

Sacramento (sak rə men′tō) The capital of the state of California. It also served as the western-most stop on the route of the pony express. (m. 251, t. 251)

St. Joseph (sānt jō′zef) A city in Missouri that was the eastern-most stop on the route of the pony express. (m. 251, t. 251)

Gazetteer

San Antonio (san an tō'nē ō) A port city located in south Texas, connected to the Gulf of Mexico by the San Antonio River. (m. 120, t. 118)

San Antonio River (san an tō'nē ō riv'ər) A river that flows southeast from the city of San Antonio, Texas, into the Gulf of Mexico. (m. 120, t. 118)

San Diego (san dē ā'gō) A port city in southern California. (m. 126, t. 232)

Senegal (sen'i gôl) A country in western Africa. (m. 179, t. 178)

Shapleigh (shap'lē) A rural community in the state of Maine. (m. 187, t. 187)

South America (south ə mer'i kə) A continent in the Southern and Western hemispheres. (m. G5, t. 52)

Southern Hemisphere (suth'ərn hem'i sfîr) The half of Earth south of the equator. (m. 59, t. 58)

South Pole (south pōl) The place farthest south on Earth. (m. G5)

T

Tampa (tam'pə) A port city in west-central Florida on the Gulf of Mexico. (m. R7, t. 193)

Tokyo (tō'kyō) The capital of Japan and its largest city. (m. 293, t. 292)

Toms River (tomz riv'ər) A suburban community in the state of New Jersey. (m. 329, t. 329)

V

Vandalia (vân dal'ē ə) The western-most city on the National Road. It is located in the state of Illinois. (m. 243, t. 248)

Veracruz (ver ə krüz') A port city on the eastern coast of Mexico. (t. 232)

Vietnam Veterans Memorial (vē et näm' vet'ər ənz mə môr'ē əl) A place in Washington, D.C., that has the names of more than 58,000 Americans who died in the Vietnam War. (m. 176, t. 173)

Virginia (vər jin'yə) A southern state on the Atlantic Ocean. It was one of the original 13 colonies. (m. 99, t. 98)

W

Washington, D.C. (wô'shing tən) Capital city of the United States. (m. 171, t. 168)

Washington Monument (wô'shing tən mon'yə mənt) A tall tower in Washington, D.C., that honors President George Washington. (m. 176, t. 172)

Western Hemisphere (wes'tərn hem'i sfîr) The half of Earth that includes North and South America. (m. 58, t. 58)

White House (hwīt hous) The home of the President of the United States, located in Washington, D.C. (m. 171, t. 166)

Biographical Dictionary

The Biographical Dictionary tells you about the people you have learned about in this book. The Pronunciation Key tells you how to say their names. The page numbers let you see where each person first appears in the text.

Adams, Abigail (ad'əmz), 1744–1818 Wife of President John Adams and mother of another president, John Quincy Adams. (p. 166)

Adams, John (ad'əmz), 1735–1826 The second President of the United States, 1797-1801. He was the first President to live in the White House. (p. 166)

Banneker, Benjamin (ban'i kər), 1731–1806 Surveyor who helped to draw plans for designing the city of Washington, D.C. in 1791. (p. 168)

Bell, Alexander Graham (bel, al ig zân'dər grā'əm), 1847–1922 Inventor who built the first working telephone in 1876. (p. 252)

Cisneros, Henry (sēs när'rōs), 1947– Mayor of San Antonio, Texas, 1981-1989. First person of Mexican heritage to be mayor of a large U.S. city. (p. 128)

Cooper, Peter (kü'pər), 1791-1883 Inventor who built the *Tom Thumb* in 1830, one of the first railroad steam engines. (p. 244)

pronunciation key

a	at	ī	ice	u	up	th	thin
ā	ape	îr	pierce	ū	use	th	this
ä	far	o	hot	ü	rule	zh	measure
âr	care	ō	old	ù	pull	ə	about, taken,
e	end	ô	fork	ûr	turn		pencil, lemon,
ē	me	oi	oil	hw	white		circus
i	it	ou	out	ng	song		

Earhart, Amelia
(âr´härt, â mēl yuh), 1898–
1937 First woman to fly
alone across the Atlantic
and Pacific oceans.
(p. 246)

Ford, Henry (fôrd),
1863–1947 Maker of the
Model T car in 1908. He
made his cars so that
many people could afford
them. (p. 245)

Franklin, Benjamin
(frang´klin), 1706–1790
American colonial leader,
writer, and scientist.
(p. 147)

Fulton, Robert (fŭl´tən),
1765–1815 Inventor who
built the *Clermont,* one
of the first steamboats,
in 1807. (p. 243)

Jefferson, Thomas
(jef´ər sən), 1743–1826
Colonial leader who wrote
the Declaration of
Independence and was
third President of the
United States. (p. 150)

Jemison, Mae
(jem´ə sən, mā), 1956–
In 1992 she became the
first African American
woman to travel in
space. (p. 246)

King, Martin Luther, Jr.
(king), 1929–1968 Leader
who worked to make
laws fair for all people.
(p. 229)

L' Enfant, Pierre
(län fän´, pē´yâr), 1754–1825
Builder who drew up the
plans for Washington,
D.C. in 1791. (p. 167)

Lawrence, Jacob (lôr′əns), 1917– Artist who made a series of paintings about the Great Migration in 1941. (p. 224)

Lin, Maya Ying (lin, mī′ə ying), 1959– Artist who designed the Vietnam Veterans memorial in Washington, D.C. (p. 174)

Lincoln, Abraham (ling′kən), 1809–1865 The sixteenth President of the United States, 1861–1865. He led the North during the Civil War and wanted to end slavery. (p. 225)

Lyons, Oren (lī′ənz, ôr′ən), 1931– A teacher and leader of the Iroquois people. (p. 74)

Madison, James (mad′ə sən), 1751–1836 The fourth President of the United States, 1809–1817. In 1787, he made a plan for three different parts of government. (p. 157)

Marconi, Guglielmo (mär kō′nē, gül yêl′mō), 1874–1937 Inventor of the wireless telegraph in 1895. (p. 253)

Morse, Samuel (môrs), 1791–1872 Inventor who built one of the earliest telegraphs in 1844. (p. 252)

Otis, Elisha (ōt′əs, e lī′shə), 1811–1861 He invented an automatic safety clamp in 1852 that led to the first elevators. (p. 246)

pronunciation key

a at; ā ape; ä far; âr care; e end; ē me; i it; ī ice; îr pierce; o hot; ō old; ô fork; oi oil; ou out; u up; ū use; ü rule, u̇ pull; ûr turn; hw white; ng song; th thin; <u>th</u> this; zh measure; ə about, taken, pencil, lemon, circus

Pocahontas (pō kə hon′təs), 1595?–1617 Daughter of Chief Powhatan who helped the English colony of Jamestown to survive. (p. 105)

Smith, John (smith), 1580?–1631 English colonial leader in Virginia who helped the Jamestown settlement to survive during hard times. (p. 102)

Powhatan (pou ə tan′), 1550?–1618 Chief of the Powhatan who lived on Chesapeake Bay near the English settlement at Jamestown. (p. 102)

Washington, George (wô′shing tən) 1732–1799 The first President of the United States, 1789–1797. During the American Revolution he led the colonial army. (p. 154)

Rolfe, John (rälf), 1585–1622 Leader of Jamestown colony who grew a new kind of tobacco that could be sold for a lot of money. (p. 105)

Wright, Orville (rīt), 1871–1948 With his brother Wilbur, he built the world's first successful airplane. (p. 245)

San Juan, Eduardo (san hwän′, əd währ′dō), 1925–1988 Designer of the vehicle that astronauts drove on the moon in 1971 and 1972. (p. 246)

Wright, Wilbur (rīt), 1867–1912 With his brother Orville, he built the world's first successful airplane. (p. 245)

Glossary

This Glossary will help you to pronounce and understand the meanings of the vocabulary in this book. The page number at the end of the definition tells where the word first appears.

A

agriculture (ag′ri kul chər) The business of growing crops and raising animals for food. Farmers are an important part of the **agriculture** business. (p. 301)

almanac (ôl′mə nak) A book that comes out every year with information on many different subjects. *Poor Richard's Almanac* was popular long ago. (p. 148)

ambassador (am bas′ə dər) A person who is sent to represent his or her country in another country. The **ambassador** studies the different cultures of the countries she visits. (p. 178)

American Revolution (ə mer′i kən rev ə lü′shən) The war fought by the American colonies to end English rule, 1775-1783. The American colonies defeated the English in the **American Revolution**. (p. 150)

artifact (är′tə fakt) A human-made object left behind by a group of people who lived long ago. The Anasazi left behind many **artifacts** at Mesa Verde. (p. 87)

assembly line (ə sem′blē līn) A line of workers and machines all working together to make a final product. Airplanes and televisions are two products made on an **assembly line**. (p. 312)

author (ô′thər) The writer of a book or other printed work. An **author** does research before writing a book. (p. 191)

B

bar graph (bär graf) A graph that uses bars of different heights to show amounts of things. The **bar graph** showed the population of three cities in Florida. (p. 134)

bay (bā) A part of a sea or lake that is partly surrounded by land. The English sailed in ships over the Chesapeake **Bay** to get to Jamestown. (p. 99)

Bill of Rights (bil uv rīts) A list of our country's most important rights and freedoms that was added to the Constitution in 1791. The **Bill of Rights** includes the right to free speech and the right to practice religion freely. (p. 159)

C

cactus (kak′təs) A plant that grows in hot, dry, sunny places. There are many **cactus** plants in the desert. (p. 122)

canyon (can′yən) A deep valley with steep sides. The river ran a few miles through the **canyon**. (p. 80)

pronunciation key

a	at	ī	ice	u	up	th	thin
ā	ape	îr	pierce	ū	use	th	this
ä	far	o	hot	ü	rule	zh	measure
âr	care	ō	old	ù	pull	ə	about, taken,
e	end	ô	fork	ûr	turn		pencil, lemon,
ē	me	oi	oil	hw	white		circus
i	it	ou	out	ng	song		

capital (kap′i təl) A place where the government of a state or country is located. People decided that the **capital** of our country should be located between the northern and southern States. (p. 166)

Capitol (kap′i təl) The building in Washington, D.C., where Congress meets to make laws. Both the House of Representatives and the Senate meet in the **Capitol**. (p. 171)

cardinal directions (kârd′ ən əl di rek′ shenz) Cardinal directions are north, south, east, and west. The airplane pilot used the compass rose to find the **cardinal directions** on the map. (p. G8)

cause (kôz) Something that makes something else happen. The **cause** of the sunburn was too much sun. (p. 290)

channel (chan′əl) A narrow waterway between two larger bodies of water. The ships sailed through the **channel** before reaching the ocean. (p. 256)

citizen (sit′ə zən) A member of a community or country. Communities need **citizens** to work together to solve problems. (p. 11)

city council (sit′ē koun′səl). Group of elected people who make the laws for a city. The **city council** meets in the town hall on Main Street. (p. 186)

Civil War (siv′əl wôr) The war between the North and the South, 1861-1865. After the **Civil War**, African Americans were free from slavery. (p. 225)

classifying (klas′ə fī ing) The grouping together of similar things. The movers **classified** the furniture into two groups: heavy pieces and light pieces. (p. 216)

cliff (klif) The high, steep face of a mountain or rock. The Anasazi lived in homes built into the **cliffs**. (p. 80)

climate (klī′mit) The weather a place has over a long period of time. Alaska has a cold **climate**. (p. 39)

coast (kōst) The land next to an ocean. There are many beaches and ports along the California **coast**. (p. 52)

coastal plain (kōs′təl plān) The flat land along a coast. The settlers built farms along the **coastal plain**. (p. 100)

colonist (kol′ə nist) Someone who lives in a colony. The **colonists** built a community at Jamestown. (p. 103)

colony (kol′ə nē) A place that is ruled by another, distant country. The King of England hoped that the **colony** at Jamestown would provide great riches. (p. 103)

communicate (kə mū′ni kāt) To share ideas, thoughts, or information with someone. Telephones help people **communicate** quickly. (p. 250)

community (kə mū′ni tē) A place where people live, work, and have fun together. It is usually made up of several different neighborhoods. Many people in Michael's **community** have fun by going to the beach during the summer. (p. 8)

compare (kəm pâr′) To see how things are alike. The students will **compare** the different jobs people have in the community to understand how they are alike. (p. 160)

compass rose (kum′ pəs rōz) A guide to the cardinal directions on a map. Mary used the **compass rose** to find that the river was south of her community. (p. G8)

compromise (kom′prə mīz) To settle an argument by agreeing that each side will give up some of its demands. In making fair laws people often work together and **compromise**. (p. 157)

Congress (kong'ris) The part of the United States government that makes laws for our country. Members of **Congress** are elected by citizens. (p. 157)

Constitution (kon sti tü'shən) The plan of government for the United States that explains what the different parts of government are and outlines the most important laws. Today the **Constitution** is still important in helping people make laws in our country. (p. 156)

consumer (kən sü'mər) People who buy goods and services. **Consumers** buy the products that are made or grown by producers. (p. 277)

continent (kon'tə nent) A very large body of land. Canada and the United States are both located on the **continent** of North America. (p. G5)

contrast (kən trast') To see how things are different. At the museum, the visitors saw the differences in Jacob Lawrence's paintings by **contrasting** them. (p. 160)

culture (kul'chər) The way of life of a group of people including that group's language, music, foods, holidays, and beliefs. The language the Iroquois speak and the dances they participate in are all part of their **culture**. (p. 25)

D

decision (di sizh'ən) The act of choosing one thing rather than another. When you choose what food to eat, you are making a **decision**. (p. 92)

Declaration of Independence (dek lə rā'shən uv in di pen'dəns) A document written by Thomas Jefferson in 1776 that explains why the colonies had decided to free themselves from England. On July 4th, Americans celebrate the signing of the **Declaration of Independence**. (p. 150)

desert (dez'ərt) A dry environment where little rain falls. A **desert** gets less than 10 inches of rainfall each year. (p. 78)

designer (di zī'nər) A person who plans how something will look. Book **designers** choose the photographs and illustrations to be used in books. (p. 283)

diary (dī'ə rē) A written record of what someone has seen, done, or thought. In her **diary** Sallie described her life. (p. 213)

domestic trade (də mes'tik trād) Trade within one country. **Domestic trade** may involve buying wheat in Kansas and selling airplanes in Washington. (p. 321)

E

economy (i kon'ə mē) The making and consuming of goods and services. Our country's **economy** needs people to buy and sell products. (p. 277)

editor (ed'i tər) Someone who works with authors and designers in all the steps involved in making a book. The **editor** decided to include a story in the book about Philadelphia. (p. 280)

effect (i fekt') Something that happens as a result of a cause. The **effect** of the sunburn was that Jane's skin hurt. (p. 290)

elect (i lekt') To choose by voting. George Washington was **elected** the first president of the United States in 1789. (p. 156)

pronunciation key

a **at**; ā **ape**; ä **far**; âr **care**; e **end**; ē **me**; i **it**; ī **ice**; îr **pierce**; o **hot**; ō **old**; ô **fork**; oi **oil**; ou **out**; u **up**; ū **use**; ü **rule**; ù **pull**; ûr **turn**; hw **white**; ng **song**; th **thin**; <u>th</u> **this**; zh **measure**; ə **about, taken, pencil, lemon, circus**

Glossary

employer (em ploi′ər) Someone who hires and pays other people to work. The **employer** had seven people working in the office. (p. 275)

encyclopedia (en sī klə pē′dē ə) A book or set of books with facts about people, places, things, and past events. Catherine looked in the **encyclopedia** for information about Senegal. (p. 190)

endangered (en dān′jerd) Plants or animals that are in danger of dying out. The black rhinoceros is one of many **endangered** animals. (p. 30)

environment (en vī′rən mənt) All the air, water, land, and the living things surrounding people. People are working to save the **environment** and its many resources. (p. 48)

equator (i kwā′tər) An imaginary line around the middle of Earth. The **equator** divides Earth into the Northern Hemisphere and Southern Hemisphere. (p. G4)

export (ek′spôrt) To sell and ship goods to another place or country. Canada **exports** fish to the United States. (p. 321)

F

factory (fak′tə rē) A place where things are manufactured. Many of the products we use are made in **factories**. (p. 312)

fertilizer (fûr′tə lī zər) Chemicals used to help plants grow. The farmer uses **fertilizers** for the crops. (p. 301)

fiction (fik′shən) Made-up stories of people, places, and events. *Alice in Wonderland* is Jill's favorite **fiction** book. (p. 190)

Fiesta (fē es′tə) An event in San Antonio, Texas that celebrates Texas' independence from Mexico. **Fiesta** means "festival" in Spanish. (p. 130)

flow chart (flō′ chärt) A chart that shows the order of steps that are followed to make a final product. The scientist used a **flow chart** to show how the rocket would be built. (p. 306)

fuel (fū′əl) Something that is burned to provide heat, light, or power. Most cars use gasoline for **fuel**. (p. 247)

G

geography (jē og′rə fē) The study of Earth's surface, bodies of water, climate, and natural resources. It is also about how people change the land around them. Knowing **geography** helps people learn about the land and water in their community. (p. 36)

goods (gůdz) The things for sale that people make or grow. Many **goods** are made in factories. (p. 274)

governor (guv′ər nər) An elected leader of a state's government. The **governor** chooses people to help run state government. (p. 186)

Great Migration (grāt′ mī grā′shən) In the early to mid 1900s, the journey of thousands of African Americans from the South to build new lives in the cities of the North. During the **Great Migration** many people traveled to large cities in the North by train. (p. 224)

grid map (grid map) A map with a set of crisscrossing lines used to find places on the map. The tour book has a **grid map** of Mexico City. (p. G11)

guide words (gīd wûrdz) The words that appear at the top of the page in many reference books. They tell the first and last subjects that appear on each page. Richard used the **guide words** in the dictionary to find the word he wanted to define. (p. 190)

H

harvest (här'vist) Ripe crops that are gathered. The **harvest** was loaded onto trucks at the end of the summer. (p. 301)

hemisphere (hem'i sfêr) Half of a sphere or globe. The United States is located in the Northern **Hemisphere**. (p. 58)

high-tech (hī' tek') The use of the latest technology to make electronic and other goods. Computers are **high-tech** products. (p. 294)

history (his'tə rē) The story of what happened in the past. At Jamestown Settlement, people learn about the **history** of the Powhatan and the English. (p. 70)

hurricane (hur'i kān) A storm with very strong winds and heavy rain. Many houses were destroyed in the **hurricane**. (p. 11)

I

immigrant (im'i grənt) Someone who comes from one country or place to live in another. Many **immigrants** to the United States came through Ellis Island. (p. 218)

import (im'pôrt) To buy goods from another place or country. Russia **imports** wheat from the United States. (p. 321)

independence (in di pen'dəns) Freedom from others. Texas won its **independence** from Mexico in 1836. (p. 126)

index (in'deks) An alphabetical list that shows where information can be found. Peter looked at the **index** on the grid map to find the Washington Monument. (p. 176)

interest (in'trist) Money paid for the use of borrowing money. Joe paid **interest** on his loan from the bank. (p. 276)

intermediate directions (in tər mē'dē it di rek'shənz) A direction halfway between two cardinal directions. **Intermediate directions** are helpful in showing the relationship between two different places on a map. (p. 50)

international trade (in tər nash'ə nəl trād) The import and export of goods between countries. **International trade** is important to many countries around the world. (p. 322)

island (ī'lənd) Land surrounded on all sides by water. The boat captain saw birds flying over the **island**. (p. 10)

J

journalist (jûr'nə list) A writer for a newspaper, magazine, or television news program. The President explained his ideas to the **journalist**. (p. 293)

K

kiva (kē'və) A special room used for religious ceremonies by some Native Americans. The Pueblo people held the ceremony in a **kiva**. (p. 84)

L

landform (land'fôrm) One of the shapes of Earth's surface. Pioneers saw many different types of **landforms** while traveling on the Oregon Trail. (p. 38)

pronunciation key

a at; ā ape; ä far; âr care; e end; ē me; i it; ī ice; îr pierce; o hot; ō old; ô fork; oi oil; ou out; u up; ū use; ü rule, u̇ pull; ûr turn; hw white; ng song; th thin; <u>th</u> this; zh measure; ə about, taken, pencil, lemon, circus

Glossary

landform map (land'fôrm map) A map that shows the different kinds of land on Earth. Mountains and hills can be seen on a **landform map**. (p. G10)

legacy (leg'ə sē) A part of our past that we value in our lives today. Celebrating Thanksgiving is a **legacy** people share from long ago. (p. 14)

line graph (līn graf) A graph that uses the rising or falling of a line to show how something changes over time. The **line graph** shows the total number of cars manufactured in the United States between 1920 and 1960. (p. 134)

living history museum (liv'ing his'tə rē mū zē'əm) A place that shows what the past was like by having people dress, talk, and do things as people did long ago. At the **living history museum**, people can eat food like Native Americans did long ago. (p. 108)

local government (lō'kəl guv'ərn mənt) The people who run a city or community. **Local governments** are often led by a mayor. (p. 186)

locator (lō'kāt tər) A small map included on a bigger, or main, map. Jeff used the **locator** to find California. (p. G9)

M

manufacturing (man yə fak'chər ing) The business of making things. People who work in **manufacturing** make many different products like cars, clothes, foods, and books. (p. 312)

map key (map kē) Something that tells what the symbols on a map stand for. Jane used the **map key** to help find the airport on the map. (p. G7)

mayor (mā'ər) A person who is the head of a city government. The **mayor** makes sure that local laws are obeyed. (p. 179)

memorial (mə môr'ē əl) Anything, such as a monument or holiday, that is set aside to remember a person or event. The Jefferson **Memorial** in Washington, D.C. honors Thomas Jefferson. (p. 172)

mesa (mā'sə) A landform that looks like a high, flat table. Native Americans grew crops on the **mesa**. (p. 80)

migration (mī grā'shən) The movement of people or animals from one place or country to another. Each year people go to the park to watch the **migration** of birds to the south. (p. 224)

mill (mil) A place where people use machines to turn natural resources into finished products. Steel and paper are products made in a **mill**. (p. 317)

mineral (min'ər əl) Natural substance found in the earth that is not a plant or animal. Iron and diamonds are examples of **minerals**. (p. 47)

mission (mish'ən) Communities set up by Roman Catholic priests to teach their religion to others. The Alamo was established as a **mission** in 1718. (p. 123)

missionary (mish'ə ner ē) A person sent by a church to spread its religion into a different country. Spanish **missionaries** taught Native Americans to speak and write in Spanish. (p. 123)

museum (mū zē'əm) A place where people can look at objects of art, science, or history. The students saw artifacts of colonial life at the **museum**. (p. 89)

N

national park (nash'ə nəl pärk) Land set aside by a government for all people to enjoy. The family was not allowed to build a house in the **national park**. (p. 28)

natural resource (nach′ər əl rē′sôrs) Something found in nature that people use. Water and soil are examples of **natural resources**. (p. 46)

nonfiction (non fik′shən) Information about real people, places, and events. A book about the life of George Washington would be located in the **nonfiction** section of the library. (p. 190)

nonrenewable resource (non ri nü′ə bəl rē′sôrs) Things found in nature that cannot be replaced, such as minerals. People are taking care to save **nonrenewable resources**. (p. 308)

North Pole (nôrth pōl) The place farthest north on Earth. Very few people live on the **North Pole**. (p. G4)

oath (ōth) A serious promise made in public. New immigrants take an **oath** of loyalty to our country when becoming citizens. (p. 235)

ocean (ō′shən) A very large body of salt water. People are finding new ways to work together to help fight pollution in **oceans** around the world. (p. G5)

oral history (ôr′əl his′tə rē) Recorded interviews with people who can tell firsthand what life was like in the past. The students listened to **oral histories** to learn more about San Antonio. (p. 219)

P

peninsula (pə nin′sə lə) Land that has water on all sides but one. Paracas is a community located on a **peninsula**. (p. 53)

pioneer (pī ə nîr′) A person who is among the first to explore an area not known to them. **Pioneers** traveled for many months on the Oregon Trail. (p. 210)

plain (plān) A large area of flat land. Long ago, many buffalo lived on the **plains** of our country. (p. 38)

plateau (pla tō′) A large area of high, flat land that is raised above surrounding land. The hikers climbed up the **plateau** and pitched their tents. (p. 38)

Pledge of Allegiance (plej uv əlē′jəns) An oath promising to be loyal and to support the government of the United States. In saying the **Pledge of Allegiance**, people are promising to be loyal to the United States. (p. 192)

pollution (pə lü′shən) Anything, such as a harmful chemical, that spoils land, water, or air. At the town meeting, people made laws to help fight **pollution**. (p. 11)

pony express (pō′nē ek spres′) A team of daring horseback riders who swiftly rode across the western United States to deliver mail. The **pony express** delivered mail from 1860 to 1861. (p. 251)

port (pôrt) A place, such as a harbor, where ships load and unload their goods. Francis liked to watch the boats being unloaded at the **port**. (p. 10)

prairie (prâr′ē) Flat or rolling land covered with tall grasses. The rich soil of the **prairie** makes it good for growing corn and other crops. (p. 210)

President (prez′i dənt) The leader of the United States government. People vote for **President** every four years. (p. 157)

pronunciation key

a **at**; ā **ape**; ä **far**; âr **care**; e **end**; ē **me**; i **it**; ī **ice**; îr **pierce**; o **hot**; ō **old**; ô **fork**; oi **oil**; ou **out**; u **up**; ū **use**; ü **rule**, ù **pull**; ûr **turn**; hw **white**; ng **song**; th **thin**; <u>th</u> **this**; zh **measure**; ə **about, taken, pencil, lemon, circus**

private property (prī′vit prop′ər tē) Land that is owned by people or companies. The mall was built on **private property**. (p. 310)

process (pros′es) To change a product into a different form so that it can be sold. Corn and other grains are **processed** to make breakfast cereals. (p. 305)

producer (prə dü′sər) Someone who makes goods or services. Farmers and car makers are two examples of **producers**. (p. 283)

product map (prod′ukt map) A map that shows the places where goods are made and crops are grown. Tanya used a **product map** to find different products that are grown in Texas. (p. 302)

public property (pub′lik prop′ər tē) Land that has been set aside for all people to use. Many parks are built on **public property**. (p. 310)

publishing (pub′lish ing) The making and selling of books, magazines, CD-ROMs, musical scores, or other informational material. This book was made by a **publishing** company. (p. 280)

R

recycling (rē sī′kling) Using something over again. Karen carried the bottles and cans to the bin for **recycling**. (p. 48)

reference (ref′ər əns) Type of book or other kind of stored information that contains facts on many different subjects. Susan looked at books in the **reference** section of the library for information on gardening. (p. 190)

renewable resource (ri nü′ə bəl rē′sôrs) Things found in nature that can be replaced. Water is a **renewable resource**. (p. 308)

research (ri sûrch′) To look for information. To do their class report, students **researched** facts at the library. (p. 190)

robot (rō′bot) Machine that does jobs instead of people. **Robots** are often used to make cars and other products. (p. 314)

rural (rur′əl) A community of farms or open country where distances are far between one place and another. Many fishing villages are located in **rural** communities. (p. 19)

S

satellite (sat′ə līt) A spacecraft that is used to connect radio, telephone, and television communications. Many of the TV programs we watch are sent by **satellites**. (p. 254)

scale (skāl) A ruler on a map that measures distance. It helps you to find out the larger, real distance on Earth. The pilot used a **scale** to measure the distance between two cities on a map. (p. 22)

services (sûr′vis əz) Work that helps others by providing something they need or want. Restaurants provide a **service** by making food for customers. (p. 274)

slavery (slā′və rē) The practice of one person owning another. President Abraham Lincoln wanted to end **slavery**. (p. 107)

South Pole (south pōl) The place farthest south on Earth. Explorers and scientists travel to the **South Pole**. (p. G4)

suburb (sub′ûrb) A community located near a city. People who live in **suburbs** often work in nearby cities. (p. 18)

Supreme Court (sə prēm′ kôrt) A part of the American government that makes sure laws follow the Constitution. There are nine judges on the **Supreme Court**. (p. 157)

symbol (sim′bəl) Anything that stands for something else. The Statue of Liberty is a **symbol** of freedom for many people. (p. G6)

T

tax (taks) Money people pay to support the government. The colonists did not want to pay **taxes** to England. (p. 150)

technology (tek nol′ə jē) The use of skills, ideas, and tools to meet people's needs. Computers are an example of a **technology** that some people use every day. (p. 81)

telegraph (tel′i graf) To send messages long distances over wires, using special codes. The ambassador sent a **telegraph** from the United States to Japan. (p. 252)

time line (tīm līn) A strip marked off evenly in periods of time that shows events in the same order as they happened. The **time line** shows important events in the history of Washington, D.C. (p. 112)

town meeting (toun mē′ting) A yearly gathering of town people to discuss and vote on community laws, rules, and other issues. At the **town meeting**, students introduced their plans for building a new park. (p. 187)

trade (trād) The buying and selling of goods and services. Different countries around the world **trade** many kinds of products with each other. (p. 320)

transportation (trans pər tā′shən) The moving of people or goods from one place to another. Buses and trains are important types of **transportation**. (p. 19)

transportation map (trans pər tā′shən map) A map that shows the routes people can use to travel from place to place. Gary used a **transportation map** to locate the subway stops in the city. (p. 248)

U

urban (ûr′bən) A community that includes the city and its surrounding areas. Many people in **urban** communities live in tall apartment buildings. (p. 17)

V

volunteer (vol ən tîr′) Someone who does a job by choice, without pay. Communities need **volunteers** to deliver food to people who can't leave their homes. (p. 130)

W

wildlife (wīld′līf) The animals that live in an area. Birds and fish are two types of **wildlife**. (p. 54)

pronunciation key

a **at**; ā **ape**; ä **far**; âr **care**; e **end**; ē **me**; i **it**; ī **ice**; îr **pierce**; o **hot**; ō **old**; ô **fork**; oi **oil**; ou **out**; u **up**; ū **use**; ü **rule**, u̇ **pull**; ûr **turn**; hw **white**; ng **song**; th **thin**; t̲h̲ **this**; zh **measure**; ə **about, taken, pencil, lemon, circus**

index

This Index lists many topics that appear in the book, along with the pages on which they are found. Page numbers after an *m* refer you to a map. Page numbers after a *p* indicate photographs, artwork, or charts.

CREDITS

Cover design by: Pentagram

Maps: Geosystems

Charts and Graphs: MMSD

Illustrations: Mike Adams: pp 246, 260, 304; Hal Brooks: pp 149; Genevieve Claire: pp 11, 28, 39, 54, 83, 100, 130, 158, 174, 195, 212, 244, 252, 276, 303; Renee Daily: pp 73, 74; Michael Hampshire: pp 116-117, 124-125; Jim Hays: pp 164-165, 208-209; Robert Korta: pp 68-69, 82, 83, 84-85, 86, 240-241; Kelly Maddox: pp 42, 71; Karen Minot: pp 322; Paul Mirocha: pp 55; Hima Pamoedjo: pp 16-19, 22, 50; Rebecca Perry: pp 314, G7, G8, G11; Rodica Prato: pp 106, 112-113; James Ransome: pp 286; Margaret Sanfilipo: pp R19-R22; Rob Schuster: pp 6, 34, 68, 97, 117, 145, 165, 184, 209, 241, 272, 298; Nina Wallace: pp 306, 307, 310; David Wenzel: pp 96-97, 144-145; Lane Yerkes: pp 216-217, 235, 289

PHOTOGRAPHY CREDITS: All photographs are by the Macmillan/ McGraw-Hill School Division (MMSD) except as noted below:

Cover and title page: Henry Francis DuPont Winterthur Museum, Washington at Verplanks, painting by John Trumbull, oil on canvas, detail, 1790/courtesy, Winterthur Museum. iii: t. George Jones/Photo Researchers; b. Lawrence Migdale. iv: b. Laurence Parent; t. Richard T. Nowitz; m. Anne Nielson for MMSD. v: l. Richard T. Nowitz; r. Anne Nielson for MMSD. vi: b.m. Anne Nielson for MMSD; b. Jeff Greenberg/The Picture Cube; t. Chermayeff & Geismar/Metaform. vii: b. Deters/Monkmeyer; m. Gary Buss/FPG International; t. Chermayeff & Geismar/Metaform. G2: t.r. Mark Wagner/Tony Stone Images; b.l. Joseph Muench. G3: t.r. Greg Mellis; m.l. Nicholas DeVore III/Photographers/Aspen; b.r. Thomas Nebbia. G2-G3: Elizabeth Wolf. G6: J.A. Kraulis/MasterFile. **Chapter 1** 2: b.l. Bob Torrez/Tony Stone; m.r. Richard Palsey/Stock Boston; t. Liz Hymans/Tony Stone; r. Lawrence Migdale; m.l. Tim Davis/Photo Researchers. 3: b. J. Sohm/The Image Works; r. Wolfgang Kaehler. 4S: Daniel R. Westergren. 6: Jim Schwabel/New England Stock Photo. 7: l. Jack Hoehn/Profiles West; r. Barry Durand/Odyssey; m. Bonnie Sue Rauch/Photo Researchers. 8: Robert Mihovil. 9: Jim Levin for MMSD. 10: Robert Mihovil. 11: b.r. The Rosenberg Library. 12: b. Joe Viesti/Viesti Associates; t. Robert Mihovil. 13: Chuck O'Rear/Westlight. 14: b. Thomas T. Taber/Madison Public Library. 14-15: m. George Jones/Photo Researchers. 14: frame Jim Levin for MMSD. 15: t.r. Matt Bradley/West Stock; b.l. Sobel/Klonsky, The Image Bank; m.r. Robert Mihovil. 16: postcard borders Jim Levin for MMSD; b. Fulton County Historical Society; t. John Neubauer/West Stock, Inc.; m. Louis Benezе/Liaison International. 17: t. David Noble/FPG; b. Bob Krist/Black Star. 18: t. Tim Heneghan/West Stock; b. Louis Bencze/Liaison International. 19: t. Darryl Jones, Fulton County Historical Society; b. Joseph Nettis/Photo Researchers. 21: Bryan Peterson/West Stock. 24: Howard Breitrose for MMSD. 25: J. P Courau/D. Donne Bryant Stock Photo. 26: t.l. Robert Frerck/Odyssey; b.r. Cameramann Int'l., Ltd. 27: Howard Breitrose for MMSD. 28: Howard Breitrose for MMSD; l. Jim Levin for MMSD. 29: Bob Thomason/Leo de Wys Inc., NY. 30: W. Hille/Leo de Wys Inc., NY. 31: t. courtesy Hollia Kemp; b. courtesy Elisabeth Turbow; m. courtesy Ned Marsen. **Chapter 2** 35: l. Uniphoto; m. Wolfgang Kaehler; r. Gabe Palmer/The Stock Market. 36: Uniphoto. 37: m. courtesy Francis Akinsulie; t. Mulvehill/The Image Works; b. Joe Sohm/The Image Works. 38: l. Luis Garcia; r. David Hiser/Photographers Aspen. 39: r. Bryan & Cherry Alexander; l. Chuck Carlton/Black Star. 41: b. Barry L. Runk/Grant Heilman; b.m.r. Trevor Wood/The Image Bank; t.r. William H. Mullins/Photo Researchers; b.r. Harold Sund/The Image Bank; t.m.r. James Randkley/Tony Stone International. 43: Terry E. Eiler/Stock Boston; l. inset Jim Levin for MMSD. 44: l. Pierre Fabre. 44-45: m. Creda Axton. 45: m.r., b.l. Pierre Fabre; t. Bettmann Archives. 46: Peter Cole/Bruce Coleman, Inc. 47: t. Hans Wendler/The Image Bank; m.r Dwight Kuhn/Bruce Coleman, Inc.; b.l. Gordon M. Kurzweil/Uniphoto Picture Agency; r. D.D. Morrison/The Picture Cube. 48: l. Peter Beck/The Stock Market; r. courtesy Tara Church. 49: b. Ken Kerbs for MMSD; t. Jim Levin for MMSD. 52: Alejandro Balaguer. 53: George Holton/Photo Researchers. 54: r. Alejandro Balaguer; l. Brian Parker/Tom Stack Associates. 56: Alejandro Balaguer. 57: Michael McDermott. 60: J.P.Meyers/Academy of Natural Sciences- Vireo. 63: Monica Stevenson for MMSD. 64: m. John Running; b. Laurence Parent; t.l. Tom Bean; t.r. Anne Nielson for MMSD. 65: t.r. Richard T. Nowitz; m.r. Anne Nielson for MMSD; b. Robert Llewellyn. 66: b.l. Michael Schwarz. 66-67: © Michael Philip Manheim. 67: t. Dorothy Littell Greco/Stock Boston; b. Cotton Coulson. **Chapter 3** 70: Richard Welch. 72: t.l. National Museum of the American Indian; b.l. David Heald/National Museum of the American Indian; b.r. Joslyn Art Museum. 74: Monty Roessel/TBS, Inc. 75: Richard A. Cooke III/Neah Bay Museum. 76-77: Chris Roberts. 77: b.r. Michael Crummett; b.l. John Running; t. Edwin L. Wisherd/National Geographic Society. 78: David Muench. 79: b. David Muench; t. David Carriere/Tony Stone International. 80: b.l. Todd Powell/Profiles West; b.r. Rod Planck/Tony Stone International; t.l. Ann Trulove/Unicorn Stock Photos. 81: George H.H. Huey. 87: David Hiser/Photographers Aspen; bkgnd. Jim Levin for MMSD. 88: Steve Rudolph. 89: Jerry Jacka Photography. 90: l. David Hiser/Photographers Aspen; r. The Image Bank. 91: courtesy Steve Rudolph. **Chapter 4** 98: Bruce Roberts. 99: Fil Hunter. 100: The Granger Collection. 101: Llewellyn. 102: The Bettmann Archives. 103: b.r. Superstock;l. Archive Photos; t.r. The Granger Collection. 104: b. The Granger Collection. 105: r. Don Henley & Savage/Dominion Photosource; b.l. The Granger Collection. 107: The Bettmann Archives. 108: Jamestown Yorktown Foundation. 109: t. Jamestown Yorktown Foundation; b.l. Robert Llewellyn; b.r. Richard T. Nowitz/Photo Researchers. 110: b.r. Fil Hunter/Time Life Books, Inc.; t.l. Fil Hunter for MMSD. 111: Robert Llewellyn. **Chapter 5** 118: Al Rendon. 119: t.r. Scott Berner/The Picture Cube; l. Bullaty-Lomeo/The Image Bank; b. Al Rendon. 120: Scott Berner/The Picture Cube. 121: t.r. Priscilla Connell/PhotoNats; b.l. The Institute of Texas Cultures, San Antonio, TX. courtesy: Vic Fritze. 122: Steve Vidler/Leo de Wys, Inc. 123: t. Richard Reynolds Photography; b. Gil Cohen/National Park Service. 126: Masahiro Sano/The Stock Market. 127: D. Donne Bryant. 128: Bob Daemmrich. 129: b.l. Ron Thomas/FPG; b.r. Sullivan/Texastock; t. courtesy Barbara Shupp. 130: Al Rendon. 131: t. courtesy Barbara Shupp; b. Jim Levin for MMSD. 132: S.A.L.E. Inc., San Antonio TX. 133: courtesy Vernon Mullins, The Children's East Community Garden, San Antonio. 139: Monica Stevenson for MMSD. 140: t.r. Santi Visalli/The Image Bank; b.r. Richard T. Nowitz; l. Anne Nielson for MMSD. 141: b.l. Anne Nielson for MMSD; r. Jeff Hunter/The Image Bank. 142: t.l. Stanley Tretick; b.l. Library of Congress. 142-143: bkgnd. Tony Stone Images. 143: t. The Bettmann Archive; b. Dennis Brack/Black Star. **Chapter 6** 146: The Bettmann Archives. 147: r. Cigna Museum & Art Collection; l. North Wind Picture Archives. 148: Joseph Boggs Beale/Modern Galleries Philadelphia. 150-151: Superstock. 152-153: m. Doug Armand/Tony Stone Worldwide. 152: b.l. NASA. 153: t.l. North Wind Pictures; b. Archive Photos; m.r. Martin Rogers/Stock Boston. 154: FPG International. 155: b.l. Archive Photos; m., t. The Granger Collection. 156: t.r. National Geographic Photographer George F. Mobley/courtesy U.S. Capitol Historical Society; b.l. Superstock. 157: r. Ken Kerbs for MMSD. t. Superstock. 158: r. Ted Spiegel. 159: Harold M. Lambert. 160-161: The Granger Collection. (on page credit). 162: The Granger Col-

lection. **Chapter 7** 166: c. White House Historical Association. Photo by National Geographic Society. 167: Photri. 168: The Granger Collection. 169: North Wind. 170: Mike Yamashita/Woodfin Camp & Associates. 171: courtesy: Ms. Bernadette Senn. 172: David Ball/The Picture Cube. 173: t. Tony Stone Images; b.l. Uniphoto Picture Agency; m. Andre Jenny/Stock South. 174: b.l. Richard T. Nowitz; r. Jim Pickerell/Stock Boston. 175: Dirick Halstead/Gamma-Liaison. 178: Nik Wheeler. 179: courtesy Dorothy Padilla. 180: b. Thierry Prat/Sygma; t. Superstock. 181: b. M & E Bernheim/Woodfin Camp. **Chapter 8** 185: b. William Whitehurst/The Stock Market; t.l. Richard Hutchings/Photo Researchers; t.r. Uniphoto; t.m. Andre Jenny/Stock South. 186: B. Howe/Photri. 187: Kevin A. Byron/ The Sanford News. 188: t. Jim Brown/Gilles Lavigne/Gino Romano; b., m. Jim Brown/Gilles Lavigne. 189: t. courtesy Wendy Wehmeyer; b. courtesy Adam Pierce. 192-193: Mark Pokemper/Tony Stone Worldwide. 193: t.r. courtesy Alberta Reid; b.r. Zigy Kaluzny/Tony Stone Images. 194: t. Ben Brink/The Oregonian; b. Ross Hamilton/The Oregonian. 195: Oakland City Council, courtesy John Russo. 196: bor. UPI/Bettmann. 197: r. Tony La Gruth/New England Stock Photography; l. Dimaggio Kalish/The Stock Market. 198: Russ Kinne/Comstock. 199: t. courtesy Suzanne Hee; m. courtesy Debbie Macon; b. courtesy Joel Rosch. 203: Robert Milazzo for MMSD. 204: t.m., t.l. Chermayeff & Geismar/Metaform; b. Jeff Greenberg/The Picture Cube; r. Andrea Pistolesi/The Image Bank; m. Anne Nielson for MMSD. 205: l. Anne Nielson for MMSD; r. Southern Stock/NASA, FL. 206: l. David Hiser/Photographers/Aspen. 206-207: bkgnd David Hiser. 207: David Hiser. **Chapter 9** 210: USDI Bureau of Land Management. 211: Oregon Historical Society. 212: The Corcoran Gallery of Art, gift of Mr and Mrs. Lansell K. Christie. 213: b.r. St. Louis Mercantile Library; m. Clackmas County Historical Society - Oregon City, Oregon; t. National Geographic Society. 214: b. Oregon Historical Society; t. The Granger Collection. 215: t. John Elk III/Stock Boston; b. Phyllis Picardi/Stock Boston. 218: Uniphoto. 219: t. Culver Pictures; b.l., b.r. Audrey Buchter. 220: b. The Jacob A. Riis Collection/Museum of the City of New York; t. Brown Brothers. 221: t. Brown Brothers; b. Lewis W. Hine/George Eastman House. 222: Nancy A. Potter/Bruce Coleman, Inc. 223: Superstock. 224: Florida State Archives. 225: Abraham Gardner/Photri. 226: t. National Geographic Society/Dr. Louis Fargo; b. National Geographic Society/Willard Price. 227: courtesy Donna Van Der Zee, photo by James Van Der Zee. 228: t. Discovery Channel/Spike Mafford; b. The Phillips Collection. 229: Superstock. 230-231: Sam Holland for MMSD. 232: Dolores Stivalet. 233: t. Victor Perez de Lara/Leo de Wys, Inc.; b. Bushnell/Soifer/Tony Stone Images. 234: t.l. Kumar S. Nochur; b.l. Nicolas Jawdosiuk; m.l. E.B. Wilson/Oyeyinka Oyelaran; r. Jim Ortner/Tony Stone International. 236: r. M. Mantel/SIPA Press; l. courtesy: Dept of Immigration. 237: Keith Soon Kim. **Chapter 10** 242: Jeff Hunter/The Image Bank. 243: Brown Brothers. 244: The Bettman Archive. 245: t., b. Brown Brothers; m. Keith Marvin. 247: Norman Owen Tomalin/Bruce Coleman. 248-249: The Granger Collection. 250: The Bettman Archive. 251: Buffalo Bill Historical Center, Cody, W.Y. 252: l. Charles Harrington, Cornell University Photo; r. The Bettman Archive. 253: t. Leonard Lessin/Peter Arnold; b.r. Charmet/Science/Photo Library/Photo Researchers; b.l. Archive Photos. 254: NASA. 255: Lawrence Migdale/Stock Boston. 256: Archive/Imapress/N'Diaye. 258: t.l., t.r. Q A Photos; b. Monica Stevenson for MMSD. 259: b. Q A Photos; t. Terminus/Gamma Liaison. 260: m. Eurotunnel Education in collaboration w/ Kent Arts and Libraries. 262-263: Benn Mitchell/The Image Bank. 263: t.l. Culver Pictures; t.r. Lori Adamski Peek/Tony Stone; b.r. Bob Winsett/Tom Stack and Associates; b.l. Bob Daemmrich/Stock Boston. 267: Monica Stevenson for MMSD. 268: b. Deters/Monkmeyer Press; t.r. Gary Buss/FPG; t.l. National Museum of American Art, Smithsonian Institution, DC Art Resource - Thomas Hart Benton, Wheat 1967, Oil on wood, 20"x21", Gift of Mr./Mrs. James A. Mitchell and Museum purchase. 269: b. Superstock. 270: l. Daniel R. Westergren; bkgnd Richard T. Nowitz. 271: t. Steven Pumphrey; b. Jerry Jacka. **Chapter 11** 273: t. Orion Press; l. Anthony Boccacio/The Image Bank; r. Doug Milner/Uniphoto; m. Sylvain Grandadam/Photo Researchers. 274: Jim Stratford. 275: l. Jim Stratford; r. Skip Flythe. 276-278: Jim Stratford. 279: Joel Seigelman. 280-281: Robert Milazzo for MMSD. 283: t. Robert Milazzo; b. Blair Seitz/Photo Researchers. 284: t.m. Dena Abergel in A Midsummer Night's Dream; m.l. Steve Joester/FPG International; b.l. photo courtesy of Denice Burnham; b.r. Zack Burris Photography. 284-285: t. Bobbie Kingsley/Photo Researchers, Inc. 285: t.r. photo courtesy of Alfredo Estrada; m. (television screen) Superstock; m. Eccles/Outline; b. photo courtesy of Kim Guyette; b.r. Henry Wolf/The Image Bank. 287: Anne Nielsen. 288-289: t. Currier & Ives/Museum of the City of New York. 288: b. Bob Daemmrich. 289: b.r. Eastcott/Momatiuk/The Image Works; t.r. R.L. Wolverto/Profiles West. 289: b.l. Robert Davis. 292: Ken Strait/The Stock Market. 293: courtesy Tsutomu Yamaguchi. 294: t. Richard Nowitz; b.r. Ronald D. Modra/Sports Illustrated/Time, Inc. 295: Michael S. Yamashita. **Chapter 12** 298: IBM. 299: r. Antonio Ribeiro/Gamma Liaison; m. McAllister of Denver/Uniphoto; l. Romilly Lockyer/The Image Bank. 300: Chester Peterson Jr. for MMSD. 301: b.l., t.r. Chester Peterson, Jr. for MMSD; b.r. John & Diane Harper/New England Stock Photo. 302: First Light (A.G.E. Fotostock). 303: m.l. David Overcash/Bruce Coleman; t.r. Chuck O'Rear/WestLight; b.l. Charlie Ott/Photo Researchers. 305: Michael Rosenfeld/Tony Stone Worldwide. 308: t. Alan Kearney/Viesti Assoc. 308-309: b. Peter Dreyer/The Picture Cube. 309: m. courtesy Andrew Romero; t.r. courtesy Dana Romero; b.r. Richard Treplow/Photo Researchers. 310: David E. Spaw/Midwestock. 311: Ron Sanford/FStop Pictures. 312: Steve Dunwell/The Image Bank. 313: t. from the collections of Henry Ford Museum & Greenfield Village. b. Brown Brothers. 314: Andy Sacks. 315: t. Frank Fisher/West Stock; b. John Riley/Southern Stock Photos. 316: l. David Ulmer/Stock Boston; r. Rob Crandall/Stock Boston. 317: Superstock. 318: H. Armstrong Roberts. 319: Marc Morrison. 320: Peter Vandermark/Stock Boston. 321: b.r. Grant V. Faint/The Image Bank; b.l. Greig Cranna/Stock Boston; t. James Kirby/Photri, Inc. 323: Uniphoto. 325: Paul Lau/Gamma Liaison International. 327: Robert Milazzo for MMSD. **Chapter SS** 330: b.l. Townsend P. Dickinson; bkgnd., t.l., b. Monica Stevenson for MMSD. 331: b.l., bkgnd. Monica Stevenson for MMSD. 332: l. From the Collection of Richard Steele/Courtesy of Ocean County Library; r. Ocean County Cultural & Heritage Commission. 332-333: bkgnd. Monica Stevenson for MMSD. 333: Monica Stevenson for MMSD. 334: b.l. courtesy of South Tom's River Elementary School; t.r. Robert J. Novins Planitarium, Ocean County College. 334-335: t., bkgnd. Monica Stevenson for MMSD. 335: b. Townsend P. Dickinson. 336: t.l. Monica Stevenson for MMSD. 336-337: bkgnd. Monica Stevenson for MMSD. 337: Clare Devine/North Dover Elementary School. 338: b.r. Jeffrey Dunn/Viesti Associates; b.m. Eric Schweikardt/The Image Bank; b.l. Andy Levin/Photo Researchers. 338-339: bkgnd. Monica Stevenson for MMSD. 339: t. Monica Stevenson for MMSD. R3: Abraham Gardner/Photri. Endpapers: Bridgeman Art Library.

(continued from page ii)

Acknowledgments
From **Ben Franklin of Old Philadelphia** by Margaret Cousins. Copyright 1952 by Margaret Cousins, renewed 1980. Random House. From **New Letters of Abigail Adams** edited w/an Introduction by Stewart Mitchell. Copyright 1947 by the American Antiquarian Society. Greenwood Press Publishers, a division of Williamhouse-Regency, Inc. From **The Great Migration** by Jacob Lawrence. Copyright 1993 by the Museum of Modern Art, New York, and the Phillips Collection. HarperCollins Publishers. "Harvest" from **Slave Songs of the Georgia Sea Islands**. "Georgia Folk Song," book by Lydia Parrish. Copyright 1942 by Lydia Parrish, renewed 1969 by Maxfield Parish, Jr. Farrar, Straus & Giroux, Inc. Reprinted by permission of Farrar, Straus & Giroux, Inc. From **"No Star Nights"** by Anna Egan Smucker. Text copyright 1989 by Anna Egan Smucker. Illustrations copyright 1989 by Steve Johnson. Alfred A. Knopf. **"It's a Small World"** by Richard M. Sherman and Robert B. Sherman. Copyright 1963 by Wonderland Music Co. Inc.